Ohio River Valley Series

Rita Kohn and William Lynwood Montell
Series Editors

RIVER JORDAN

African American Urban Life in the Ohio Valley

JOE WILLIAM TROTTER JR.

THE UNIVERSITY PRESS OF KENTUCKY

Publication of this volume was made possible in part by a grant from
the National Endowment for the Humanities.

*F
520.6
.N4
T76
1998
Jan.1999*

Editorial and Sales Offices: The University Press of Kentucky
663 South Limestone Street, Lexington, Kentucky 40508-4008

98 99 00 01 02   5 4 3 2 1

Frontispiece: "In River Jordan."
The Rev. George W. Wyatt of Cincinnati's Antioch Baptist Church
prepares for baptismal ceremonies in the Ohio River around World War I.
From W.B. Dabney, *Cincinnati's Colored Citizens* (1926)

Library of Congress Cataloging-in-Publication Data
Trotter, Joe Wiliam, 1945-
River Jordan: African American urban life in the Ohio Valley /
Joe William Trotter, Jr.
    p. cm.—(The Ohio River Valley series)
Includes bibliographical references and index.
ISBN 0-8131-2065-9 (cloth : alk. paper). — ISBN 0-8131-0950-7
(paper : alk. paper)
    1. Afro-Americans—Ohio River Valley—Social conditions. 2. City
and town life—Ohio River Valley—History. 3. Ohio River Valley—
Social conditions. 4. Ohio River Valley—Race relations.
I. Title. II. Series.
F520.6.N4T76 1998
977'.00496073—dc21   97-43458

To Aunt Velma Tillman Anderson

in memory of

Uncle Melvin Clarence Anderson

Contents

Figures, Maps, and Tables

Tables

Series Foreword

The Ohio River Valley Series, conceived and published by the University Press of Kentucky, is an ongoing series of books that examine and illuminate the Ohio River and its tributaries, the lands drained by these streams, and the peoples who made this fertile and desirable area their place of residence, of refuge, of commerce and industry, of cultural development, and, ultimately, of engagement with American democracy. In doing this, the series builds upon an earlier project, "Always a River: The Ohio River and the American Experience," which was sponsored by the National Endowment for the Humanities and the humanities councils of Illinois, Indiana, Kentucky, Ohio, Pennsylvania, and West Virginia, with a mix of private and public organizations.

The Always a River project directed widespread public attention to the place of the Ohio River in the context of the larger American story. This series expands on this significant role of the river in the growth of the American nation by presenting the varied history and folklife of the region. Each book's story is told through men and women acting within their particular place and time. Each reveals the rich resources for the history of the Ohio River and of the nation afforded by records, papers, and oral stories preserved by families and institutions. Each traces the impact the river and the land have had on individuals and cultures and, conversely, the changes these individuals and cultures have wrought on the valley with the passage of years.

As a force of nation and as a waterway into the American heartland, the Ohio and its tributaries have touched us individually and collectively. This series celebrates the story of that river and its valley through multiple voices and visions.

River Jordan: African American Urban Life in the Ohio Valley reveals the impact that Pittsburgh, Cincinnati, Louisville, and Evansville had on blacks and the effects those people had on the cities themselves. Within the mainstream we witness the emergence of a distinctive black economy, culture, and political structure. Joe William Trotter draws upon traditional and new sources to bring dimension to each center's African American population and depicts how, throughout two centuries, individuals and institutions emerged from the shadows to bring diversity and vibrancy to their own and to the region's history. *River Jordan* presents the picture as it is, inviting us to assess the manifestations of the American story of people of color.

Rita Kohn
William Lynwood Montell

Preface

This book builds upon the recent explosion of scholarship in African American urban history. Although class, gender, and cultural issues require much more research, the existing scholarship provides the intellectual foundation for a new African American urban synthesis.[1] Accordingly, based primarily upon existing scholarship, this book is conceived and presented as a partial contribution to a larger synthesis. The Ohio Valley is an excellent place to start because it holds great symbolic significance in African American history. It not only represented the boundary between slavery and freedom during the antebellum era, but the division between the Jim Crow South and the urban North during the industrial age. Indeed, African Americans frequently referred to the Ohio as the "River Jordan" because it symbolized their passage from southern bondage to the "land of hope" or "promised land" farther north.

River Jordan examines African American life in four Ohio Valley cities—Pittsburgh, Cincinnati, Louisville, and Evansville—from the American Revolution to the mid-twentieth century. By exploring the development of black urban life in a regional context, connected by the Ohio River, this book not only aims to broaden our understanding of black life in urban America, it also addresses the overall aim of the Ohio River Valley Series, i.e., to illuminate the "impact of the Ohio River in the context of the larger American story."[2]

As a work of synthesis, this book seeks several specific objectives. First and most important, it emphasizes the role of black workers in the transformation of black urban life under the impact of commercial and later industrial capitalism. While documenting the deleterious impact of racial and class inequality on black life, the book gives particular attention to the migration of rural southern blacks into Ohio Valley cities, their participation in the urban political economy, and their role in the development of black urban communities and the struggle for social justice. Second, this study documents the gradual emergence of the black middle class and its small elite, including the nature of their relationship with black workers and their role in the growth of cross-class black institutions and social and political movements. Third, for both elite and working-class blacks, this book explores the development of interracial alliances at different points in time, accenting both the limitations and advantages of class and racial consciousness under different phases of urban capitalist development.

Finally, this study also highlights similarities and differences in the social history of Ohio Valley cities and shows how these factors influenced the development of African American life. The four cities exhibited significant differences in demographic make-up, economic base, and political and cultural traditions, which underlay important contrasts in inter- and intra-class and race relations from city to city. In Pittsburgh, for example, during the emancipation era, African Americans gained a footing in the manufacturing sector (i.e., iron and steel production) much earlier than blacks in Cincinnati, Louisville, and Evansville. With heavy concentration in the metal industries, however, the occupational structure of blacks in Pittsburgh was less diversified than elsewhere; thus, blacks in the "City at the Point" experienced higher unemployment rates than their counterparts in other Ohio Valley cities.

African Americans faced the brunt of slavery and later dejure segregation in the southern city of Louisville, Kentucky. Despite Louisville's slave past and the post-Reconstruction rise of Jim Crow, the city's black population retained the vote and encountered fewer incidents of mob violence and lynchings than their brothers and sisters farther south. Conversely, during the antebellum period, despite prohibitions on slavery, African Americans faced the most violent attacks on their lives and property in Cincinnati, Ohio. Moreover, during the era of the Great Migration in the twentieth century, the Ku Klux Klan gained its most significant political victories in Evansville, Indiana. In 1924, the Klan captured city hall and dominated the party of Lincoln until the onset of the Great Depression. At the same time, the city of Louisville, which the historian George Wright characterizes as the site of "polite racism," excluded the Klan from use of public facilities and undercut its promotion of white supremacy.

Black community formation also varied significantly along temporal, spatial, color, class, and gender lines. As elsewhere, until the late nineteenth century, a light-skinned elite and its children catered to an exclusive white clientele and took the lion's share of opportunities for education and economic development open to African Americans. The steady movement of rural southern blacks into Ohio Valley cities added a regional dimension to African American life and exacerbated class conflicts. For their part, black women from different class backgrounds, but particularly the poor and working class, faced greater limitations than black men on their efforts to move up in the occupational structure and take leadership positions within the black community.

In short, this study demonstrates that the rise of black urban communities in the Ohio Valley, as elsewhere, was an exceedingly complex process. Yet, several key themes emerge quite clearly regardless of place. First, as elsewhere in nineteenth- and twentieth-century America, Ohio Valley blacks faced racial hostility from whites and class, color, and cultural fragmentation among themselves. Second, despite significant social cleavages within the black community as well as ongoing ethnic and racial conflicts with whites, African Americans succeeded in building substantial bridges across such social chasms and creating new communities in Ohio River cities. Third, the long-term transformation of southern agricultural workers into a new urban working class stood at the forefront of Ohio Valley community development and social conflict.

In helping to make this book possible, I am pleased to acknowledge the help of numerous people. As a work of synthesis, this book builds upon the work of several scholars, as indicated by the list of references. I am, however, especially indebted to books and/or essays by Dennis C. Dickerson, George C. Wright, Henry Louis Taylor Jr., Darrel E. Bigham, David A. Gerber, Laurence Glasco, John Bodnar, Roger Simon, Joel A. Tarr, and Michael P. Weber, to name only a few. I also wish to extend a special thanks to my friends and colleagues Earl Lewis and Laurence Glasco for reading the manuscript at a late date and offering timely suggestions for revision. Although I was unable to address some of the most significant of their suggestions, their comments helped me to understand better both the promise and the limits of works of synthesis, especially this effort on the Ohio Valley.

Graduate students also aided this book as both research assistants and seminar participants. For research assistance—bibliographical and interlibrary loan—I owe a debt to Donald Collins, Matthew Hawkins, Charles Lee, and Ancella Livers. For help on the statistical data and photographs, respectively, and I am also indebted to Kate Aberger and

Tywanna Whorley. Through their thoughtful participation in my upper division African American history course, my undergraduate students— Sami Badia Albania, Xavier Cain, Erin Galloway, Richard Gilmore, Teresa Marx, Gina L. Schuyler, Pascale C. Tufau, and Heather Walker—also facilitated the publication of this book.

For their consistent and generous support of my research activities and the programs of the Center for Africanamerican Urban Studies and the Economy (CAUSE), I am indebted to Steve Schlossman, chair of the Department of History; Peter N. Stearns, dean of the College of Humanities and Social Science; Mark Kamlet, dean of the H. John Heinz III School of Public Policy and Management; Philip B. Hallen, president of the Maurice Falk Medical Fund; Barbara Lazarus, associate provost for Academic Projects; Everett Tademy, director, Equal Employment Opportunity office; Provost Paul Christiano, President Emeritus Richard M. Cyert; and former president Robert M. Mehrabian. At Carnegie Mellon, I am also grateful to Elaine Burrelli, administrative assistant to CAUSE, for her typing of the manuscript. Her careful work on several drafts of this book is greatly appreciated.

As always my wife, LaRue, and my brothers, sisters, nephews, and nieces represent an ongoing source of love, encouragement, and inspiration. As residents of Cincinnati, my nephew Carson Trotter III and his wife, Meredith, and their two children, Vittoria and Alexis, provided more inspiration for work on this project than they realize. In some measure, I hope that his book will enable them to understand better the connection between the old and the new Ohio Valley. Such knowledge, I hope, will also enable them to strengthen their bonds of family and community. Finally, for their unconditional confidence in LaRue and me, this book is dedicated to Aunt Velma Anderson in memory of Uncle Melvin Clarence Anderson. As residents of New Orleans near that other great river in African American life, the Mississippi, their lives and the lives of their families are also inextricably interwoven with River Jordan.

PART ONE

African Americans and the Expansion of Commercial and Early Industrial Capitalism, 1790-1860

1

African Americans, Work, and the "Urban Frontier"

African American life in the Ohio River Valley had its beginnings in the development of commercial and early industrial capitalism. While African Americans arrived with whites during the colonial period, the social changes that stimulated black population growth were unleashed by the American Revolution. Like the larger white population, however, the black population grew slowly until the 1820s, when steamboat, canal, and road-building projects transformed the region from a local distributor of agricultural and forest products to a national center of commerce and industry. While class and ethnic conflicts also punctuated these developments for whites, African Americans faced the added burdens of slavery and race. They not only faced formal bondage in early Pittsburgh and antebellum Louisville, but the legacy of slavery and racial subordination in Cincinnati and Evansville. Still, blacks in the Ohio Valley slowly gained a foothold in the economy, developed a series of creative responses to class and racial inequality, and established the social and institutional foundations for the spread of black urban communities in the wake of the Civil War and Reconstruction. In order to fully understand these changes in African American life, a perspective on the origins of Ohio Valley cities is indispensable.

African Americans and the Origins of Cities in the Ohio River Valley

Located at the confluence of the Allegheny, Monongahela, and Ohio Rivers, Pittsburgh emerged at the socioeconomic and political center of the early Ohio Valley region. It played a key role in the expanding inter- and intra-regional movement of trade, people, and ideas. Although Pittsburgh was part of the commonwealth of Pennsylvania, initial interest in the region emanated from colonial Virginia. As early as 1753, George Washington had surveyed the area for Governor George Dinwiddie and promoted the settlement of Pittsburgh "at the point." In his journal, Washington wrote: "I spent some time in viewing the rivers, and the Land in the fork; which I think extremely well situated for a Fort, as it has the absolute command of both rivers. *The Land at the point* [my italics] is 20 to 25 feet above the common surface of the water and a considerable bottom of flat, well timbered land all around it, very convenient for building."[1]

In the wake of the American Revolution, some contemporary observers believed that Pittsburgh would "never be very considerable." Others, more correctly, predicted future success. As a German traveler put it, "From its advantageous site, it must be that Pittsburgh will in the future become an important depot for the inland trade."[2] Following Washington's "discovery," the British established Fort Pitt and engaged in stiff warfare with the French and Indians. Before long, however, the British gained control of the point and set the larger spatial context for the growth of Pittsburgh as a multiethnic and increasingly multiracial city.

African Americans entered the Ohio Valley with colonial soldiers, explorers, and Native Americans. During the French and Indian wars, the Virginia Assembly provided for the enlistment of free blacks, slaves, and Amerindians. The law stipulated, however, that all such persons "shall appear without arms, and may be employed as drummers, trumpeters or pioneers, or such other servile labor, as they shall be directed to perform."[3] As early as the 1750s, George Washington enlisted slaves and free blacks in his scouting expeditions to the Ohio River. In a letter to one captain in the colonial army, Washington urged the employment of "both mulattoes and negroes . . . as pioneers or hatchet men."[4]

Over the next half century, advertisements for the sale or recapture of runaway slaves became quite common. Still, by the early 1790s, only 160 slaves lived in Allegheny County. Merchants, landowners, lawyers, ministers, elders of the church, and artisans employed a few slaves in their households, shops, and fields. According to Pittsburgh writer Hugh Henry Brackenridge, many western Pennsylvanians "held and abused slaves" but would not "for a fine cow have shaved their beards on Sunday." Even as the number of slaves increased, state legislation undercut the growth of slavery and led to the gradual emancipation of all Pennsylvania blacks. Passed in 1780, the Gradual Abolition Act outlawed the importation of

The Ohio Valley

new slaves into the commonwealth and provided that all persons born slaves after enactment of the law would be free at age twenty-eight. By 1800, according to U.S. Census figures, only ten slaves lived in the town of Pittsburgh and by 1810 all blacks in the city, about 185 persons or 3.8 percent of the total population, were free.[5]

Cincinnati developed some 450 miles downstream from Pittsburgh. Unlike Pittsburgh, however, the federal government played a key role in the early development of Cincinnati, the state, and its black population. In the Northwest Ordinance of 1787, the federal government prohibited slavery north of the Ohio River. Although migrants to the area initially settled along the Miami River, they soon discovered the advantages of the Cincinnati location. Under the leadership of John Cleves Symmes, a New Jersey-based land company spearheaded the Euro- and African American settlement of Cincinnati. The first settlers arrived in late 1788. According to Symmes, they "landed safe on a most delightful high bank of the Ohio, where they founded the town of Losantiville," i.e., "village opposite the mouth" of Licking River, which soon became Cincinnati.[6] By late January 1789, the group had erected log cabins to accommodate eleven families and twelve bachelors. During the same year, the federal government built a fort, which until it closed in 1803 played a key role in the settlement of the city. Although the *Northwest Centinel* reported a few blacks in Cincinnati before 1800, no estimates of the total are available. Indeed, as late as 1800, no blacks appeared on the city's first census returns, and, by 1810, only eighty blacks showed up in the official count. For its part, as late as 1820, Evansville reported only a dozen blacks, making up less than 1 percent of the city's small total.[7]

From Pittsburgh to the Mississippi, the Ohio River flowed almost a thousand miles. Only the "falls" at Louisville offered a major obstruction to downstream travel. Created by a fossilized coral reef that crossed the river at odd angles, the falls of the Ohio interrupted the river's flow, producing violent rapids which made travel by boat exceedingly hazardous. The river dropped nearly twenty-two feet within a distance of about two miles. Visitors frequently remarked on the violent character of the river at the falls. "The ear is stunned with the sound of rushing waters . . . and the sight of waves dashing, and foaming, and whirling among the rocks and eddies below, is grand and fearful."[8] Some observers referred to the falls as this "boiling place."[9]

Settlers moving down the Ohio River had to disembark at the falls, travel overland to another spot on the river, and resume travel beyond the rapids. Although there were several possible town sites at the falls, Louisville's position at the mouth of Beargrass Creek and its fertile rural hinterlands gave it a distinct advantage over its competitors. As one contemporary observer put it, Louisville stood "at the head of ascending and the foot of descending navigation . . . all the wealth of the western country must pass through her hands."[10]

Like blacks in Pittsburgh, African Americans entered the falls area during the colonial struggles of the mid to late eighteenth century. As early as 1751, two black men—one a slave and the other a "servant"—had traveled to the vicinity of the falls with the explorer Christopher Gist. By 1782, George Rogers Clark had established Fort Nelson at Louisville and, partly with the assistance of slaves, gradually consolidated the position of white settlers in the area. Ten years later, when Kentucky gained statehood, it approved the institution of slavery and stimulated the in-migration of slaveholding residents and black bondsmen. By 1810, Louisville's black population had increased to nearly five hundred. Thus, as slavery declined in Pittsburgh, it took on a new life in Louisville, making up over 98 percent of the total black population, which in turn comprised about one-third of the city's total.[11]

No less than for other groups, African American life was deeply embedded in the larger city-building process. Each Ohio Valley city developed early plans which later influenced the urban landscape. As early as 1764, British soldiers and settlers gave Pittsburgh its initial town plan. Laid out in four squares along the Monongahela River, the first Pittsburgh town plan established the physical context for future growth. Two decades later, the Penns of Philadelphia built upon the first plan when they laid out the entire area from the old fort at the western end of "the point" to Grant Street on the east. When the state legislature approved borough status for the city in 1794, the city again elaborated upon its original town plans.

During the first decades of the nineteenth century, the city's population largely filled out the "land at the point." Whereas only about 3 percent of the region's population resided in the urban core in 1800, Pittsburgh's urban center gained an increasing share of the region's total population. A number of towns emerged in close proximity to the city and added to the urban total. Allegheny City on the north side of the Allegheny River became the most important of these sites. Other signifi-

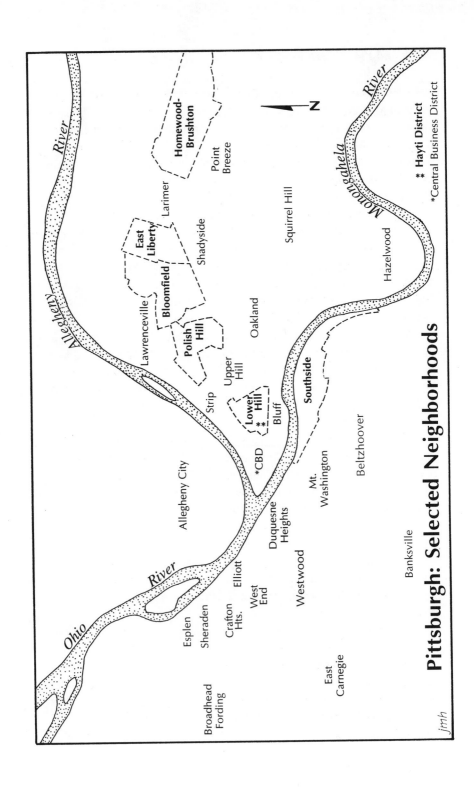

Pittsburgh: Selected Neighborhoods

Ohio River

Allegheny River

Monongahela River

N

Broadhead Fording

Esplen

Sheraden

Crafton Hts.

West End

Elliott

Westwood

Duquesne Heights

East Carnegie

Banksville

Mt. Washington

Beltzhoover

Allegheny City

CBD*

Lower Hill
**

Bluff

Strip

Lawrenceville

Upper Hill

Oakland

Polish Hill

Bloomfield

East Liberty

Shadyside

Larimer

Southside

Hazelwood

Squirrel Hill

Point Breeze

Homewood-Brushton

** Hayti District

*Central Business District

jmh

cant settlements included Birmingham and East Birmingham on the south side of the Monongahela River and Northern Liberties, Pitt Township, Oakland, Lawrenceville, and Peebles Township in the east end.[12]

Like Pittsburgh, Cincinnati's early plan and especially the river and hills shaped its early growth. Whereas Pittsburgh had its "point," Cincinnati occupied a terraced basin along the banks of the Ohio River, surrounded by several steeply rising mountains. The terrace had three interlocking levels: the Bottoms, from the river to about Third Street; the Basin, which ascended sharply from about Fifth Street for nearly five miles up the Mill Creek Valley; and the Hilltops, a chain of hills that reached over four hundred feet above the river level. During the first half of the 1800s, the population settled mainly within one-half mile of the river. Until the 1820s, this was a highly compact area that housed all activities within close proximity. Little specialization of land use or differentiation by class or ethnicity characterized this early city. Commercial, manufacturing, residential, and leisure activities clustered together near the public landing, as did the variety of people, including African Americans, who engaged in such activities.[13]

In 1784, the Court of Kentucky had surveyed and laid out the town of Louisville. A year later, the state turned the land over to the city's trustees and empowered them to divide and sell it at "the best price that can be had." Trustees ordered a new survey and, more so than other cities, soon sold nearly all available lots. By 1810, the city had little land for public parks, markets, and public buildings.[14] Like other Ohio Valley cities, Evansville would pursue a similar but belated pattern. Until the 1830s, the entire population of Vanderburgh county, Evansville included, numbered just over 2,600.[15]

Ohio River Valley cities soon became major marketing centers for agricultural and forest products from nearby rural areas. As farms expanded along the Ohio River, farmers produced larger volumes of grain crops for markets at Cincinnati, Pittsburgh, and Louisville. By supplying settlers and traders as they moved downriver from Pittsburgh to New Orleans, these cities also slowly linked the region to national and international trade. Western products, mainly from the Ohio Valley, entering the Gulf port's inland trade rose from less than $3.6 million in 1801 to $5.3 million in 1806, and to $8.0 million in 1816.[16]

Ohio Valley cities not only became processing and shipping centers for agricultural and forest products, but stimulated and housed the de-

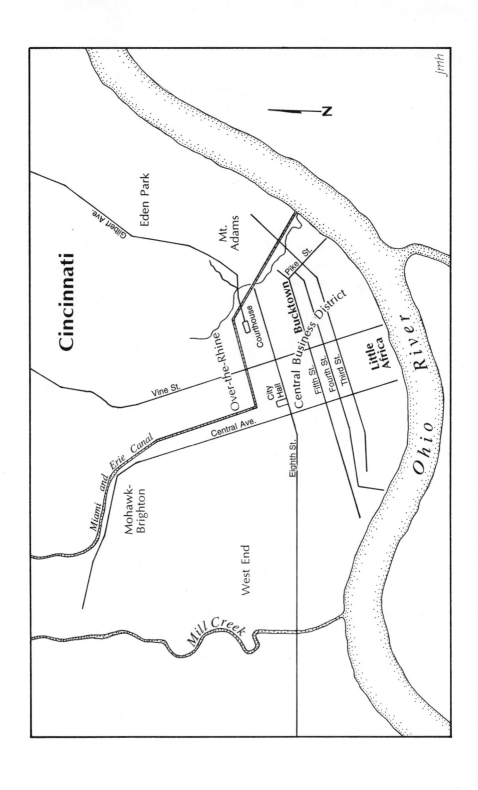

velopment of new manufacturing industries as well. Such industries supplied the growing western markets and the increasing numbers of migrants who journeyed down the Ohio River. Under the influence of merchant capitalists and nascent manufacturing elites, the cities' wharves, warehouses, boatyards, artisan shops, hauling services, and coal- and ironworks expanded. Although diverse manufactories emerged in each of the cities, Pittsburgh emerged as the leading manufacturing and commercial center before the advent of the steamboat. As early as 1792, Alsatian immigrant George Anshutz founded Pittsburgh's first iron furnace a few miles outside the city limits. A decade later, the city's rolling mills began operations, followed by nail factories and ironworks, which in turn provided an expanding market for pig iron from country furnaces. In addition, the rich energy resources of the hinterlands fueled the city's textile and glass manufactories as well as copper and brass foundries. The number of manufacturing firms increased from an estimated 163 in 1803 to 257 in 1817.[17]

The arrival of the steamboat during the 1820s opened a new chapter in the economic and social history of the Ohio River Valley. Steamboats not only increased regional trade along the Ohio, but opened the ocean-going trade via the Mississippi River and the Gulf of Mexico. The speed of these vessels lowered costs, particularly on the arduous upriver return trip, when workers had used ropes to pull and drag boats upstream at the slow rate of ten to twelve miles per day. Whereas a barge set a record of seventy-eight days for the fifteen-hundred-mile return trip from New Orleans to Cincinnati in 1811, the steamboat cut the return from New Orleans to Louisville, just ninety miles south of Cincinnati, to twenty-five days in 1817. Although a variety of problems had to be ironed out, the steamboat soon proved its superiority over the earlier flatboats and keelboats.[18]

Under the growing impact of the steamboat, Cincinnati displaced Pittsburgh as the principal city along the Ohio River. As the volume of trade passing through the city escalated, Cincinnati claimed the title "Queen City of the West." Its entrepreneurs had embarked upon their shipbuilding careers with the completion of the city's first steamer, made in 1817 for a New Orleans firm, and a second 176-ton vessel made for a local owner in 1818. Cincinnati built twelve of the seventy-one steamboats constructed before 1820, but thereafter outstripped all competitors in the number of steamboats produced. The boat- and shipyards also

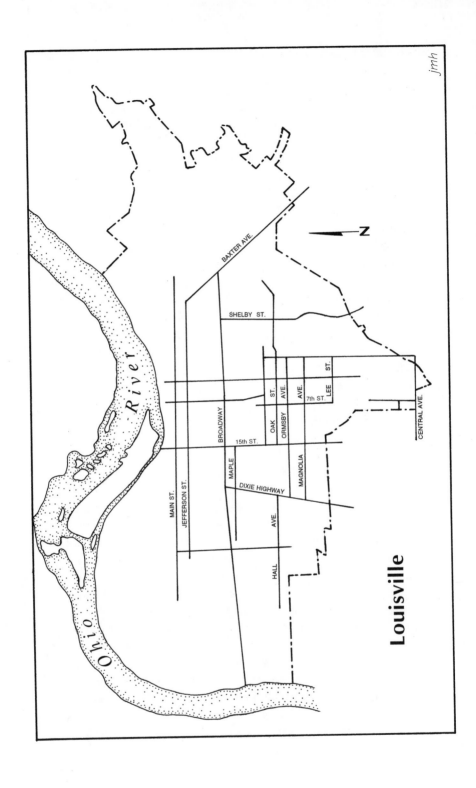

Louisville

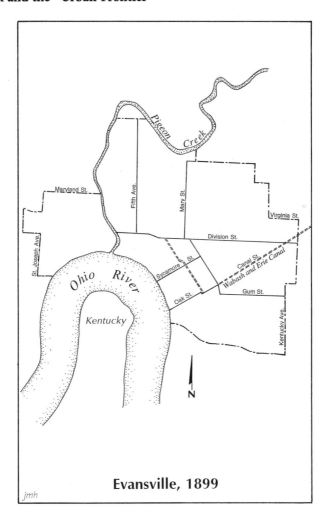

Evansville, 1899

jmh

stimulated demands for steam engines, iron foundries, rolling mills, forges, machine shops, and machine tool shops. These industries not only produced spin-offs into manufacturing of sugar mills for New Orleans sugar planters, for example, but also reinforced the city's foothold in earlier industries: flour-milling, woodworking, whiskey distilling, slaughtering, meatpacking and tanning. Indeed, by the 1840s, the city's meatpacking business gave the "Queen City" its popular image— "Porkopolis." Still by 1860, Cincinnati ranked third among the nation's industrial cities and was the leading manufacturing center in the West. Between 1841 and 1851, the value of the annual product of the city's industries rose from $17.7 million to $54.5 million, and Cincinnati ranked sixth in the hierarchy of American cities, first among cities of the West, and fourth in the nation's manufacturing output. According to an English visitor, manufacturing was transforming Cincinnati into "one of the wonders of the New World."[19]

Transportation improvements also connected Cincinnati to the Great Lakes and large eastern markets. In 1832, a series of canals connected the Miami River to Lake Erie and brought the huge Hudson River and New York City markets within the orbit of Ohio River entrepreneurs. A decade later, rising numbers of eastern investors found Cincinnati an attractive market and invested in rail lines, linking the city to St. Louis on the Mississippi and the major ports of the Atlantic seaboard via the Baltimore and Ohio. Still, throughout the antebellum period, Cincinnati faced south and received her wealth and well-being from supplying plantation owners with foodstuffs to enable them to keep their own land planted in cotton and sugar. As historian Constance McLaughlin Green put it, "The city's commercial ties with the Southern states were too old and strong to be broken by anything less than the Civil War. Her steamboats and down into the fifties flatboats too, gave her cheaper shipping than could canals or railroads of the day. Up to 1861 she remained a river city, her expanding industry strengthening and enlarging her commercial domain."[20]

Although Cincinnati emerged as the "Queen City of the West," the steamboat and other transportation innovations helped to transform the entire Ohio Valley region. In Pennsylvania, the state completed construction of the Mainline Canal in 1834, and capitalists later built numerous rail lines linking Pittsburgh to Philadelphia and other cities and regions to the east and north. By 1850, the number of industries rose to more than 750 in the city (and 1,200 in the county). The value of production from the city's manufacturing firms jumped from less than $1.0 million in 1803 to $2.6 million in 1815, and to nearly $17.0 million in 1850. Pittsburgh merchants and manufacturers not only operated within a regional area, covering western Pennsylvania, northern West Virginia, and eastern Ohio, but also increasingly exported products to national and international markets via the Ohio River to New Orleans on the Mississippi and the Gulf of Mexico.[21]

In Louisville, the number of barges and total tons of cargo steadily increased during the first two decades of the nineteenth century, but the arrival of the steamboat heightened this process. During the 1820s, the number of steamboats arriving in the city increased from 196 in 1823 to 300 in 1824 and to over 1,000 annually by 1829. The value of the city's commerce rose to $13 million. The Louisville and Portland Canal in 1830 eased travel around the falls and further stimulated the city's growth as a transshipment center. The rapid expansion of warehouses symbolized the town's growing dependence on the transfer business. Before river transport and canal building proceeded very far, however, Louisville gradually turned to railroad construction. After failure of plans to build railroad lines into Ohio and Indiana, the city looked south. In addition to building local roads in Kentucky and Tennessee, Louisville capitalists joined hands with their Nashville counterparts and built the Louisville and Nashville Railroad. By the late 1850s, the road linked the two cities and promised broader entrée into the lower South.[22]

Although the transshipment of goods and people emerged at the center of Louisville's economic development, other industries soon developed as well. During the first decade of the century, entrepreneur Richard Steele hoped to build an iron factory at the falls and take advantage of slave labor. In 1812, Paul Skidmore operated an iron foundry and made steam engines on a small scale. Three years later, the Tarascon brothers initiated a huge Merchant Manufacturing Mill, while a New England investor opened a large distillery. By 1815, the opening of the State Bank of Kentucky also signaled the city's gradual emergence as a commercial and manufacturing center. By the 1850s, Louisville had become the twelfth largest industrial center in the nation and number one in the South.[23]

Although Evansville continued to lag behind developments in Pittsburgh, Cincinnati, and Louisville, it experienced an economic "takeoff" during the 1840s and 1850s. The advent of steamboats, canal-building, and rail lines enabled the city to exploit its rural and extractive resources, particularly coal and hardwood. In 1847, the city received its charter and grew rapidly through the 1850s. By 1857, local elites established a Board of Trade. Although the city's iron foundries and flour, and lumber mills expanded, Evansville remained dependent on commerce for its economic growth.[24]

Merchants and manufacturers played key roles in the development and transformation of Ohio Valley cities. Although some scholars posit

an antagonism between commercial and early industrial capitalists, recent scholarship suggests an early and growing consonance of interests
between the two. Pittsburgh's early bankers, merchants, and manufacturers—predominantly American-born white men of English-speaking and
Scots-Irish backgrounds—were not entirely self-made men. Most had
gained business experience as part of family-owned mercantile and manufacturing establishments. As historian John Ingham notes, "practical iron
manufacturers" initiated the city's American Iron Works (later Jones &
Laughlin) but turned for capital to the merchant elites Benjamin F. Jones
and Samuel Kier, who in turn enlisted the even greater resources of merchant James Laughlin. By the 1850s, these men had class interests that
increasingly set them apart from the expanding numbers of workers that
they employed.[25]

Unlike Pittsburgh, some of Cincinnati's leading manufacturers were
people of German descent. German entrepreneurs like Martin Baum,
Albert van Stein, and others, particularly the manufacturing partnership
of Gross and Dietrich, found significant economic opportunities in the
Queen City. Moreover, according to historian Steve Ross, Cincinnati's rising manufacturing elite worked themselves up from the ranks of the
craftsmen rather than from privileged positions within an older commercial elite. A survey of the top 10 percent of the city's manufacturers in
1850 revealed that nearly 75 percent had been artisans of one kind or another. The following manufacturers, for example, had begun their careers
as journeymen: engine builders David Griffey, Amos Holadbird, and Jabez
Reynolds; furniture makers Henry Boyd, Robert Mitchell, and Frederick
Rammelsberg; soap and candle makers William Procter and James
Gamble; and clothing manufacturers Jacob Kornbluh and Sebastian
Myer.[26] Commercial and manufacturing elites also emerged at the forefront of urban development in Louisville and Evansville. One contemporary observer described Louisville's elite as "a circle, small 'tis true . . .
but within whose magic round abounds every pleasure that wealth, regu-
lated by taste, can produce."[27] While Louisville's early nineteenth century elite would resemble its Cincinnati and Pittsburgh counterparts,
dependence on slave labor would distinguish Louisville from other Ohio
Valley cities. When entrepreneurs Richard Steele and his brothers planned
to build an iron mill in the city, they selected Louisville because of special advantages "in working with slaves."[28]

As elsewhere in early- to mid-nineteenth century America, signifi-

cant demographic and cultural changes influenced the rise of commercial and nascent industrialism in the Ohio Valley. Migration from the old
northeastern states and the rapid influx of European immigrants stimulated tremendous population growth. Between 1820 and 1850,
Pittsburgh's population increased from an estimated 8,000 to 46,000;
Cincinnati's rose from just over 9,600 to 115,000, Louisville's increased
from a little over 4,000 to 43,200, and Evansville's jumped from less than
2,000 to over 11,400. Although natural increase and annexation of outlying territory added to the population over time, most of the increase
came from rural-to-urban migration and immigration from overseas.[29]

Along with the acceleration of white migration from the northeastern states, the rapid influx of European immigrants from abroad precipitated growing ethnic diversity. During the 1830s and 1840s, rising
numbers of immigrants came from Ireland and Germany, supplemented
by people of Welsh, Scots-Irish, Swiss, and French descent. By 1850, German immigrants increased from negligible numbers to between 10 and
15 percent of Pittsburgh's total, while the Irish increased by more than
ten thousand and made up about 21 percent of the total. In Cincinnati,
the German-born population increased from only 5 percent in 1820 to
an estimated 15 to 20 percent of the total by the 1850s; by 1860, over 40
percent of Cincinnatians were of German birth or German parentage.
Supplementing the expansion of the German population was the influx
of people from Ireland. Rising to nearly 12 percent of the city's total between 1850 and 1860, the Irish brought the city's immigrants or persons
with immigrant parents to well over 50 percent of the total. Louisville
also attracted a significant number of immigrants of Irish and German
descent. By 1850, immigrants made up about 33 percent of the city's total population, much higher than most southern cities. At the same time,
immigrants from Germany played a growing role in the economy of
Evansville.[30]

The rapid growth of the region's immigrant population paralleled
as well as complicated the development of a huge predominantly white,
landless, wage-earning proletariat. Although the process would vary over
time and from industry to industry, by 1850 a variety of firms experienced increasing size, capitalization, and use of white manual laborers as
wage-earners. Commercial transactions, industrial production, and transportation along the cities' waterways, canals, and roads required expanding numbers of workers. In Pittsburgh, the number of industrial workers

rose from an estimated 300 in 1803 to nearly 3,000 in 1826 to nearly 8,900 in the city (and 15,017 in the county) in 1850. An estimated 33 percent of the city's white male workforce occupied unskilled jobs, 30 percent worked in skilled positions, and 8.7 percent were small manufacturers, including some self-employed artisans. By the mid-1840s, Cincinnati counted nearly 110 industrial firms employing nearly 1,300 workers producing an annual product worth over a million dollars. In Cincinnati, between 1826 and 1840, the number of employees in commerce and transportation rose sharply from about 1,300 to 3,800, but the number engaged in manufacturing increased most dramatically, from 3,000 to 10,287. By 1850, Cincinnati employed 29,401 workers in its shops and factories, almost equaling the combined total for Pittsburgh, Louisville, St. Louis, and Chicago (30,147).[31]

Although white women worked mainly as domestic servants and laundresses, industrialization gradually transformed their role in the economy. The growth of the garment industry brought growing numbers of white women and children into the workplace. In Cincinnati, by 1850, women made up 60.2 percent of clothing employees, 52.3 percent of textile operatives, and 16.2 percent of boot and shoe factory workers. In Pittsburgh, as historian Maureen Greenwald notes, although the iron and steel industries dominated the manufacturing economy, the employment of women in the production of cotton cloth and clothing goods "made women a very important part of the manufacturing sector as a whole."[32] By 1850, the Pittsburgh cotton mills employed an estimated fifteen hundred people, mainly single Irish women whose incomes played an important role in the livelihood of their families.

During the early nineteenth century, most manufacturing firms were small, averaging little more than two to three workers per firm. Organized mainly around the traditional craft structure of masters, journeymen, and apprentices, these firms offered white journeymen and apprentices board, opportunities for interaction with the master craftsmen and their families, and substantial hope for proprietorship. As firms increased in size, became more highly capitalized, and depended increasingly on wage laborers, however, white journeymen found it more difficult to move up the hierarchy and become owners of property and small shops. As this process unfolded, master craftsmen and manufacturers gradually developed a new class consciousness which increasingly set them apart from their workers. In Cincinnati, for example, they gradually transformed the previously multiclass Ohio Mechanic Institute into an arm of industry rather than one of labor and industry. At the same time, earlier more intimate relationships between employers and employees gradually gave way to more impersonal and conflicting relationships. The earlier pattern of housing and boarding journeymen and apprentices with the master's family broke down; workers now paid for board on a cash basis and negotiated a higher wage in order to find housing on their own.[33]

As their numbers increased and their status deteriorated, white workers became increasingly articulate in their own interests. From the early nineteenth century on, such workers gradually formed unions in the clothing, textile, and iron industries. In Pittsburgh, by the late 1830s, white workers had organized unions in some sixteen different crafts. These unionizing activities culminated in the 1850s with the formation of the Sons of Vulcan by iron puddlers. Workers used their unions to make increasing demands on their employers. As early as 1804, for example, shoe workers struck for higher wages and by 1809 had negotiated a wage scale with employers, who later initiated criminal conspiracy proceedings against their workers. In 1848 and again in 1850, workers struck the city's large cotton textile and iron mills.[34]

Despite the growing homogenization of life in the working class and the growth of class consciousness, ethnic differences punctuated the proletarianization process. According to a sample of two hundred Pittsburgh workers from the U.S. manuscript census of 1850, nearly 70 percent were immigrants. The largest percentage came from Ireland (33.5), the next highest from Germany (25), and the lowest from the British Isle (10.0) and other places (1.0). In Cincinnati during the 1840s and 1850s, immigrant men and women increased from 35.3 to nearly 69 percent of the total labor force.[35] Ethnicity not only marked the origins of the city's industrial workers but influenced their position in the expanding urban labor force. The Germans and the Irish occupied the lowest rungs of the early industrial ladder. As historian Nora Faires suggests, in economic terms Germans and Irish immigrants shared a similar status—few owned substantial amounts of property and most worked as manual laborers. Even so, Germans faced somewhat less economic discrimination from American-born white employers and gained more access to skilled jobs than their Irish counterparts. Such inequality precipitated conflicts that

fragmented the working class along ethnic lines. Ethnic class conflicts were
by no means confined to the workplace. They spilled over into the larger
residential, institutional, social, and political life of the region.[36]

To be sure, certain technological innovations helped to link diverse
parts of Ohio river cities. In the 1840s, for example, introduction of the
omnibus in Pittsburgh offered commuter passenger service to different
parts of the city and facilitated spatial integration of the outlying areas.
As early as 1833, officials divided Pittsburgh into four wards. Four years
later, the city added Northern Liberties and created a fifth ward. Between
1845 and 1846, the annexation of Pitt Township added four more wards.
By annexing adjacent territory, Pittsburgh increased its land mass from
a relatively small number of acres during the early nineteenth century to
1,130 in 1846. Similarly, as historian Zane Miller notes, "technological
innovations in the means of intracity transportation" also constituted the
dynamics behind "a spate of annexations" in Cincinnati by the 1850s.[37]
Cincinnati increased from about one square mile in 1800 to six square
miles in 1860. Although Ohio Valley cities increased their territorial
boundaries, they remained by later standards walking or pedestrian cities. Most people walked to and from their residences to places of work
and business. Work and residence, elites and workers, immigrants and
the American-born, all remained closely interlinked in a relatively small
area.

Despite the tight-knit spatial structure of early nineteenth-century
cities, ethnic and class segregation nonetheless slowly emerged in the late
antebellum period. Merchants, manufacturers and bankers not only occupied the best spots near the cities' business and government establishments, but gradually took advantage of commuter service to outlying
areas, while the working classes and poor clustered in the least desirable
spaces near the central city. In Cincinnati, the principal commercial and
manufacturing establishments occupied the bank and terrace closest to
the Ohio River. To the rear of the terrace and taking up parts of the central sections of the Basin proper were the expanding retail and financial
districts of the city, flanked by the city's two major elite neighborhoods
on the east and west. At the same time, growing numbers of elite residents moved to the Hilltop area well beyond the city limit, taking advantage of emerging streetcar commuter service. Most of the city's
American-born white Protestants resided in "a broad circle" just beyond
the central sector. Beyond this "native" section, according to one histo-

rian, lived "the submerged classes," including the Germans who lived in an area called "Over-the-Rhine" at the foot of the northern hills. Irish and African Americans inhabited the Ohio River bottoms, close to the wholesale houses and factories.[38]

Irish Catholics, Germans, and Jews also had their own relatively distinct settlement patterns. In Pittsburgh, Irish Catholics settled in three major areas: close to the developing Central Business District (CBD), near St. Paul's Cathedral; in the Hill District, a decidedly poor area and home for single male common laborers, including African Americans; and in the lower Strip District, where Irish industrial workers lived close to the English, Scottish, and Welsh workers. While the Germans concentrated primarily in the eastern wards of Allegheny City, they also clustered in the lower Strip District and Lawrenceville along the Allegheny River and the Uptown area along the Monongahela River. German Jews also lived in Allegheny City, in the area called "Dutchtown," but they concentrated around the CBD in Pittsburgh and slowly exited Allegheny City over time.[39]

The community life and politics of Ohio Valley cities were sharply stratified along ethnic and class as well as racial lines. In Cincinnati, for example, as elites formed their own voluntary organizations and abandoned earlier cross-class organizations like firehouses and taverns, workers established their own taverns, pool halls, bowling alleys, theaters, and voluntary associations. At the same time, in addition to the development of class-based organizations, each group built separate ethnic institutions and sought to influence the city in their own interests. Such organizations not only excluded blacks, but limited access to other white ethnic groups as well. In Pittsburgh, English Protestants founded the Presbyterian Church, Germans founded Catholic as well as Protestant Lutheran and Methodist churches, Irish Roman Catholics created a Catholic parish centered around St. Paul's Cathedral, and German Jews founded Rodef Shalon and Tree of Life. A similar pattern emerged in Cincinnati, where Jews established their first congregation in 1824, the city's Catholics created a new diocese in 1821, and Protestants established nearly a half dozen churches as early as 1815.[40]

Ethnic conflicts also shaped municipal politics, schools, and the struggle for city services. Local politicians often subordinated class issues, like the deleterious impact of early industrialization on workers' lives, to a series of highly emotionally charged cultural questions: Catholicism versus Protestantism, Sunday closing laws, temperance, and language and Bible reading in schools. In Cincinnati, such campaigns often brought radical workingmen advocates like H. T. Ogden together with conservative manufacturers like Miles and Greenwood. Formed in Philadelphia in 1844, the Cincinnati chapter of the OUAM (Order of United American Mechanics) opened in 1847 claiming as members "true born sons of America." The organization aimed to protect members from the "degradation brought upon us by the constant influx of . . . the pauper labor of Europe." Such sentiment sometimes culminated in violence. In the election of 1855, for example, a mob of three hundred to four hundred native-born whites attacked Germans in the Over-the-Rhine section, killing two people and wounding others. Ethnic hostilities also spread into the Irish community.[41]

Despite intense class and ethnic fragmentation, diverse ethnic and class groups used notions of white superiority, citizenship, and republicanism to help bridge social cleavages and mitigate the effect of conflict among whites. According to Steve Ross, under the growing impact of nascent industrialism after 1830, many white Cincinnatians sought to alter the role and uses of republican ideology to defuse rising class conflict. Proponents of new republicanism argued that the old republicanism, which emphasized landownership and farming as the bedrocks of virtue, no longer reflected the reality of growing numbers of landless American citizens who sought their independence as producers in the nation's shops, stores, and manufactories. The virtuous republic could now inhere in manufacturing and commerce as well as the Jeffersonian yeomanry. In short, spokesmen for the new virtuous republic "skillfully combined liberal capitalism, the producer ideology, and local republican rhetoric to create a new republican synthesis which stressed the cooperation of producers, eschewed class conflict, and held that the inequalities which plagued society were merely temporary."[42]

Although the new civic elites divided the society into producing and nonproducing classes, they defined the producing classes broadly enough to include almost all white men. In their view, merchants, clerks, clergymen, physicians, lawyers, farmers, and artisans were producers who added to the commonwealth. Accenting the role of producers, republican ideology maintained that the system of production, distribution, or exchange was not inherently unjust. Only greed, excessive individual acquisition, corruption, and monopolies undermined the commonwealth. Thus, only the wealthiest white landed people, who lived on inherited wealth, remained outside the purview of virtue. In this way, spokesmen reconciled commercial and early industrial capitalism with a producer ideology that emphasized just reward for labor or for those who produced "something useful."[43]

According to the new ideology, white men not only played roles as producers, they also filled the equally important role of citizen. As citizens in a larger polity, proponents argued, white men could rectify imperfections in the economic sphere. By defining the political sphere as a classless arena for the promotion of the common good, the civic elites used the polity as a vehicle to unite white men as equal citizens in the interest of the general welfare. Thus, unlike Europe or even parts of the eastern United States, white workers often articulated their faith in the state as an instrument of social justice. Although republican ideology more often empowered white elites at workers' expense, it nonetheless facilitated white racial solidarity and reinforced the racial subordination of African Americans. It was within this broader context of class and ethnic fragmentation and solidarity that the African American experience in the Ohio Valley unfolded.

2

Disfranchisement, Racial Inequality, and the Rise of Black Urban Communities

Under the impact of commercial and early industrial capitalism, the African American population in the Ohio Valley gradually expanded. Although they had entered the region during the late colonial era, blacks faced numerous difficulties gaining a foothold in the economy and society of the area. From the outset, white political leaders, employers, and workers erected barriers that hampered the migration, employment, and settlement of blacks in Ohio Valley cities. Yet, by the 1850s, African Americans would gain a significant but precarious place in the urban economy, establish all-black institutions, and launch new movements to secure their own freedom as well as the liberation of slaves in the South. A close look at the obstacles that they faced reveals the depths of their achievements during the antebellum era.

Migration, Work, and the Growth of the Antebellum Black Population

African Americans confronted debilitating ideological and legal constraints on their access to the job market in Ohio Valley cities. Rooted deeply in the social forces unleashed by the intensification of capitalist development, anti-black sentiment and social practices emerged above and below the Ohio River. In Louisville, as in other parts of the South, whites described free blacks as "lazy, worthless, and less fortunate than slaves."[1] Northern journalists and political leaders also referred to free blacks and slaves alike as being "as depraved and ignorant a set of people as any of their kind."[2] On one occasion, for example, the Ohio legislature reported free blacks as "more idle and vicious than slaves" and urged strong measures to prevent their migration into the state. Similarly, an Indiana Supreme Court Judge opposed the migration of what he called, "a low, ignorant, degraded multitude of free blacks." The free black, the Indiana Colonization Society argued, "adds nothing to the strength, and little to the wealth" of the state and nation.[3] As nonslaveholding whites moved into the territories in rising numbers, they were exceedingly hostile to slavery. They believed that the use of slaves would spawn a large free black population that would in turn compete with whites for land and other resources. Furthermore, according to Northern whites, Southerners released their most troublesome and unproductive blacks onto the Northwest territory. Thus, antislavery sentiment, intertwined with antiblack beliefs, hampered the in-migration of free blacks.

Although the Northwest Ordinance prohibited slavery north of the Ohio River, the state constitutions and laws of Ohio and Indiana contained discriminatory provisions against free blacks. In 1804, the Ohio legislature passed a law requiring free blacks and mulattoes to provide proof of their freedom upon entering the state. In 1807, the state intensified such restrictions by prohibiting free blacks and mulattoes from settling in the state unless they posted a $500 bond to guarantee their ability to support themselves.[4]

The Indiana legislature passed an even harsher series of measures against free blacks. In 1815, Indiana passed a law imposing a $300 annual poll tax on all adult black and mulatto men. In 1831, the state required free blacks to register and post bond to guarantee "good behavior" and viable employment against becoming "public charges."[5] In 1851, such antiblack sentiment culminated in the adoption of a new Indiana state constitution, which barred blacks from settlement altogether. According to Article 13, "no negro or mulatto shall come into, or settle in the State, after the adoption of this constitution."[6] For its part, in 1818, Kentucky prohibited the immigration of free blacks into the state from elsewhere. In 1834, the state also passed a law requiring free blacks to post bond in order to remain in the state.[7]

A variety of extralegal forms of intimidation, including the use of violence, reinforced legislative enactments. Although only the Southern states passed curfew laws requiring that free blacks leave the city streets by 9:00 or 10:00 at night, Northern states and cities routinely enforced such restrictions and curfews informally. Additionally, when a group of

white Ohioans met a group of free blacks from the South and forced them
to return, Congressman William Sawyer requested three cheers for the
whites who resisted black migration. He also predicted that white men
would arm themselves all along the Ohio River to prevent the influx of
blacks.[8] On another occasion, Sawyer postulated that, "The United States
were designed by the God in Heaven to be governed and inhabited by
the Anglo-Saxon race alone."[9] By the 1850s, according to another Ohio
Valley legislator, both north and south of the Ohio River the "prejudice
against the Negro [was] worse than it [had] been, and it [was] idle to sup-
pose that this sentiment [would] ever decrease as long as the two races
remained together."[10]

Despite stiff restrictions on their efforts to migrate into the region,
gain work, and settle down, African Americans slowly gained a foothold.
Similar to whites, expanding job opportunities attracted free black men
and women to Ohio Valley cities. Between 1820 and 1850, Pittsburgh's
black population rose from 286 to 1,959 (2,525, including Allegheny City),
Cincinnati's from 433 to 3,237, and Louisville's from 1,124 to 6,970.
Vanderburgh County's black population, mainly Evansville, also slowly
increased from 12 in 1820 to 230 in 1850 (See Table 1).[11]

As elsewhere, on the eve of the Civil War, Ohio Valley blacks were
disproportionately mulattoes and women. The population reflected the
dynamics of interracial sex, particularly between white men and black
women. While available statistics suggest a somewhat lower ratio of mulattoes to blacks in Louisville and Evansville, mulattoes made up well over
50 percent of the black population in Pittsburgh (74 percent), Allegheny
City (60 percent), and Cincinnati (54 percent). The sex ratio was about
even in Cincinnati (1.07), but disproportionately female in Louisville
(1.20), Pittsburgh (1.10), and Evansville (1.20). While the tendency of
some Southern masters to manumit their children by slave women and
assist their resettlement elsewhere partly accounts for this phenomenon,
it is only part of the story.[12]

As the so-called "Cotton Kingdom" expanded during the first third
of the nineteenth century, Southern blacks, both slave and free, faced increasing restrictions on their humanity, which fueled the northward migration of fugitives and free blacks. As early as 1806, in the aftermath of
the Haitian Revolution, Virginia passed a law requiring any slave set free
after May of that year to leave the state or face reenslavement. In the wake
of Denmark Vesey's slave plot in 1822 and Nat Turner's rebellion in 1831,

Southern whites tightened restrictions on free blacks and slaves. By 1850, nearly three-quarters of Cincinnati's black population came from the slaveholding states, mainly Virginia and Kentucky, which contributed well over 50 percent of the total. Although most blacks came to Pittsburgh from outlying rural and urban areas within the state, a sizable minority, 25 to 28 percent, migrated from the Upper South states of Virginia and Maryland. Evansville's small black population originated in rural Kentucky and Tennessee, supplemented by Deep South states and in-migration from other parts of Indiana. In Louisville, although the majority of the blacks were born in the South, nearly one-third came from other Southern states, particularly Virginia, the Carolinas, and Maryland.[13]

Contemporary observers frequently commented on the lowly place of black men and women in the region's workforce. In 1815, Cincinnati physician Dr. Daniel Drake described blacks as "disciplined to laborious occupations" and "prone to the performance of light and menial drudgery."[14] Another observer, a local editor, believed that the "evils of slavery ... infected" Cincinnati and relegated blacks to "certain kinds" of labor "despised as being the work of slaves."[15] In 1827, a black visitor described his disappointment upon arriving in the city: "I thought upon coming to a free state like Ohio I would find every door thrown open to receive me, but from the treatment I received by the people generally, I found it little better than in Virginia. . . . I found every door was closed against the colored man in a free state, excepting the jails and penitentiaries."[16] Although some white abolitionists encouraged the employment of black artisans, blacks repeatedly complained, "We have among us carpenters, plasterers, masons, etc., whose skills as workers is confessed and yet they find no employment not even among [white] friends."[17] During the 1830s, a black cabinetmaker lost his job when white workmen threw down their tools and refused to work with a black man.[18] By 1850, the percentage of black men holding jobs as craftsmen, including carpenters, tailors, blacksmiths, masons, plasterers, coopers, and shoemakers, stood at an estimated 13.2 percent in Louisville, 8.2 percent in Cincinnati, and 3.9 percent in Pittsburgh (minus Allegheny City). Even fewer African Americans gained jobs in business and the professions as teachers, physicians, and lawyers. Among blacks listed in entrepreneurial pursuits, most were listed as peddlers, traders, hucksters, market men, dealers, and so on, all at the lowest rung of the mercantile ladder.[19]

As whites restricted African American access to the skilled trades,

Table 1. African American Population in Ohio Valley Cities, 1800-1850

	1800		1810		1820		1830		1840		1850	
	No.	%	No.	%	No.	%	No.	%	No	%	No.	%
Pittsburgh	102	6.5	185	3.8	286	3.9	473	3.7	710	3.3	1,959	4.2
Cincinnati	20	2.6	82	3.2	433	4.4	1,090	4.3	2,240	4.8	3,237	2.8
Louisville	77	21.4	495	36.4	1124	28.0	2,638	25.5	4,049	19.0	6,970	16.1
Evansville*	---		---		12	0.6	48	1.8	112	1.8	230	2.0

Source: Adapted from Leonard P. Curry, *The Free Black in Urban America 1800-1850* (Chicago: Univ. of Chicago Press, 1981), pp. 245-46.
*Vanderburgh County

business, and professional pursuits, blacks took jobs as day laborers and domestic servants in rising numbers. In Cincinnati, by the late antebellum years, five occupations—boatman, barber, cook, laborer, and waiter—claimed 66 percent of the black male workforce. Similarly, by 1850, nearly 70 percent of Pittsburgh's African American men worked as day laborers, coachmen, waiters, whitewashers, and servants. In Louisville, nearly 60 percent of black men worked in jobs defined as unskilled, semiskilled, and personal service, while Evansville's small black population had 85 percent of its numbers in such jobs. In each city, black women gained employment primarily as housekeepers, washerwomen, and seamstresses.[20]

While Louisville also used slaves and free blacks as janitors, laborers, handymen, and household servants, the line between male and female labor as well as child and adult labor blurred considerably in "the city at the falls." Louisville employers regularly advertised for slaves, whom they rented, leased, and owned. In one ad, a Louisville firm sought "100 women and boys for brick-yards, draymen, etc., 40 men and boys for ropewalks, 40 men and boys for hotel waiters, and 50 boys and girls for tobacco stemmeries."[21] Louisville not only employed blacks in general labor jobs, but as skilled workers, including carpenters, mechanics, and brick masons. In 1838, a Louisville owner reported a profit of $636 from the rental of three skilled slaves. Louisville's free blacks, like slaves, also worked in a variety of occupations, including skilled crafts; but unlike slaves, free blacks invariably worked at lower wages and in less skilled positions than their free white and black slave counterparts.[22]

Yet, free blacks were not entirely victimized by such work. Ohio River blacks often took such jobs and challenged white rhetoric about their "improvidence," "depravity," and "ignorance." African Americans not only used such work as a route to their own freedom, but as a vehicle for securing the freedom of loved ones. As early as 1834, a Cincinnati census revealed that an estimated 1,129 of the city's blacks had known slavery. Well over a third had purchased their own freedom at a cost of $215,522, or about $450 per person. Others reported working and saving to purchase family members and friends. According to the Reverend Charles B. Roy, a black New York minister and newspaper editor, these black men and women had the "proper materials in their character to become industrious, economical, and reputable citizens."[23]

Race, Public Policy, and Civil Rights

As elsewhere in commercial and early industrial America, African Americans not only faced restrictions on their role as producers; they also confronted constraints on their access to citizenship. As white men from diverse ethnic backgrounds gained the franchise and participated in an expanding democratic polity, African Americans faced an accumulating series of legal and extralegal barriers on where they could live, acquire public accommodations, seek social services, secure an education, and obtain justice before the law. By the second half of the early nineteenth century, antiblack sentiment and social practices gained increasing expression in disfranchisement legislation, an organized movement to rid the region and nation of all free blacks, and the eruption of violent attacks on the black community itself. To be sure, as discussed in Chapter 1, significant class and ethnic conflicts shaped the experiences of Ohio Valley whites. Yet, over time, white elites, workers, and various nationality groups increasingly adopted notions of white superiority and republicanism. They used these ideas as mechanisms for creating white racial solidarity and holding the line on the struggles of African Americans for full citizenship.

Closely related to efforts to bar blacks from the region, state laws curtailed African American access to courts of law, legislative assemblies, education, and the franchise. By the 1830s, Ohio Valley states had blurred the legal distinction between slaves and free blacks. Indiana and Ohio prohibited free blacks from testifying in courts against whites, serving in the militia, voting, and, in the case of Indiana, marrying across racial lines. In 1839, the Ohio legislature redefined the right of petition as a privilege for free blacks, proclaiming that blacks and mulattoes "who may be residents within the State, have no constitutional right to present their petitions to the General Assembly for any purpose whatsoever, and that any reception of such petitions on the part of the General Assembly is a mere act of privilege or policy and not imposed by any expressed or implied power of the constitution."[24]

Ohio modified its "black laws" in 1849. It allowed blacks to attend separate schools and testify against whites in court, but still denied blacks legal residence and the right to vote.[25] In 1837-38, the Pennsylvania constitutional convention restricted voting to white males, twenty-one years of age and older. Until then, African Americans voted in Pittsburgh and elsewhere in the state. Enemies of black suffrage buttressed their case with the decision of a Bucks County Court of Quarter Sessions, which held that "a negro in Pennsylvania had not the right of suffrage."[26]

The line between freedom and bondage was even less distinct in Kentucky. Free blacks gained the right to vote in the constitution of 1792. Seven years later, however, the state constitution curtailed their rights considerably, applying much of the state's slave code to free blacks, who, like slaves, were subject to death for crimes like manslaughter, arson, rebellion, and rape of a white woman. Unlike free whites, free blacks were also subject to the whip "well laid on" their bare backs; they could not testify in court against whites in capital cases; and, like slaves, they faced the slave patrols, which regularly searched their quarters without warrants.[27] More so than blacks north of the Ohio, Louisville's free blacks also had to carry their "free papers" at all times. Otherwise, they could easily slip back into bondage.

Legal and extralegal practices also limited African American access to housing, public accommodations, and social services. As early as 1842, Cincinnati's white residents mobilized to prohibit blacks and mulattoes "from purchasing or holding real estate" within the city limits.[28] Throughout the early to mid-nineteenth century, African Americans lived in widely dispersed neighborhoods, near whites from a variety of ethnic and nationality backgrounds. Yet, by the late antebellum years, they faced increasing segregation in certain sections of the city. In Pittsburgh, for example, blacks clustered in a contiguous area, known as the "Hayti" district, which covered parts of the Third, Sixth, and Seventh wards, near the CBD. The city's index of dissimilarity, a statistical measure of segregation by race, increased from 10.2 percent in 1820 to 46.5 percent in 1850.[29]

In Cincinnati, most blacks lived in a waterfront area called "little Africa." Two and a half decades later, they had moved beyond Fifth and Sycamore Streets on the East End to an area disparagingly called "Bucktown." These areas represented the most dilapidated low-rent areas in the city. According to Leonard Curry, one of every fourteen blacks occupied alley dwellings. Still, landlords made extraordinary profits from free blacks, who faced restrictions on their access to housing elsewhere in the city. In 1830, one journalist highlighted the interracial mixture of the neighborhood and the existence of housing exploitation in the area: "Heaven preserve the shanties . . . and supply proprietors with tenants

from whom the rent can be screwed, without respect to color or character."[30]

By 1850, Cincinnati blacks inhabited a variety of clusters on the edge
and in the center of town. According to historians Henry Louis Taylor
and Vicky Dula, Cincinnati's antebellum African American community
occupied 106 clusters, i.e., two or more families living in the same dwell-
ing with another African American family, next door to another black
family, or a few doors away from other black households.[31] While the size
of clusters varied greatly, the average contained five households and
twenty-seven people. In each cluster, however, African Americans shared
space with white neighbors of different ethnic and class backgrounds:
Irish and German workers in the East End Factory and Central Waterfront Districts; middleclass, American-born whites and Germans in the
Central Core; and Germans in the Over-the-Rhine area. Out of eleven
wards, well over 50 percent of the city's African American population resided in adjoining sections of the First, Fourth, and Ninth. Within this
area, over 30 percent of blacks inhabited the area straddling the line between the First and Ninth wards. As a result of some dispersal from the
1830s on, however, the index of dissimilarity dropped from 43.9 in 1830
to 37.5 in 1850.[32]

In Louisville, free blacks lived intermingled with household slaves in
an increasingly segregated enclave. The core black neighborhood emerged
in a four-block area between Ninth, Chestnut, Eleventh, and Walnut
streets. Along with five adjacent blocks, this area accounted for 25 percent of the city's free black population. Conversely, most of Evansville's
small black population clustered near the waterfront, "between the mouth
of Pigeon Creek and Main Street."[33] As we will see, although whites may
have referred to the major black concentrations as "Bucktown," "Little
Africa," "Hayti," and other pejorative terms of the day, blacks also recognized those areas as centers of black institutions as well as residence and
work. According to historians Taylor and Dula, it was the emergence of
black institutions in these areas that helped to focus subsequent community-building activities of African Americans and gave an otherwise widely
dispersed black population a sense of cohesion, solidarity, and identity.
As they put it, "This clustering of institutions created a 'commons' for
black Cincinnati during the pre-ghetto era. The commons served as a fo-
cal point of social interaction for blacks."[34]

Closely interconnected with the growth of residential segregation were increasing constraints on African American access to public accommodations, social services, and education. Restaurants, theaters, hotels, and other public accommodations routinely barred African Americans or served them on a segregated and unequal basis, but discriminatory educational policies proved most damaging.[35] In 1834, Pennsylvania passed its Public Education Act, which established a system of common schools for the entire state and required school districts to establish schools for educating all school-age children when petitioned to do so by parents, guardians, or friends of the school-age population. In Pittsburgh, several wards soon established schools for white children, but none for blacks. Although the law itself was silent on the question of black education, only during the 1850s, following protests from the black community, would the state legislature establish segregated schools for blacks and whites. The law required the establishment of a black school in areas where twenty or more black students resided.[36]

Like Pennsylvania, when the Ohio legislature authorized tax levies for public education in 1825, it was silent on blacks. By 1829, however, when Cincinnati established its public school system, a new state law forbade blacks from attending public schools, but exempted them from the school tax levy. In 1847, the state supreme court ruled that children who were more than half white could attend the public schools, but only persistent protests by black leaders led to the establishment of separate schools for black children, paid for by black taxpayers and governed by a black board of directors elected by blacks. Still, it took a state supreme court ruling to force Cincinnati officials to comply. Even then, the city resisted enforcement; only in 1858 did the city's first black public school open its doors. Thus, as late as the 1850s, when nearly 72 percent of the city's white school-age children attended school, only about 38 percent of black children were so enrolled. Custom and law also excluded blacks or relegated them to segregated and unequal access to education in Kentucky and Indiana. Although Kentucky law permitted the education of slaves and free blacks, when Louisville established public schools in the 1820s, it excluded blacks. For its part, Indiana excluded blacks from its public school laws of 1852 and 1855.[37]

Racism gained its most powerful expression in organized efforts to rid the region and nation of free people of color. Formed in 1816, the American Colonization Society (ACS) symbolized the movement to remove free blacks from the country. Branches of the organization soon spread throughout the Ohio Valley. Although its constitution advocated "voluntary recolonization" of blacks in Africa, ACS members believed that blacks and whites could not peacefully coexist as free people on American soil. Moreover, according to some of its spokesmen, the removal of free blacks from the U.S. represented a viable program of racial uplift for African peoples on the continent. New World ex-slaves would presumably bring democratic institutions to Africa and open up the continent for American "civilization," commerce, and industries.[38]

In September 1826, influential religious, business, and professional people formed the Pittsburgh chapter of the American Colonization Society. The local organization remained active for twelve to fifteen years, declined, and then resurfaced in 1836. The initial roster of officers included Henry Baldwin, a Democratic lawyer, president; the Reverend Robert Bruce, pastor of the First Associate Presbyterian Church; the Reverend Elisha P. Swift, pastor of the Second Presbyterian Church; the Reverend John Black, pastor of the Reformed Presbyterian Church; the Reverend Charles Avery, the cotton mill owner; Rev. Joseph Stockton, pastor and first principal of the Pittsburgh Academy; Walter Forward, attorney and state representative; and Neville B. Craig, editor of the *Pittsburgh Gazette*, vice president. During its revival, Neville Craig pledged $500 for its support; Benjamin F. and James Bakewell, Pittsburgh glass manufacturers, donated $50; and Baird, Leavitt, and Company pledged $100.[39]

Although the colonization society idea persisted throughout the antebellum era, it declined by the 1840s, as the abolitionist and antislavery movements gained momentum. As late as 1852, however, some white Pittsburghers urged the federal government to use surplus revenue to recolonize free blacks in Africa. In other words, as the city opened its doors to growing numbers of immigrants from Ireland and Germany, it sought to reverse the flow of Africans and their descendants. The expulsion of free blacks also gained support in Louisville, Cincinnati, and Evansville. The editor of the *Evansville Daily Journal* argued that colonization was the only means by which to make the ex-slave's freedom "compatible with his happiness and best interests."[40]

The same racist sentiment that underlay efforts to secure a peaceful and voluntary removal of free blacks led others to adopt violent methods to secure the same ends. In 1834, a white mob entered the "Hayti" district of Pittsburgh and threatened residents with violence. A decade later, a white mob attacked members of a black band after a performance at the Temperance Ark in Allegheny City. An abolitionist paper, the *Spirit of Liberty Weekly,* blamed the incident on "alcohol and a deep-seated hatred" for black people. In Louisville, the patrols regularly conducted midnight raids on the homes of free blacks and threatened inhabitants with bodily harm if they did not leave the city. When free black homeowners complained of such attacks, authorities advised them to "leave the state."[41] In Evansville between July and early August of 1857, a mob attacked the small black settlement on two separate occasions, forcing several blacks out of the city.[42]

The most destructive incidence of violence broke out in Cincinnati. In the Queen City, African Americans faced riots in 1829, 1836, and 1841. On 22 August 1829, whites complained that the Black Laws were not being enforced. Following a ward election that revolved around these issues, the township trustees announced their intention to enforce the restrictive laws. The city's black population appealed for delay in the enforcement effort. According to one black who later left the city, "If the act is enforced, we, the poor sons of Aethiopia, must take shelter where we can find it. . . . If we cannot find it in America, where we were born and spent all our days, we must beg it elsewhere."[43]

White citizens became impatient with apparent delays and launched an attack on the black community. Nearly three hundred whites attacked the homes of some thirty to forty free blacks, who defended themselves by firing into the mob, killing at least one rioter and wounding others. In the riot of 11 April 1836, however, a night of violence left several blacks dead when a mob entered the black community and indiscriminately attacked people, burned buildings, and forced large numbers to leave their homes. Only the intervention of the governor and the declaration of martial law brought the riot under control.[44]

In 1841, during an economic downturn and the hot summer months of August and September, racial violence erupted when whites attacked black churches and businesses on Sixth and Broadway. Unlike their response to most antebellum riots, African Americans selected Major J. Wilkerson, a twenty-eight-year-old "self-made man of color," to organize an armed defense of the community. For a while, heavily armed black men pushed the white mob out of their community, leading to white as well as black casualties. Unfortunately, whites were able to regroup, move an iron cannon into place, and fire upon the black community. When officials finally declared martial law, guardsmen and mobsters herded black people into the square at Sixth and Broadway. Although many had posted bond for their release, they were detained. Authorities arrested some three hundred black men, who were violently attacked by members of the mob en route to jail.[45]

Before the mob spent its energy, additional attacks on black homes, churches, and businesses took place. In the wake of the riot, the value of black private property holdings dropped by an estimated $150,000. In the short run, many blacks became disillusioned and left the city; others remained but became more cautious and fearful to assert their rights and struggle against injustice. Before long, however, the black community regrouped and took a stand for its rights in the Queen City. Indeed, as one observer later recalled, "The colored men were imprisoned because it had been thoroughly shown by their conduct that they had become so determined to protect themselves against whatever odds, that great and serious damage might be expected were they again assaulted."[46] Similarly, as resident John Mercer Langston put it, "the riot and its repressive aftermath failed to hush the voices of the eloquent colored men themselves who through such experience were learning what their rights were and how to advocate and defend them."[47]

During the 1850s, federal policies strengthened state and local restrictions on the lives of free blacks. To be sure, federal policy was not uniformly hostile. In 1842, the U.S. Supreme Court ruled in the *Priggs v Pennsylvania* case that states could not enact legislation purporting to uphold or hamper federal statutes.[48] This ruling resulted in passage of many personal liberty laws by state legislatures, which prohibited state and local officials from aiding Southern slaveholders in recovering property in slaves. Such policies, however, were overshadowed by passage of the Fugitive Slave Act of 1850, which increased penalties for aiding and abetting runaways. On the pretense of seeking runaways, slave catchers and kidnappers regularly entered Ohio Valley cities seeking to entrap free blacks as well as runaway slaves for sale in the Deep South, where huge profits rewarded their efforts.

As hostility toward African Americans intensified, blacks declined in proportion in Ohio Valley cities. Between 1820 and 1850, only Evansville's small black population slightly increased its share of the total from 1.8 to about 2.0 percent of the total. Cincinnati's black population dropped from a high of 4.8 percent of the total in 1840 to a low of 2.8 percent in 1850. Similarly, Pittsburgh's black population declined from nearly 4.0

percent in 1820 to about 3.3 percent in 1840, before rising again to 4.2 percent in 1850. Louisville's black percentage of the total also steadily declined, but unlike Cincinnati and Pittsburgh, the city's black population represented a much higher percentage of the total, about 16 percent in 1850, a decline from a high of 36.4 percent in 1810 and 28.0 percent in 1820 (see table 1).

Under the impact of the fugitive slave law and the climate of fear and uncertainty that it generated, African Americans left Ohio Valley cities in significant numbers. Between 1850 and 1860, Pittsburgh's black population dropped from 1,974 to 1,149 (not including Allegheny City, which increased slightly from 561 to 689). Delany estimated that over 150 blacks left Pittsburgh during a six-month period in 1855. Following mob violence in Evansville, Vanderburgh County, a contingent of blacks moved to Gibson County, north of Evansville, and established a settlement called Lyles Station, apparently named for the black resident Daniel Lyles whose family evidently led the exodus. The county's black population dropped from 230 in 1850 to 128 in 1860. Louisville's black population also slightly declined between 1850 and 1860, but free blacks increased their proportion of the total from 22 to 28 percent. Although Cincinnati's black population also declined as a percentage of the total, it expanded in absolute numbers during the troubled decade of the 1850s.[49]

Politics, Institutions, and Community Building

Ohio Valley African Americans were by no means passive in the face of class and racial subordination in the white republic. As elsewhere, Ohio Valley blacks built new community-based institutions, forged alliances with sympathetic white allies, and launched broad political assaults against racial discrimination. In response to the 1829 riot in Cincinnati, prominent black citizens sent a petition to the state legislature, seeking repeal of what they called "those obnoxious black laws."[50] These developments were deeply rooted in the emergence and expansion of the black working class and the corresponding growth of the small black middle class. Under the impact of commercial and early industrial capitalism, the most prominent members of the black middle class served white clients or employers in the urban economy. Yet, they gained their principal influence and prestige through participation in cross-class institutional, cultural, and political activities within the black community. A close look at the rise of the black middle class helps to illuminate the dynamics of black community life, culture, and politics during the antebellum era.

Well-educated, skilled, and relatively better paid laborers emerged at the top of the antebellum black class structure. In Pittsburgh and Allegheny City, the value of black real property had increased to $110,015 in 1850. Laborers, stewards, cooks, and caterers accounted for seven and barbers accounted for three of the thirteen blacks who owned property in excess of $12,000. A similar pattern prevailed in 1860, although the amount of wealth declined slightly, and the number of wealthholders increased and became more diverse, including a banker, pattern finisher, musician, porter, grocer, and "a private Gentleman."[51]

In 1850, Cincinnati listed the value of black property holdings at $317,780. Out of eighty-eight African Americans who held property of $1,000 or more, close to half worked as laborers, stewards, butlers, and cooks. Three of Cincinnati's most renowned residents and property-holders were Richard Phillips, a huckster ($13,000); Joseph J. Fowler, another huckster ($18,000); and John G. Gaines, a stevedore ($3,000). At the same time, Louisville's black population listed real estate valued at $95,650. Louisville also claimed one of only about nineteen blacks in urban America who owned property in excess of $20,000. Despite its small size, Evansville's black population also numbered a few propertyholders. The hotel-keeper, James Carter, the most renowned of these propertyholders, owned real estate valued at $1,500 in 1850. Another black propertyholder, Joseph Smith, a carpenter, owned property valued at $1,400. In all, however, twelve black families in Evansville owned real estate valued at less than $10,000. Black property ownership, however, was not exclusively a male affair. In 1850, women made up 31.1, 16.9, and 10.5 percent, respectively, of black propertyholders in Louisville, Cincinnati, and Pittsburgh. In Evansville, the widow Mrs. Sina [Lena?] McDaniel owned the single largest amount of black real and personal property— $4,000 in 1860, or about one-third of the total.[52]

African American propertyholders offered inspiring stories of individual and group success and entrepreneurship. The barber trade provided black men their most promising opportunities to earn a living, purchase real estate, and increase their standing in Ohio Valley cities. Black editor William Dabney later celebrated the mid-nineteenth century black barber and barbershop: "Barber shops were the greatest places for gossip and the white customers were generally well informed as to the doings

An interior view of William Glover's barbershop in Evansville. Whereas most black barbers lost their white clientele by the late nineteenth century, Glover's shop continued to serve white clients into the 1920s. Courtesy Special Collections, University of Southern Indiana, Evansville

of Negro society. The Negro barber, as a workman, was an artist. The razor in his hands became an instrument that made sweet melody as it charmed away the grass that grew on facial lawns."[53] As Cincinnati displaced Pittsburgh as the Queen City of the West, one local resident recollected: "If there has ever existed in any colored community of the United States, anything like an aristocratic class of such persons it was found in Cincinnati. In fact the entire Negro community of the city gave striking evidences in every way at this time of its intelligence, industry, thrift and progress; and in matters of education and moral and religious culture, furnished an example worthy of the imitation of their whole people."[54]

Serving an elite white clientele, some black barbers, cooks, and caterers gained a substantial economic footing in antebellum Ohio Valley cities. Supplemented by a small number of schoolteachers and ministers who combined their professional activities with the pursuit of a trade or business, these people accounted for a disproportionate share of the black community's income. In Pittsburgh, as historian Laurence Glasco points out, "Barbering was the most prestigious occupation open to blacks, who operated most of the downtown barbershops that catered to the city's elite."[55] The Quaker-educated free black, Lewis Woodson, for example, operated several shops in the city's leading hotels, including the Anderson, the St. Charles, and the Monongahela House. Other African American business and community leaders—John Vashon, John Peck, and Lemuel Googins—also operated barbershops serving a white clientele. Similarly, Louisville's Washington Spradling commenced his career as a barber and gained a reputation as "an expert shaver." Spradling invested his earnings in real estate, which reached a value of $30,000 by 1850. Some of the barbers would also train their sons and transform the job into a family tradition.[56]

Because some black entrepreneurs had been slaves, their careers were even more poignant. The barber William W. Watson became the most well-known propertyholder of antebellum black Cincinnati. In 1832, Watson received his freedom when a family member purchased him from his owner. Within less than a decade he owned his own barbershop and bathhouse, which catered to a predominantly white clientele in the CBD. He also owned two brick houses and lots within the city and another 560 acres of farmland in nearby Mercer County. His property holdings stood at an estimated $5,500. In her rationale for *Uncle Tom's Cabin*, Harriet Beecher Stowe, who lived in Cincinnati during her research for the book, named Watson and five other former slaves as examples of the race's capacity for "conquering for themselves comparative wealth and social position by their strength of character, energy, patience and honesty."[57]

Unfortunately, however, sympathetic whites also reinforced and fomented the growth of class divisions among African Americans. As the riot of 1829 took its toll on the black community, the poorest and most destitute blacks received less sympathy from whites than their elite brothers and sisters. In its report on the riot's aftermath, the *Cincinnati Gazette* sympathized with the black elite:

It has driven away the sober, honest, industrious, and useful portion of the colored population. The vagrant is unaffected by it. The effect is to lessen much of the moral restraint, which the presence of respectable persons of their own colour,

Fountain Lewis Sr. arrived in Cincinnati and gained a job in the barbershop of a Frenchman during the early 1840s, later taking over the business when his employer left the city. The senior Lewis and later his son catered to a predominantly white clientele until the early twentieth century. Barbers like Lewis occupied a prominent place in mid-nineteenth century cities. From W.P. Dabney's *Cincinnati's Colored Citizens* (1926)

imposed on the idle and indolent, as well as the profligate. It has exposed employers of coloured persons to suits by common informers, where no good or public motive was perceptible. It has reduced honest individuals to want and beggary, in the midst of plenty and employment; because employers were afraid to employ them. It has subjected men of color who won property to great sacrifices. It has furnished an occasion for the oppressor and common informer to exhibit themselves, and commence their depredations on the weak and defenseless, under cover of law. It has demonstrated the humiliating fact, that cruelty and injustice, the rank oppression of a devoted people, may be consummated in the midst of us, without exciting either sympathy, or operative indignation.[58]

Although mid-nineteenth century black elites owed their livelihood to white clients, their lives were closely intertwined with those of black workers and the poor. As mulatto and dark-skinned blacks alike gained a foothold in the economy, their industriousness did not insulate them from racist attacks. On the contrary, their progress generated as much resistance and hatred as their alleged intemperance and improvidence. In 1834, an English visitor to Cincinnati remarked that whites discussed African American efforts at self-help and improvements "with a degree of bitterness that dictated a disposition to be more angry with their virtues than their vices."[59] In 1841, a white working man pontificated that: "White men . . . are naturally indignant . . . when they see a set of idle blacks dressed up like ladies and gentlemen, strutting about our streets and flinging the 'rights of petition' and 'discussion' in our faces."[60] Such attitudes underlay a variety of practices that curtailed the rights of all blacks and helped to forge bonds across intraracial class and color lines. Moreover, unlike some communities where mulattoes sought an independent existence separate from blacks, Ohio Valley mulattoes identified with their darker-skinned brothers. In 1844, for example, the mulatto leader John Gaines rejected the idea of a separate school for mulatto children: "This I anticipate would be fraught with evil consequences . . . It would not only divide the colored children, but create prejudices too intolerable to be borne."[61]

African Americans in the Ohio Valley developed a variety of cross-class institutions and social movements. As elsewhere, the African American church emerged at the forefront of black institution-building and political activities. In Pittsburgh, African Americans founded Bethel African Methodist Episcopal Church (AME) in 1800, when James and George Coleman and Abraham Lewis "gathered a small group of children and five adults for a Sunday school service in the basement of an alley apartment."[62] Named after "Mother Bethel" AME in Philadelphia, the Pittsburgh church represented the gradual spread of the AME into the Ohio Valley. By the mid-1840s, blacks in Pittsburgh and Allegheny City had built no less than five additional churches—including Presbyterian and Baptist bodies.

In Louisville, African Americans also built independent churches. Under the leadership of Henry Adams, a Georgia-born migrant who arrived in Louisville in 1829, African Americans broke away from the white First Baptist Church and formed the "Colored" or "African" Baptist Church in 1842. Later renamed the Fifth Street Baptist Church, it had 475 charter members at its formation. Although the church retained ties to the white body, it managed its own "internal affairs" in its "own way."[63] By 1844, another group of Louisville blacks broke from the white First Baptist Church and founded the Second Colored Baptist Church. By the

1830s, although black Methodists outnumbered their white counterparts and pushed for independent congregations, they were less successful than their Baptist brethren. Nonetheless, blacks in Louisville founded the Fourth Street Methodist Church (later Asbury Chapel) in 1829 and Quinn Chapel AME (circa 1840).[64]

In 1824, Cincinnati blacks broke ranks with the white Methodist church and established the Bethel AME Church. Under the leadership of itinerant missionary Moses Freeman and teacher Owen Nickens, the black community protested against racial discrimination within the predominantly white body. Among other practices, they abhorred the practice of relegating blacks to the back of the line during communion services. When blacks seceded from the white body, Nickens received the title of "local" preacher. The group worshiped at a variety of private homes and even workshops before purchasing an edifice in 1834 on Sixth Street, east of Broadway. The congregation eventually pooled its resources, skills, and labor and built its own church.[65]

Although the city's black Baptists retained ties to the white body, they also established separate congregations. In 1831, black Baptists formed the Union Baptist Church and soon built their own brick edifice. Partly under the leadership of its influential parishioner, barber William W. Watson, black Baptists purchased a new edifice in 1830. Located on Baker Street, the new edifice was formerly occupied by white parishioners and held a great deal of symbolic value for blacks. By 1848, the church had paid off its debt on an edifice that cost $19,000. In 1843, another pillar of Cincinnati's black religious community emerged with the formation of the Zion Baptist Church, under the pioneer minister missionary, Wallace Shelton.[66]

Black institution-building activities were not confined to Louisville, Pittsburgh, and Cincinnati. As early as 1843, African Americans in Evansville formed the "Evansville African Methodist Church." Under the leadership of trustees Joseph Turner, Paul Henderson, Primos Lofton, and George Johnston, blacks leased a quarter acre of land and soon commenced Sunday services and a Sunday school. By the 1850s, another AME church opened in Vanderburgh County.[67]

The black church not only played a role in the religious life of the community; it also served as a springboard for the development of other black organizations. African American church leaders and lay people repeatedly articulated their vision for black liberation in religious terms.

As the statement of the board of managers of Cincinnati's Colored Education Society put it in 1837, "Ethiopia shall soon stretch out her hand to God, is the declaration of infinite goodness and wisdom. It must take place, and will doubtless be effected by human agency."[68] Some contemporaries believed that black churches had "done more to educate the heart and mind for freedom's blessing . . . than every other means combined."[69] Building upon the institutional foundation of the black church, itself rooted in the transformation of the black class structure, African Americans established a plethora of fraternal orders, social clubs, militia groups, schools, newspapers, and social welfare, civic, civil rights, and political organizations. In 1845, attorney Salmon P. Chase of Cincinnati, a future senator, governor of Ohio, and chief justice of the U.S. Supreme Court, vividly described this process in Cincinnati's black community: "Debarred from the public schools, you have established schools of your own; thrust by prejudice into the obscure corners of the edifices in which white men offer prayer, you have erected churches of your own . . . Excluded from the witness box, you have sought that security which the law denies."[70]

Using their expanding community institutions as sites of organization, planning, and strategy, African Americans resisted racial and class inequality in the social, economic, political, and cultural life of the region. The fight against disfranchisement, exclusion from public schools, slavery, and the activities of the American Colonization Society emerged at the center of their concerns. When Pennsylvania moved to disfranchise black citizens in 1837, African Americans in Pittsburgh and Western Pennsylvania filed one of the most militant protests, "Memorial of the Free Citizens of Colony of Pittsburgh and Its Vicinity Relative to the Right of Suffrage" in July 1837. Over seventy-five blacks signed the petition exhorting the state to restore the franchise to black people. In a supplement, the petition cited the contributions that blacks had made to the state and argued forcefully that African Americans were as worthy and entitled as whites to exercise the vote. The Memorial" stated in part that:

Enough has been exhibited, to satisfy any unprejudiced mind that the colored population appreciates their present privileges; and are endeavoring to sustain themselves honorably, and respectably in the community in which they live. Whatever of ignorance or degradation there is among us, owes its existence chiefly to our former condition in life. Slavery, that unright[eous] and unnatural state in which many of us were raised, deprived us of every means of moral cultivation, and caught its own sordid interest in shutting out every ray of intellectual light. The fathers of this commonwealth abolished this wicked system; and the wisdom of their deed is evinced in the fact that as we further recede from the fetters of the slave, we are better prepared to sustain the honours and high responsibilities of freemen.[71]

In January 1841, John Peck became president of a group that launched a new effort to gain the franchise. A week later the group met at Bethel AME Church and proposed a statewide convention to continue the fight for suffrage. In August 1841, a statewide convention met at the same church, with John B. Vashon, Lewis Woodson, A.D. Lewis, and Martin Delany taking leadership roles.

Closely intertwined with their fight for suffrage, African Americans also waged a struggle against the institution of slavery in the South. Their resistance to slavery gained its most powerful expression in the underground railroad. Because the western states opened later than those in the east and because they bordered the slave states of Virginia, Kentucky, and Pennsylvania, slaveowners regularly passed through Ohio Valley cities like Cincinnati, Pittsburgh, and Evansville. Slaveowners often stayed overnight in the cities' hotels with their slaves. Thus, black hotel employees played a pivotal part on the underground railroad. They reported on the arrival of planters and slave catchers, informed slaves of their opportunities for gaining freedom, and facilitated contact with conductors. In June 1848, for example, blacks working at the Pittsburgh Merchants Hotel helped two female slaves escape from a visiting planter. Black riverboatmen played a similar role. In early August 1841, a letter from a Cincinnati fugitive to his enslaved wife revealed the names of William O'Hara, the barber, and "George" Casey, presumably William Casey, a riverman. In the letter, the fugitive informed his wife and her friends that black boatmen would guide them to abolitionists.

By the 1850s, Ohio Valley blacks had organized an elaborate communications and escape network. Designed to free fugitives by aiding their escape further north or by concealing their residence within local black communities, the underground railroad depended upon the cooperation of large numbers of Ohio River blacks. On one occasion, Martin Delany arranged a mass meeting to protest the illegal kidnapping of two Beaver County children, ages four and seven. Attendees agreed to raise funds for a reward for the arrest of the kidnappers and the return of the children. When the federal government passed the Fugitive Slave Act, blacks met at an AME church to discuss ways to resist the measure. Indeed, African Americans took great pride in their resistance activities. As Cincinnati agent John Hatfield put it, "I never felt better pleased with anything I ever did in my life, than in getting a slave woman clear, when her master was taking her from Virginia."[72]

African Americans in the Ohio Valley linked their fight against slavery with the fight against colonization. As early as January 1817, Pennsylvania blacks met in convention at Philadelphia and rejected the notion of colonization; they denounced it as "a scheme" of Southern slaveholders to rid the nation of free blacks and secure the institution of slavery. Two months later, John B. Vashon wrote to William Lloyd Garrison emphasizing the United States as the home of free blacks. He also stressed the need to remain and fight the colonization movement and the institution of slavery itself. Nearly two decades later, in 1835, blacks in Pittsburgh had another mass meeting to protest the colonization movement. Under Vashon's leadership, the group condemned colonization as a tactic designed to expel educated blacks. The gathering also opposed any colony of blacks outside the U.S., whether in Africa, Canada, or Haiti. In 1849, Cincinnati's Rev. Wallace Shelton again counseled blacks to reject colonization: "Stay where you are . . . and never leave this land as long as one chain is to be heard clanking, or the cry of millions is to be heard floating on every breeze."[73] Across the state and nation, other blacks took the same stand.

Blacks fought equally hard for educational opportunities. In 1837, the Pittsburgh AME Church hosted a meeting to discuss black education and plan ways to improve it. After conducting a survey of black education in the city, the group expressed dissatisfaction that the city did not fund a single black school. The following year, the school board allotted funds for the city's first black public school. In Cincinnati, African Americans attacked the state's "Black Laws," which denied them access to education and other civil rights. Their effort bore partial fruit in 1849, when the state legislature approved public funds to educate black children. Under the leadership of Peter Clark, the black educator, socialist, and civil rights leader, African Americans pushed for implementation of the new legislation. Although the city of Cincinnati dragged its feet, three years later African Americans secured public funding and opened a black school. Black teacher Owen T. B. Nickens, from Virginia, abandoned his privately run school for blacks and took over the publicly funded school for blacks in the eastern district of the city. At about the same time, African Americans in Cincinnati formed the Colored Education Society (CES) and supervised three private schools for black children, two supported solely by black funds. Although the state ignored their request, a movement for black education also developed in Evansville before the onset of the Civil War. For its part, the city of Louisville continued to exclude African Americans from public education. As a result, African Americans at "the falls" directed their efforts toward building private schools in their churches and homes.[74]

The struggle for social justice was not an all-black affair. African Americans cultivated and achieved the support of white allies who assisted the fight against the ACS, slavery, and restrictions on black education. In Pittsburgh, prominent supporters of African Americans included Jane Grey Swisshelm, editor of the *Saturday Visitor*, an abolitionist paper; F. Julius LeMoyne, president of the Pittsburgh Anti-Slavery Society; and Neville B. Craig, editor of the *Pittsburgh Gazette*, the city's first daily paper. In Cincinnati, African Americans received the aid of Levi Coffin, a Southern-born Quaker, and renowned conductor on the underground railroad who moved to Cincinnati in 1847. Under the leadership of Connecticut-born Theodore Dwight Weld and Augustus Wattles, white faculty and students at Cincinnati's Lane Seminary published the antislavery *Philanthropist* and supported the underground railroad. The abolitionist movement also gained some support among Cincinnati lawyers and jurists. In 1841, for example, attorney Salmon Chase represented the fugitive slave Mary Towns in the Hamilton County Court. Before facing charges as a runaway, Towns had lived in Cincinnati for a decade. The judge accepted Chase's defense of Towns; "freedom and not slavery," he declared, was the rule in Ohio.[75]

At the local level, whites offered their strongest support for black education. In addition to schools operated by Lane Seminary and the Ladies Anti-Slavery Society, Gilmore High School represented one of Cincinnati's most outstanding examples of white philanthropy in behalf of black education. In 1844, wealthy British clergyman Hiram S. Gilmore established the institution, employed five teachers, and taught some three hundred black students a variety of subjects, including Latin, Greek, art, and music. Some students paid fees, others attended free, and some received partial support to make their attendance possible. By 1848, Gilmore turned the school over to one of his teachers. Paradoxically, in Pittsburgh, one of the most consistent supporters of black education was also a colonizationist. Cotton manufacturer Charles Avery, part owner of the Eagle Cotton Mill, not only supported efforts to recolonize blacks in Africa; he also funded Allegheny Institute and Mission Church, an institution of higher education for African Americans in Allegheny City. Built on land near his home, the school combined education in the classics with training in the trades. Upon his death in 1858, Avery left $25,000 for the continuation of the school's work under the name of Avery College. A lay preacher in the Methodist church, Avery also articulated the view that blacks were "the biological and social equals of whites."[76] More so than others in the ACS, he apparently took seriously the notion of voluntary recolonization.

Interracial cooperation sometimes included city officials. In Pittsburgh, when a white mob threatened the black community with violence in 1834, the mayor dispatched the Duquesne Grays, a white militia group, to disperse the crowd. After another racial incident in 1839, Mayor John R. McClintock, described as a "law and order" mayor, cooperated with black leader Martin Delany; they created special interracial teams of black and white officers to put down the disturbance. Whereas the mayor of Philadelphia feared black militia and fraternal orders and restricted their ability to use city streets for their parades, in Pittsburgh, the black Hannibal Guards and Free Masons paraded in the streets during the 1850s without incident. Moreover, Allegheny City and Pittsburgh blacks regularly and publicly celebrated British Emancipation Day or August First. Even in violent Cincinnati, African Americans regularly commemorated the West Indies Emancipation Day. On such occasions, speakers spoke boldly and clearly about the need for liberation. In August 1841, one speaker warned "all oppressors in every nation that the day is at hand when the hand of Almighty God will sunder the chains of the oppressed in every land."[77] For their part, Cincinnati authorities sometimes upheld the claims of blacks over whites. In the racial outbreak of 1829, for example, the police arrested ten blacks and seven whites for their part in the conflict, but the mayor fined the whites and released the blacks, affirming that they had acted in self-defense. As one historian concludes, "In this instance, at least, the black community appears to have been totally victorious."[78]

Even as African Americans worked to build interracial alliances, they confronted a variety of internal tensions and conflicts. Class, color, gender, cultural, ideological, and political differences repeatedly threatened racial solidarity. As elsewhere in America, in the Ohio Valley African Americans of light-skinned color gained economic opportunities and privileges denied to their darker-skinned counterparts. Although the vast majority of all blacks worked in jobs at the floor of the urban economy, dark skinned blacks occupied a notch below their lighter-skinned counterparts. This light-skinned privilege was not only revealed in economic and class terms, but in legal and political status as well. An example of this occurred on two occasions during the 1840s, when the Ohio State Supreme Court sanctioned the right of mulattoes to vote, arguing that they were not "Negroes." When Democrats gained control of the Ohio legislature and passed a law in 1850 disfranchising anyone with a "distinct and visible admixture of African blood," the Ohio Supreme Court again defended mulatto men, insisting that the law could not disfranchise males with over 50 percent white ancestry.[79]

In addition to cleavages along color lines, African Americans faced significant gender conflicts. African American women played a key role in the community life of Ohio Valley cities. In addition to their church-based activities, they spearheaded the formation of antislavery societies, temperance unions, and sewing circles. They also raised funds for black male-dominated fraternal, religious, social, and political organizations. In Cincinnati, under the leadership of Elizabeth Coleman and Sarah Earnest, for example, the Anti-Slavery Sewing Society produced clothing for runaway slaves and aided their escape from bondage. African American women also swelled the ranks of those attending the black political and civil rights conventions. Yet black women were often disfranchised. Consequently, at one of the early conventions, black women passed and delivered a resolution to the men: "Where as we the ladies have been invited to attend the Convention and have been deprived of a voice, which we the ladies deem wrong and shameful. Therefore, resolved, That we will attend no more after tonight, unless the privilege is granted."[80] As a result of the women's protest, the men introduced and passed a resolution "inviting the ladies to share in the doings of the Convention."[81]

Ohio Valley blacks also faced important ideological and political differences. Some blacks eschewed protest despite worsening conditions. When a group of Cincinnati blacks petitioned the legislature for redress and protection during the riot of 1829, leaders of the Methodist Episcopal Church abstained from endorsing the document. As one spokesperson explained, "All we ask is a continuation of the smiles of the white people as we have hitherto enjoyed them."[82] Other blacks moved to Canada. Between 1843 and 1847, Martin Delany published a black newspaper called the *Mystery*. Although living in Pittsburgh, he also served as co-editor of the *North Star* with Frederick Douglass. In 1849, Delany and Douglass parted ways. Douglass retained his commitment to an interracial abolitionist movement, including close cooperation between blacks and whites like William Lloyd Garrison and Harriet Beecher Stowe. By the late 1840s, however, Delany moved increasingly toward a black nationalist stance.[83] He also advocated pride in blackness, urged independent actions, and gradually adopted the notion of emigration to a new homeland for African Americans. In his book on the question of black "destiny," he repeatedly claimed: "Mexico, Central America, the West Indies, and South America, all present now opportunities for the individual enterprise of our young men, who prefer to remain in the United States, in preference to going where they can enjoy real freedom, and equality of rights." Delany insisted that African Americans act independently on the question of emigration. "Go or stay—of course each is free to do as he pleases—one thing is certain; our Elevation is the work of own hands."[84] Although Delany would eventually advocate the Niger Valley area as a site of settlement, he rejected the ACS and resisted settlement of Liberia as a viable solution to the problems facing African Americans.[85]

As Delany moved toward emigration ideas, other blacks broke ranks with Garrisonian and Douglass abolitionists on different grounds. As early as July 1850, the Reverend Lewis Woodson opposed Garrisonian abolitionists. When Frederick Douglass visited Pittsburgh and spoke at the Wylie Street African Methodist Church, Woodson disrupted the antislavery gathering by his persistent challenges to Douglass's ideas, calling the renowned abolitionist an infidel. Woodson objected to the Garrisonian beliefs that the church aided and abetted slavery and that abolitionists should abrogate religious affiliation. Woodson later became president of a new Christian Anti-Slavery society formed in Pittsburgh during the late 1850s.[86] Conversely, while African American leaders like Delany and Woodson worked to reconcile emigration, civil rights, and abolitionist ideas on their own terms, some blacks accepted the overtures of the ACS. Between 1846, when Liberia became an independent Republic, and 1849, over a thousand blacks left the United States for Africa. Of these one hundred ninety-seven settled in Pennsylvania's Bassa Cove colony, founded in 1835 when the Pennsylvania Colonization Society broke away from the parent body. In November 1857, five Pittsburgh blacks left for Africa on the ship *M.C. Stevens* from Baltimore. Three years later fifteen Allegheny County blacks departed for Africa on the same ship.[87]

Although African Americans faced significant internal conflicts and differences, their difficulties in securing a position in the urban political economy as a group helped to mitigate such friction. While blacks catering to white elites amassed resources, power, and prestige that enabled them to protect themselves better than their working-class and poor counterparts, their industriousness and social contacts failed to fully shield them from racist attacks. As noted above, African Americans from different socioeconomic and cultural backgrounds took jobs at the bottom of the urban economy and transformed them into instruments of freedom for themselves, relatives, and friends, but their industriousness attracted no less hostility than their assumed ignorance, laziness, and irresponsibility.

White men from a variety of class, ethnic, and national backgrounds coalesced around racism and notions of republicanism. Such attitudes and social practices undercut the opportunities and rights of all blacks and reinforced bonds across class, color, and cultural lines within the black urban community. Only the onset of the Civil War and the rapid expansion of industrial capitalism would bring blacks more fully into the economy and polity as citizens as well as producers. Building upon their antebellum communities, ideas, and strategies for social change, African Americans would play a key role in their own transformation from a subordinate proletariat to new workers and citizens.

PART TWO

Emancipation, Race, and Industrialization, 1861-1914

3

Occupational Change
and the Emergence of a
Free Black Proletariat

The expansion of industrial capitalism influenced the transformation of African American life in the Ohio Valley region and in the nation. Symbolized by the emergence of the giant U.S. Steel Corporation in 1901, a few large companies gained a growing proportion of the region's economy, wealth, and power. Under the impact of industrial capitalism, the African American population not only increased, but made up a slightly larger proportion of the total; gained greater access to the industrial sector; and claimed citizenship rights under new amendments to the U.S. and state constitutions. Yet, social injustice would soon gain new expression in jobs, housing, and the institutional and political life of Ohio Valley cities. During the Civil War, the black Cincinnati teacher William Parham foresaw the struggle ahead: "When this war is over the next war will be against prejudice . . . we shall need all the talent that we have among us or can possibly command."[1] Like the old era of disfranchisement and slavery, the new era of emancipation and citizenship would challenge blacks to develop fresh modes of social struggle and resistance.

At the war's beginning, few Ohio Valley whites perceived the struggle as an opportunity to emancipate slaves. Indeed, by remaining loyal to the Union, Ohio Valley whites hoped to contain slavery where it existed and maintain the status quo for free blacks. When Ohio blacks petitioned Governor David Todd for permission to raise a black regiment, he replied, "Do you not know . . . that this is a white man's government; that white men are able to defend and protect it?" At the local level, when Cincinnati blacks planned public demonstrations to support the Union's war effort, municipal officials prohibited such meetings. For their part, white workers, particularly Irish immigrants, attacked black workers on the docks and destroyed their property in nearby neighborhoods in Cincinnati and Evansville.[2]

Despite initial rejection by white public officials and citizens, African Americans took the initiative and transformed the war between the states into a war for black liberation. From the outset of hostilities, African Americans volunteered their services to the Union army. In Pittsburgh, for example, black men formed the Hannibal Guards on 18 April 1861. In a letter to General J.S. Negley, commander of Western Pennsylvania, black men offered to raise a full company of black troops for the fight against the Confederacy. Although disfranchised, they also claimed U.S. citizenship: "We consider ourselves American citizens and interested in the Commonwealth of all our white fellow-citizens, although deprived of all political rights, we yet wish the government of the United States to be sustained against the tyranny of slavery, and are willing to assist in any honorable way or manner to sustain the present administration."[3]

As Ohio Valley blacks offered their services to Union officials, southern blacks voted for freedom with their feet. In rising numbers, fugitive slaves and free blacks left the Confederate states and moved into Union territory. Under the impact of wartime migration, Louisville's black population dramatically increased from 6,800 to nearly 15,000, Cincinnati's rose from about 3,730 to 5,900, Pittsburgh's from less than 2,000 to 3,200; and Evansville's from no more than 100 to about 1,400 (see table 2).

As the black population increased, military, municipal, and corporate officials hired as well as coerced blacks to work on defense projects. In the city of Louisville, authorities tightened restrictions on the movement of slaves and free blacks. According to the *Daily Journal*, blacks "were picked up by the hundreds on the streets, and all of the lazy idle characters set to work." African Americans constructed fortifications to defend the city from Confederate attacks. In Cincinnati, less than two months after the riots against local blacks, municipal officials also turned to African Americans to protect the city from approaching Confederate troops.[4] According to a governor's report, city officials forced black men to work on fortifications: "The police acting in concert and in obedience to some common order, in a rude and violent manner arrested the colored men wherever found—in the street, at their places of business, in their homes and hurried them to a mule pen on Plum Street, and thence across the river to the fortifications, giving them no explanation of this conduct and no opportunity to prepare for camp life."[5]

When General Lewis Wallace (later author of *Ben Hur*) received word of these abusive tactics, he demolished the camp and set up headquarters for the voluntary recruitment of the "Black Brigade." In order to gain the confidence of the black men (about four hundred in all), he permitted them to return home. The following morning seven hundred men volunteered for service. According to Brigade historian Sara Jackson: "There was no occasion when the men had to be compelled to work or disciplined. They showed a high degree of interest in the work they were doing, and some made valuable suggestions." Upon discharge after three weeks of intensive labor, Colonel Dickson praised the Black Brigade for laboring "faithfully, building miles of roads, rifle pits and magazines, and clearing acres of forest land." Although they served as laborers only, the men presented the white officer a sword as a token of their high regard for his leadership. In addition, the Brigade's spokesman expressed the hope that when the sword was unsheathed, "it will be drawn in favor of freedom."[6]

Although black workers served the war effort as laborers, it was not until the summer of 1862 that President Abraham Lincoln authorized the enlistment of black troops. Six months later, when Lincoln issued the Emancipation Proclamation on 1 January 1863, the use of black troops escalated. Along with the continuing activity of African Americans on their own behalf, Lincoln's Proclamation helped to transform the civil war into a war of liberation for slaves and free blacks.[7]

Between 1863 and war's end, Ohio Valley blacks gradually increased their numbers in the Union army. In Pittsburgh, twenty-seven black men appear on the Allegheny County Roll of Honor for service in the Civil War. Their ranks included seventeen privates, three corporals, and seven sergeants. Pittsburgh also contributed black soldiers to the 54th and 55th Massachusetts Volunteer Infantries as well as to units in other states. Near the war's end, antebellum black activist Martin Delany also enlisted in the U.S. Army and became a major in the 104th U.S. Colored Infantry. By August 1864, the city of Evansville had enlisted two hundred black troops and sent them to Indianapolis for assignment. The city continued to enlist black soldiers through the duration of the war. As the city's black population increased, the local draft marshal proposed the appoint-

Martin R. Delany, born near Charles Town, Virginia (now West Virginia) ca. 1812, had moved with his family by the mid-1820s to the Pittsburgh region, where he founded the newspaper the *Mystery* and fought against slavery in the south and discrimination in the north. Near the end of the Civil War, he became a major in the 104th U.S. Colored Infantry. Courtesy Charles L. Blockson, author of *African Americans in Pennsylvania* and *The Underground Railroad in Pennsylvania*

ment of a special recruiting officer for the "Ethiopians." In addition to large numbers in Kansas and Massachusetts regiments, over five thousand Ohio blacks served in the Union army, as part of the 127th Ohio volunteers.[8]

Kentucky contributed the largest number of black soldiers to the Union army. More than twenty-eight thousand Kentucky slaves and free blacks enlisted in the Union forces. Their experiences also mirrored the separate and unequal basis on which black soldiers fought. Kentucky officials delayed the use of black troops longer than elsewhere. Only in March 1864 did the state drop its opposition to black enlistment. Even then, Confederate sympathizers used intimidation, violence, and murder to prevent blacks from joining Union forces. For their part, in order to meet the city's quota of enlisted men, Union officials and municipal authorities regularly arrested African Americans, offering them enlistment in the Army as an option to prison. Upon gaining access to Union ranks, black soldiers received unequal pay, restrictions on promotion, and maltreatment from white officers.

Whereas Lincoln's Emancipation Proclamation freed slaves in the rebellious Confederate states, only the ratification of the Thirteenth Amendment on 18 December 1865 emancipated slaves in Kentucky and other loyal slaveholding states. Following enactment of the Thirteenth Amendment, African Americans gradually gained access to citizenship rights, including the franchise with passage of the Fourteenth (1868) and Fifteenth Amendments (1870).[9] Despite access to full citizenship rights, freedom produced mixed results for Ohio Valley blacks. By the mid-1880s, African Americans would face a new and more complicated pattern of exclusion, segregation, and discrimination in the socioeconomic, institutional, cultural, and political life of the region.

Urbanization in the Ohio Valley: The Maturation of Industrial Capitalism

More so than in the antebellum years, industrialization shaped the development of black life in postbellum Ohio Valley cities. As elsewhere, industrialists responded to rising national demands for manufactured products. Although all Ohio Valley cities expanded between the Civil War and World War I, Pittsburgh became the hub of industrialization in the nation and region. In addition to the water power of the three rivers and access to iron ore, Pittsburgh manufacturers exploited the rich coking coal of Connellsville. By the turn of the century, industrialists in western Pennsylvania operated nearly a thousand coal mines and more than thirty thousand beehive coke ovens.[10] By 1901, when several industrialists and finance capitalists merged their interests and created the U.S. Steel Corporation, the Pittsburgh region accounted for a third of the nation's steelmaking capacity and produced over 40 percent of its output. By World War I, Pittsburgh elites—Carnegie, Frick, Phipps, Hillman, and the Mellons—had established a commanding economic base.[11]

While Pittsburgh expanded its position as the number one steel producer, Cincinnati lost ground to other industrial centers during and following the Civil War. The city failed to make the transition to the railroad as rapidly as it did to the steamboat. By 1880, Cincinnati ranked seventh among the nation's industrial cities, a drop from third place in 1860. Following the opening of the city-owned Southern Railway in 1877, however, Cincinnati gained direct access to the growing southern cities of Knoxville, Charleston, Atlanta, and Birmingham. As a result, by the mid-

1880s, Cincinnati ranked first in the production of carriages, furniture, whiskey, and a few other items; second in clothing, boots, and shoes; and quite high in leather, metal products, and cigars. At the same time, its value of manufacturing increased from $17.9 million in 1860 to $50 million in 1880 and to $104.5 million in 1890. Still, compared to Pittsburgh, Cincinnati's economy remained more dependent on trade and commerce than heavy industry.[12]

Louisville's economy flourished during the Civil War. As a major staging base for the Union army, the city offered the Louisville and Nashville Railroad a lucrative business transporting Union troops and supplies. In the war's early aftermath, Louisville merchants also increased their fortunes when the city became a center for federal, philanthropic, and commercial efforts to reconstruct the South. Louisville business leaders tried to rekindle their ties to the Confederate states, emphasizing the city's efforts to promote a humanitarian response to the Deep South after the war. As the *Louisville Courier-Journal* put it, "Since the close of the war, our merchants have acted toward those of the South in a spirit of truest magnanimity."[13] The paper also criticized Northern merchants and industrialists as exploiters of the South's misfortunes: "This generous example has scarcely had one imitator in the opulent cities of Cincinnati, Philadelphia, New York, or Boston, whose merchants have enjoyed and grown fat on the customs of the South in years past."[14]

Indeed, Northern capitalists increased their grip on the city's economy, as symbolized by the takeover of the Louisville and Nashville Railroad. In order to retain control over Louisville and regain a measure of autonomy for the South, however, Louisville elites soon adopted the new South creed of industrialization. Henry Watterson, editor of the *Louisville Courier-Journal,* emerged as a key spokesperson for the new ideas, which emphasized making the South receptive to Northern capital as the first step toward a more independent and viable future. Spurred by Northern capital, the city gradually expanded as a regional banking, transportation, and commercial center. By the 1880s, in its value of products, Louisville ranked seventeenth in the nation and second in the South.[15]

During and following the Civil War, Evansville expanded as a major economic link between the three-state region of the lower Ohio River. The city added significant manufacturing enterprises—agricultural implements, furniture, cigars, stoves, and flour—to its prewar agricultural processing activities. By the early 1890s, the emergence of the city's renowned Swans Down Cake Flour symbolized its growing participation in the regional and national economy. By the turn of the twentieth century, Evansville was not only a world leader in hardwood timber, but claimed the world's largest furniture factory and one of the nation's largest cotton textile mills. Although on a smaller scale, like Pittsburgh and Cincinnati, it also exploited its rural iron and coal deposits, operated over a dozen foundries, several machine shops, and a rolling mill.[16]

The rapid expansion of industrial and finance capitalism demanded growing numbers of workers. Between 1860 and 1910, as elsewhere in industrial America, the population of Ohio Valley cities dramatically increased. Pittsburgh's population rose from slightly less than 50,000 to nearly 534,000, Cincinnati's from just over 161,000 to nearly 364,600, Louisville's from an estimated 68,000 to about 224,000, and Evansville's from less than 22,000 to nearly 60,000.[17] As early as 1875, a Louisville writer spoke for the urban Ohio Valley when he wrote, "The secret of substantial and steady growth is found in workshops teeming with mechanics and laborers."[18] Ten years later, Louisville claimed an estimated 22,000 operatives, producing goods valued at $50 million in some 1,300 manufacturing firms. Pittsburgh's manufacturing workforce rose from 24,000 in 1859 to nearly 155,000 in 1899. In Cincinnati, the number of industrial workers increased from about 29,400 in 1860 to over 37,300 in 1870 to nearly 52,400 during the 1880s. Evansville wage earners jumped from a handful in 1860 to an estimated 5,000 in 1900.[19] As elsewhere, by World War I, Ohio Valley industrialists had organized new and diverse manufacturing firms, replaced small, family-owned companies with large corporations, and hired growing numbers of industrial workers.

Migration and immigration fueled the region's population growth and industrial expansion. Between the Civil War and the turn of the century, with the exception of Louisville (with less than 10 percent foreign-born), immigrants comprised a rising proportion of the region's population. By 1910, respectively, in Pittsburgh, Cincinnati, and Evansville, immigrants and their children made up about 66, 58, and 30 percent of the total population; by World War I, immigrants and their offspring continued to account for a large though declining proportion of Ohio Valley cities; again, respectively, 62, 41, and 22 percent. With the exception of Pittsburgh, however, most of these cities continued to attract large numbers of Irish and Germans rather than South, Central, and Eastern Europeans.[20] Still, as immigrants and their children, especially those from South, Central, and Eastern Europe, increased, they entered the least skilled, most difficult, and lowest paid segments of the labor force. By 1907, at the Homestead Works, for example, 40 percent of American-born whites, 46 percent of British-born whites, 51 percent of Scots, and 24 percent of Irish workers occupied skilled jobs. Conversely, only 5 percent of the Polish, 1 percent of the Italians, and less than 2 percent of other immigrants held skilled positions. In Cincinnati, Evansville, and Louisville, American-born whites, German, and Irish workers also obtained the best jobs in the expanding industrial workforce.[21]

Despite the growing ethnic stratification of the workforce, industrialization ushered in new and deeper class divisions between workers and their employers. The size and capitalization of manufacturing firms increased much faster than they had during the antebellum years. In Pittsburgh, mean firm size rose from less than thirteen workers in the pre–Civil War era to nearly twenty-eight workers in 1880. Between 1869 and 1899, in the rapidly growing blast furnaces and steel mills, respectively, mean firm size rose from 71 to 176 and from 119 to 412 employees. At the same time, capital investments in blast furnaces and rolling mills rose from roughly $145,000 to $643,000 and from $156,000 to $967,000.[22]

Along with size and capitalization, new technological and managerial developments reinforced the earlier trends toward depersonalization, conflict, and exploitation in the workplace. The earlier iron industry had become increasingly specialized. Blast furnaces, forges, and rolling and finishing mills moved away from small centralized shops to larger establishments specializing in a specific operation. During the late nineteenth and early twentieth centuries, industrialists applied new technology—including the Bessemer converter, open hearth furnace, and steam and electric power—and reintegrated production processes. Industrialists also introduced new cost-accounting and managerial techniques, hired more foremen, and subjected workers to stricter supervision from the top down. Moreover, firms now perceived skilled workers as potential recruits to the new managerial structure. Such practices intensified internal distinctions within the working class.[23]

As these processes escalated, workers intensified their activism at the point of production and deepened their class consciousness. As elsewhere in industrial America, worker activism gained expression in socialism, trade unionism, and the Knights of Labor (KOL), before the emergence of the conservative American Federation of Labor (AFL) during the 1890s.

Although the socialists gained a substantial following during the 1820s and again during the early twentieth century, internal struggles over tactics, combined with attacks from industrial elites and their spokespersons, undermined the socialist initiative, which emphasized overhauling the industrial structure and promoted government ownership of the means of production. On the other hand, while trade unionists advocated use of the strike as a keystone of workers' struggle for economic justice, the Knights of Labor rejected both the strike and the wage system. Instead, the KOL, which expanded during the 1880s, advocated the creation of a series of producer cooperatives as alternatives to wage labor. Moreover, the KOL emphasized organization across ethnic, racial, and occupational lines. Unfortunately, with the emergence of the AFL, during the 1890s skilled craftsmen gained primary attention. The majority of workers, defined as "unskilled," who were predominantly new immigrants and increasingly African Americans, endured neglect.[24]

Before the rise of the AFL, workers in the Ohio Valley offered a powerful challenge to the triumph of industrial capitalism. Their activism had a major impact on the Pittsburgh region. Building upon their antebellum experiences in the Sons of Vulcan, iron puddlers joined other craftsmen and formed the Amalgamated Association of Iron and Steel Workers in the early postbellum years. The most dramatic and violent conflicts broke out in the "Railroad War" of 1877 and the Homestead Steel Strike of 1892. Despite the determined struggle of workers in these confrontations, however, companies used a combination of strategies—including the use of strikebreakers, the coercive power of the state, and private detectives—to undermine worker unity, crush their unions, and defeat their demands for equity.[25]

Ohio Valley workers nonetheless articulated an alternative vision of the social order. During this period, white workers redefined their relation to capital and the state. For them, their struggle was just. It embodied the "real" meaning of the Declaration of Independence and the beginnings of the American republic. While white workers continued to believe that "uncorrupted" capital and the state were positive forces, they now expressed the view that elite political leaders, "capitalists, monopolists, and corporations used their power to oppress labor." White workers also appropriated the civic language of law and order, which elites had used so well in the past. Workers now used similar language in their own struggle against employers and oppressors. In short, as historian Steven

Ross puts it, "White workers created a new public language which merged the roles of worker and citizen in new and profound ways."[26]

Unfortunately, even as white workingmen mobilized on their own behalf, they maintained blind spots on issues of gender and color. White men from a variety of ethnic and national backgrounds gained industrial jobs in growing numbers, but white women worked in a narrow range of jobs in domestic, personal service, and the needle and garment trades. By World War I, however, rising employment in white-collar jobs—especially in clerical, nursing, social work, and teaching—helped to offset the dearth of opportunities for white women in the industrial sector. Still, before World War I, white women faced significant limitations on their roles as citizens and producers.[27] As African Americans sought to carve out their own place as workers and citizens, these larger social conflicts would play an important role in their lives.

Freedom, Opportunities, and Limits on the Growth of the Black Working Class

Following the Civil War and Reconstruction, African American life in the Ohio Valley was linked even more closely to the fate of Southern blacks. By the late nineteenth century, Southern blacks faced new and more intense forms of class and racial inequality. Labor exploitation, intimidation, mob violence, lynchings, and disfranchisement all proceeded apace. As Southern race relations entered the nadir, African Americans increasingly viewed the urban North as a Mecca. Southern blacks frequently recalled living and working on poor land, barely able to eke out a living for themselves and their families. Moreover, in the southern wage-labor market, African American men averaged $2 to $3.50 per week on farms and in small towns, compared to $5 to $9 per week in large Southern cities like Louisville, and $6 to $14 per week in the industrial North.[28]

As Southern blacks responded to economic opportunities in the urban North, the black population in the Ohio Valley rapidly increased. Between 1880 and 1910, Pittsburgh's black population rose from just over 4,000 to more than 25,600, Cincinnati's from about 8,200 to 19,650, Louisville's from 20,900 to 40,500, and Evansville's from about 2,700 to over 7,500 in 1900, before dropping to 6,300 in 1910. The black population not only increased, but represented a slowly rising percentage of the total: from 4 to about 5 percent in Pittsburgh, 2.3 to 5.3 percent in Cincinnati, 10 to 18 percent in Louisville, and from less than one to 9 percent in Evansville (see table 2). Unlike the antebellum black population, black men made up a higher percentage of the postbellum migration than women. By 1910, the black male population out-numbered women in Pittsburgh (13,351 to 12,272), Cincinnati (9,905 to 9,734), and Evansville (3,696 to 2,570). Only in Louisville did black women continue to outnumber black men (20,920 to 19,602), but even here the gap narrowed considerably between 1890 and 1910.[29]

Although annexation and natural increase added to the numbers, migration accounted for the lion's share of black population growth. African Americans continued to come mainly from the Upper South and border states of Virginia, Maryland, Tennessee, and North Carolina. According to available statistics, an estimated two-thirds to three-quarters of blacks in Pittsburgh, Cincinnati, and Evansville were born in other states, mainly Kentucky, Virginia, North Carolina, and Tennessee. For its part, Louisville attracted migrants from its own rural farms and villages as well as from other Upper South and border states.[30]

African Americans entered the Ohio Valley as an alternative to the labor exploitation and racial subordination that they faced at home, but they soon faced new obstacles. As before, industrialists viewed black workers as "inefficient, unsuitable, and unstable." Although industrialists like steel magnate Andrew Carnegie made generous contributions to black colleges and developed close relations with Booker T. Washington and other elites, they turned to Europeans to fill their labor needs.[31] By 1910, Pittsburgh's iron and steel mills employed nearly three hundred thousand workers, but African Americans comprised only about 3 percent of the total, compared to 29 percent for American-born whites and 68 percent for immigrants. In Cincinnati, African Americans made up an estimated 1 percent of the city's metalworkers, while Evansville's black population declined as a result of limited job opportunities. Although black men and women gained jobs in Louisville's tobacco factories, they were excluded from the higher paying skilled and supervisory jobs.[32]

As elsewhere, Ohio Valley employers hired blacks mainly in domestic, personal service, and general labor sectors of the economy. While such jobs revolved around the arduous tasks of lifting, hauling, cleaning, and cooking, they were carried out in a variety of settings: in private homes, hotels, factories, department stores, restaurants, theaters, train stations (and on trains), boat ports (and on boats), office buildings, hospitals,

Table 2. African American Population in Ohio Valley Cities, 1860-1910

	1860		1870		1880		1890		1900		1910	
	No.	%	No.	%	No.	%	No.	%	No.	%	No.	%
Pittsburgh*	1,830	2.8	3,205	2.5	6,136	3.9	10,357	3.3	20,355	4.5	25,623	4.8
Cincinnati	3,731	2.3	5,900	2.7	8,179	3.2	11,655	3.9	14,482	4.4	19,639	5.4
Louisville	4,903	10.0	14,956	14.8	20,905	16.9	28,651	1.8	39,139	19.1	40,522	18.1
Evansville	96	0.8	1,480	6.5	2,686	9.2	5,553	10.9	7,405	12.5	6,266	9.0

Source: Hollis Lynch, *The Black Urban Condition: A Documentary History, 1866-1971* (New York: Thomas Crowell Co., 1973), appendix A; Ann G. Wilmoth, "Pittsburgh and the Blacks: A Short History 1780-1875" (Ph.D. diss., Pennsylvania State University, 1975), p. 210; John Bodnar, Roger Simon, and Michael P. Weber, *Lives of Their Own: Blacks, Italians, and Poles in Pittsburgh, 1900-1960* (Urbana: Univ. of Illinois Press, 1982), p. 30; Dennis C. Dickerson, *Out of the Crucible: Black Steelworkers in Western Pennsylvania, 1875-1980* (Albany: State Univ. of New York Press, 1986), p. 17.

*Includes Allegheny City, which was annexed in 1906.

schools, churches, and clubhouses. Some blacks worked in the newest and most fashionable hotels, offices, or bank buildings, with their spacious rooms, high ceilings, marble walls, and overhead fans, but most labored in jobs and surroundings with few amenities and low pay.[33]

Although domestic service jobs were somewhat insulated from the periodic downturns that sent large numbers of industrial workers to the streets, such jobs were nonetheless insecure and represented abiding constraints on the economic aspirations of Ohio Valley blacks. Moreover, under the impact of hard times, unemployment, technological change, and hardening racial attitudes, white workers coveted certain jobs in the service sector and moved to displace blacks. Black caterers, waiters, and barbers serving a white clientele faced increasing competition from European immigrants. In Louisville, as early as 1885, an Irishman not only exploited prevailing racist ideas about the benefits of racial separation, but reversed the rhetoric. Since black barbers retained wealthy white customers by serving blacks and whites on a segregated basis, the Irishman protested that, "It is nothing more or less than selling [their] birthright for a few dollars. If their barbers had race pride at heart they would step down and out of business."[34] According to black writer Wendell Dabney, African Americans were unprepared for the immigrant assault on their barbering stronghold: "White men came into the barber business. The Negro barbers laughed. More white men came. Less laughing. The white man brought business methods... He gave new names to old things. Sanitary and sterilized became his great words, the open sesame for the coming generation. ... Old customers died and then their sons 'who know not Joseph'. ... Negro barber shops for white patrons melted as snow before a July sun."[35] Additionally, as Americans moved toward European-style service in barbering, catering, and restaurants, they increasingly emphasized qualifications, including literacy, training, and expertise, which also heightened the displacement of blacks by whites.[36]

African Americans faced even stiffer competition in the industrial sector. White workers barred blacks from their unions and reinforced the exclusionary practices of industrialists. According to one white steel unionist, compelling whites to work with black men "was itself cause sufficient to drive ... [white workers] into open rebellion."[37] The Sons of Vulcan, the Associated Brotherhood of Iron and Steel Heaters, and the Iron and Steel Roll Hands Union; the Railroad Brotherhoods; the Boilermakers Union; the International Association of Machinists; and the

Plumbers' Steamfitters' Union all restricted membership to white workers either formally or informally. In addition, although the National Labor Union, formed in 1866, and the Knights of Labor (KOL), formed three
years later, encouraged the inclusion of diverse ethnic and racial groups,
they also permitted white locals to establish segregated bodies, that discriminated against black workers. Similarly, when the American Federation of Labor supplanted the KOL after 1886, it initially organized black
and white workers together, but soon relinquished the fight for racial inclusion and permitted segregation and exclusionary practices.[38]
    State and local governments strengthened the racial policies and prac-
tices of labor unions and employers. The railroad industry offers a key
illustration. In the early post–Civil War years, Ohio Valley blacks gradually gained skilled jobs as railroad firemen, engineers, conductors, switch-
men, flagmen, and brakemen, particularly in Cincinnati and Louisville.
As the railroad brotherhoods increased their bargaining power in the industry, they negotiated contracts that hampered the employment of blacks
in skilled jobs by defining certain general labor jobs (e.g., porter) as black
jobs and skilled positions as white jobs. Companies routinely circum-
vented the union by hiring blacks under the rubric of porter, but assign-
ing them brakemen duties, for example. As this practice increased, the
white brotherhoods campaigned for "full crew laws," designed to eliminate the practice of hiring workers for one job category and then assign-
ing them to the duties of another. In 1902, the brotherhood gained a
victory when the Ohio legislature passed a "full crew" act. In Cincinnati,
implementation of the new law led to the immediate firing of nearly thirty
black porter-brakemen, some longtime company employees. By the late
nineteenth century, African Americans faced increasing confinement to
a narrow range of railroad jobs, as laborers and service workers with few
opportunities beyond the role of porter on trains or sleeping cars. Other
white workers (e.g., plumbers), also strengthened their exclusionary practices by obtaining state and municipal ordinances requiring special li-
censes to practice their crafts, usually under the guise of sanitation and
safety precautions.[39]
    Discriminatory labor, state, and management practices also height-
ened the deleterious impact of technological change on black workers'
lives. In Ohio River cities, for example, the decline of the steamboat undercut black employment in the river trades. In Cincinnati, the percentage of black men in steamboat jobs dropped from 13 percent in 1860 to

less than 2 percent of the black male workforce in 1890. The white percentage also declined, but less dramatically, from 4 to 2 percent. As the internal combustion engine made motorized travel cheaper and more effective, African Americans in Ohio Valley cities also lost jobs in the horse-drawn teamster, cabbie, and hauling trades. In the steel industry, too, by World War I, mechanization started to erode African American access to such skilled jobs as puddler.[40]

Although Ohio Valley blacks found it exceedingly difficult to expand their footing in the industrial economy, they nonetheless gradually made inroads on new jobs. Although slight, this achievement was most prominent in the steel industry of western Pennsylvania. As European immigration fueled the rise of a new labor movement, employers reevaluated the potential of black workers. As early as 1881, the steel employers' *Iron Age* commented favorably on the skills of southern black boilers, heaters, and rollers. Less than ten years later the magazine reported: "Wherever the Negro has had a chance to acquire the necessary skill . . . he has shown himself capable." In rapid succession, as white workers walked out on strike, steel companies employed black strikebreakers: the Pittsburgh Bolt Company (1875), the Black Diamond Steel Works (1875), the Solar Iron Works (1887-89), Carnegie Steel (later U. S. Steel) (1892, 1901), and the McKees Rocks Pressed Steel Car Company (1909). As labor historians Sterling D. Spero and Abram L. Harris noted, "Almost every labor disturbance . . . saw Negroes used as strikebreakers. . . . In every instance the Negroes brought in were men trained in the mills of the South."[41] Company officials would later refer to black workers as "strike insurance."[42]

Strikebreaking was not merely a consequence of employers dividing black and white workers. It also represented black workers' resistance to labor union discrimination. In the iron and steel industry, where blacks were used most often and effectively to break the back of white labor, African Americans had developed deep antebellum work traditions, which facilitated their responses to inequality in both racial and class terms. The Tredgar Iron Works in Richmond, Virginia, employed nearly one thousand slaves during the Civil War. Although whites stereotyped black workers as lazy, inefficient, and incapable of performing skilled work, black iron- and steel-workers mastered a variety of jobs, including skilled jobs as puddlers and iron and steel heaters. When U.S. Steel took over the Tennessee Coal and Iron Company in 1907, African Americans made up about 25 to 30 percent of the labor force in the Birmingham district of

Alabama. Understandably, white workers in northern steel centers like western Pennsylvania feared African Americans as potential competitors.[43]

Although African Americans gained steel industry jobs as strikebreakers, they were not entirely alone in this regard. When white puddlers struck one company, white heaters and rollers stayed on the job and later cooperated with black strikebreakers and ensured the return of the mills to productivity. In the Pressed Steel Car Company strike in McKees Rocks of 1909, companies imported interracial contingents of black and immigrant strikebreakers, making it difficult for strikers to target black workers as the single cause of their problems.[44] Blacks gradually expanded their footing as regular recruits. The number of black steelworkers in Pittsburgh and Allegheny City increased from only 213 in 1890 to 789 in 1910. The pre–World War I generation of black steelworkers included men like Jefferson Jackson from King George County, Virginia; James Clagget from Mt. Zion, Maryland; and William Marbley from Beilton, West Virginia. These men found employment at the Duquesne, Carnegie, and Clairton steel companies, which later became part of the U.S. Steel Corporation.[45]

Blacks worked in a broad range of iron and steel occupations. As historian Dennis Dickerson notes, they not only held jobs at the bottom rungs of the occupational structure as custodians and common laborers; some gained prestigious and skilled jobs. John Harley, a black graduate of the University of Pittsburgh, became a draftsman at the Crucible Steel Company. Another black graduate of the University of Pittsburgh, William Dennon, joined the engineering department at the Farrell plant of U.S. Steel. William Nelson Page, another early black migrant, served as private secretary to W.G. Glyde, general manager of sales for Carnegie Steel. At the Black Diamond Steel Works in Pittsburgh, African Americans held such important skilled positions as plumber, engineer, die grinder, and puddler. At the Clark Mills in Pittsburgh, about 30 percent of the firm's 110 black employees worked in skilled jobs—as rollers, roughers, finishers, puddlers, millwrights, and heaters.

By 1910, skilled workers made up about 27 percent of Pittsburgh's black iron and steel workforce. Indeed, for a short period, immigrants from southern and eastern Europe had fewer of their numbers in skilled jobs with less average pay than African Americans. A 1910 survey of iron- and steelworkers in Pittsburgh recorded an average weekly wage of $14.98

for black workers, compared to weekly earnings of $12.21 for Polish workers. Skilled black workers often supervised their less skilled white counterparts. As Richard R. Wright, a close contemporary observer of the mills noted, "[At] one mill . . . where the two chief rollers were Negroes . . . several white men [worked] under them."[46]

Although African American workers developed strikebreaking as one strategy for gaining jobs in a class- and race- divided labor market, they repeatedly balanced rather than displaced one strategy over another. They knew, for example, that employers were no more likely to support their interests than were white workers. Thus, black workers also formed all-black locals and worked to close ranks with organized white labor. As early as 1881, black boilers formed the Garfield Lodge No. 92 at the Black Diamond Steel Works. Complementing the Pittsburgh local was the formation of Sumner Lodge No. 3 in Richmond, Virginia. When black workers struck the Black Diamond Works in 1881-82, white union officials supported their search for work at other mills during the shutdown. When employers turned to Richmond for black strikebreakers, the Sumner Lodge foiled their effort. By gaining jobs in other mills with the support of white workers and by joining hands with black workers in Richmond, African American workers demonstrated a resolve to organize across geographical as well as racial lines. Moreover, during the 1880s, a few African Americans joined the Pittsburgh Knights of Labor assembly. One black, Jeremiah Grandison, later represented the group at the founding convention of the AFL. African Americans also belonged to the coal miners' unions in western Pennsylvania, including first the Knights Assembly and later the United Mine Workers of America.

The organizing activities of black workers attracted the attention of white labor leaders. Unfortunately, such leaders invariably hoped to control and channel such activities in the interests of white workers. Such spokesmen conveniently overlooked the existence of white as well as black strikebreakers and repeatedly exhorted blacks on the merits of honoring white picket lines. In 1913, for example, the president of the Amalgamated Association, John Williams of Pittsburgh, declared that African Americans were eligible to join the union. Yet Williams emphasized the necessity of educating blacks in the "principles and ideals" of the labor movement. He refused to concede that white workers had as much to learn, perhaps even more, from their black counterparts.[47]

Emancipation ushered in a new era in African American life. Along with the federal government, Ohio Valley states amended their constitutions, removed the word "white," and confirmed the new status of blacks as citizens. Racial and class barriers did not fall easily. Blacks faced new obstacles in the economy, politics, and culture of Ohio Valley cities. The new urban industrialists and their workers retained allegiance to notions of white superiority and black inferiority. As such, they devised social practices that limited African American access to jobs and the full fruits of their own labor. Although state and municipal governments no longer endorsed overt discrimination against African Americans, their policies and procedures nonetheless reinforced racial inequality and underscored the limits of African American freedom, citizenship, and participation in the expanding urban-industrial economy. Still, by World War I, Ohio Valley blacks had increased their numbers and broadened their foothold in the region's economy. Based upon these new demographic, economic, and political changes in their lives, African Americans would also escalate their community-building activities and launch new movements for social justice. In the process, they would also face new challenges to their own solidarity.

4

The Persistence of Racial and Class Inequality: The Limits of Citizenship

African Americans not only confronted obstacles in the labor market of postbellum Ohio Valley cities, they also faced new restrictions on their lives as citizens. Although they could now vote, petition the legislature, and demand justice before the law, blacks soon discovered the limits of citizenship. While whites accepted some changes in the old order, they gradually erected new barriers in the social, cultural, and political life of the region. At the same time, residential segregation intensified and re-inforced the separation of blacks and whites in other areas of urban life. By 1889, Cincinnati's *Commercial Gazette* confirmed a regional and na-tional trend when it declared, "The color line is everywhere."[1] The racial subordination of African Americans was nonetheless inextricably inter-woven with the transformation of class relations under industrial capi-talism. Thus, as elsewhere, the responses of Ohio Valley blacks to social inequality would reveal a complicated mixture of class and race con-sciousness.

Ohio Valley cities either excluded or segregated blacks in virtually every aspect of life. As early as 1872, Allegheny County whites excluded blacks from the city's orchestra, railroad sleeping cars, and service at the Monon-gahela House, Hare's Hotel, the Lincoln Club, and "any A No. 1 restau-rant . . . except as a waiter."[2] In 1880, a popular Cincinnati restaurant denied service to George Washington Williams, the city's first black state assemblyman. Williams refused to eat his food in the kitchen or take it outside. By the 1890s, the *Evansville, Daily Journal* abandoned its earlier attacks on racial intolerance in the South and now blamed African Americans for mob violence, including lynchings for alleged sexual offenses against white women. According to the *Journal*, the "crimes of negroes" explained the lynchings. "The home," the paper said, "must be sacred."[3] Whereas some black elites continued to associate with whites and worship in their churches during the 1890s, rising hostility from white parishioners forced them to form their own congregations by the early 1900s.[4]

As the system of de facto segregation expanded in other Ohio Valley cities, Louisville followed the Jim Crow practices of its southern counterparts. The state of Kentucky and its municipalities mandated racial segregation on railroad cars, in public schools, and in a broad range of social services. Trains arriving from Louisville and other southern cities often reached Cincinnati carrying "white only" signs. Yet, according to historian George Wright, Louisvillians adopted a pattern of "polite racism."[5] During the entire period, the city retained biracial use of public parks, defeated proposals for Jim Crow streetcars, accepted the enfranchisement of blacks, and rejected mob violence as an instrument of social control. In Louisville and other Ohio Valley cities, the police played a key role in reinforcing the unequal and hostile racial order. After investigating reports of police brutality in Louisville, the NAACP concluded that the policemen assume that "the Negro [has] no rights, civil or political, that a police bully [is] bound to respect."[6]

Residential segregation accompanied and reinforced the separation of blacks and whites in the social, institutional, and cultural life of the region. Ohio Valley homeowners, realtors, politicians, and civic and social welfare leaders advocated racial separation in the housing market. As early as the 1880s, white Louisvillians urged their city council to pass an ordinance confining blacks to a "colored district." In 1900, under the headline, "Like to have a darky neighbor," the *Pittsburgh Leader* opposed open housing. Even when black homeowners maintained fine homes in or near white neighborhoods, white home-buyers, and even house-renters, avoided such areas. In 1900, a young married couple rejected a rental house because there was "a settlement of very respectable colored folks close by." Residential segregation received its strongest legal support in 1914, when the city of Louisville enacted a housing segregation ordinance requiring the separation of blacks and whites in the city's residential areas.[7]

Despite such resistance, African Americans gradually moved into previously all-white areas, usually contiguous to their antebellum settlements. In Pittsburgh, for example, whereas the pre–Civil War black community concentrated in the Third, Sixth, and Seventh wards, over 50 percent of the black population now lived in six wards: the Third, Fifth, Eighth, Eleventh, Twelfth, and Twenty-second. Even more so than before, the Hill District represented the center of the African American community. The number of blacks in the Hill District increased from fewer than 1,000 in the 1850s to 8,300 in 1900. Other Pittsburgh blacks lived in the upper Hill, the Strip District, and East Liberty.[8]

In Cincinnati, as early as 1870, the area called "Bucktown," located in the Thirteenth Ward on the East End, represented the largest concentration of blacks. To the southwest along the Ohio River was "Little Africa." Extending along Front Street, between Walnut and Ludlow near the docks, this area covered sections of the Second and Fourth wards and contained subsections called the "Levee," "Sausage Row," and "Rat Row." A third black neighborhood emerged on Cincinnati's West End. Called "Little Bucktown," this area was located along Sixth Street, between Freeman and Baymiller, in the Fifteenth and Sixteenth wards. By 1910, as industry and commerce pushed residents out of the old East End community, Cincinnati's black population moved from the old Bucktown area of the East End to the western edge of the CBD. The black population in this area increased from an estimated 3,500 in 1890 to about 8,000 in 1910. Located several blocks above the Ohio River banks, the area around West Fifth and Central Avenue emerged as the core of this West End community.[9]

Similar concentrations of blacks emerged in Evansville and Louisville. By 1900, nearly 65 percent of Evansville's black population lived in the First, Second, and Seventh wards. Ten years later, districts 141 to 145 of the Seventh Ward alone contained over 40 percent of the city's total black population. In Louisville, too, by 1910, African Americans concentrated most heavily in a few wards, particularly wards Nine and Ten near the CBD. These two wards housed the largest numbers and percentages of black residents.[10]

Despite increasing residential segregation before World War I, African Americans lived in neighborhoods with large numbers of whites. In Cincinnati, the West End contained the largest single concentration of blacks, but African Americans accounted for less than 30 percent of the total. Similarly, in the Hill District of Pittsburgh, whites outnumbered

A view of "Taylor Alley" in Cincinnati's black community described by contemporaries as "Little Bucktown." Despite negative depictions of their communities, African Americans gradually built new institutions and transformed their space in the city. From W.P. Dabney, *Cincinnati's Colored Citizens* (1926)

blacks by more than five thousand. In Evansville, blacks constituted less than 25 percent of their neighborhoods. Finally, in Jim Crow Louisville, African Americans also lived interspersed among whites. On the city's periphery, African Americans made up less than 5 percent of the total and, in seven other wards, they represented 15 to 25 percent of the total.[11]

As in the antebellum years, the growth of residential segregation was not only a matter of shifting black-white relations. It was also intertwined with changing ethnic and class relations among whites. Indeed, the industrial city became even more fragmented than its antebellum commercial and early industrial counterparts. As elsewhere in urban-industrial America, Ohio Valley cities made the transition from the "walking city" of the early to mid-nineteenth century to the sprawling metropolis of the late nineteenth and early twentieth centuries. Ohio Valley cities increased in population size, added new land through annexations, replaced old horsecar transportation systems with new electric mass transit systems, and ushered in highly specialized land use patterns. Together, these changes led to the increasing spatial separation of home, work, commerce, finance, and industry, symbolized by the rapid expansion of the Central Business District. The transformation of the city's spatial structure also reinforced segregation of urbanites along class, ethnic, and racial lines.[12]

As African Americans faced stiff restrictions on where they could live, work, and gain social, institutional, and cultural services, they transformed their increasingly segregated urban environment into a community. Key to this process was the reorientation of black entrepreneurial activities from white elite to black, predominantly working class, clients. By World War I, as elsewhere, a new black middle class emerged in Ohio Valley cities. Black barbershops, beauty salons, hotels, rooming houses, groceries, restaurants, funeral homes, dance halls, newspapers, and pool rooms all significantly expanded. In Pittsburgh, advertisements in the local black weekly revealed the range of black businesses: five restaurants, three tailors, funeral directors, insurance agents, billiard rooms, an industrial school for girls, a chauffeur school for boys, a hotel, and a large "colored grocery" store.[13] Despite its small size, Evansville's black population also developed a coterie of businesses serving the black community by 1910: seventeen barbershops and two hairdressing parlors, five boarding houses and two residences that furnished rooms, two restaurants and two lunch stands, five groceries, a tailor shop, and a funeral home among others.[14]

Louisville developed the most impressive record of black businesses. As white-oriented black businesses declined, by the late 1890s, the *Indianapolis Freeman* reported the expansion of businesses serving Louisville's black community: three newspapers, carpenter shops, blacksmith shops, two tailor shops, twenty restaurants, ten salons, twenty barbershops, and several funeral homes. By 1910, another survey of the city's black businesses revealed "too many grocery stores, restaurants, and barbershops to count, two drug stores, and a large office building completely occupied by black businessmen." Ohio Valley black business people also formed local chapters of Booker T. Washington's National Negro Business League, which promoted the principles of racial solidarity and self-help.[15]

Closely intertwined with the growth of black enterprises was the expansion of blacks in the professions. The number of teachers, preachers, musicians, entertainers, doctors, and lawyers gradually expanded. In Cincinnati, as early as 1874, William Parham, superintendent of the city's black schools, became the first black to receive a law degree from the Cincinnati Law School. Other blacks gained degrees from the city's Eclectic Medical School. Although a handful of blacks gained medical and law degrees in other Ohio Valley cities, Louisville blacks developed the most impressive showing in the professions. As early as 1871, Henry Fitzbutler, the first black to receive a medical degree from the University of Michigan, became Louisville's first black doctor. Two decades later, Louisville had thirteen physicians, eight lawyers, fifty-nine ministers, and over one hundred teachers. During the early twentieth century, as elsewhere in the South, Louisville's roster of black professionals continued to expand, with black teachers representing the mainstay of the new black middle class. Paradoxically, as the Jim Crow system broadened opportunities for black teachers in Louisville, the dismantling of segregated schools in Pittsburgh (1875) and Cincinnati (1887), threatened to undercut the position of black educators. In Indiana, where the state retained local option to segregate or integrate, Evansville retained segregation and the number of black teachers slowly increased, though few in numbers.[16]

Entrepreneurial and professional activities not only represented the growth of a dynamic business district within the heart of the black community, they also reflected the rise of an African American cultural district. In these areas, African Americans developed a plethora of religious, fraternal, social, cultural, and political institutions and organizations. Although African Americans developed their own dance halls, theaters, and other popular forms of commercial entertainment and leisure, the church emerged as the core of the cultural and institutional development of the black district. Baptist and AME churches dominated the religious and institutional life of Ohio Valley blacks. In Pittsburgh, black churches increased from an estimated half dozen during the 1850s to nearly twenty-eight by the early 1900s; the Hill District accounted for about 50 percent of these churches. In Cincinnati, black Baptist churches rose from six in 1874 to thirteen (plus eight in outlying areas) in 1900. Membership in the city's black Baptist congregations also increased, from 1,027 in 1870 to 2,011 in 1900. Between 1906 and World War I, membership in the city's Antioch and Zion Baptist churches, respectively, rose from 450 to 1,005

Rev. J. D. Rouse served as pastor of Evansville's Liberty Baptist Church between 1882 and 1929. Courtesy Special Collections, Willard Library, Evansville, Indiana

and from 307 to 1,000. Between 1874 and 1876, black Methodists in Evansville built Alexander Chapel, which occupied a new edifice and claimed some 325 members by 1889. At the same time, the city's Liberty Baptist Church experienced the most explosive growth, rising from only a few members in its Baptist Lecture Room on Chestnut Street during the Civil War to eight hundred members in a new brick edifice by 1890. In Louisville, African Americans not only developed an extensive roster of Baptist churches, but pooled their resources and established the Kentucky Normal and Theological Institute, which offered elementary, secondary, and college courses, as well as theological instruction. Opened in 1879, the school later added training in law and medicine to its curriculum.[17]

Compared to Baptists, the AME built few new churches. The AME

Evansville's Alexander Chapel African Methodist Episcopal Church, located near Fifth and Walnut Streets. This edifice, which the congregation built in 1889, stood until the advent of urban renewal during the 1960s. Courtesy Special Collections, University of Southern Indiana, Evansville

church's centralized hierarchy encouraged the concentration of resources in one or a few buildings, whereas the decentralized structure of the Baptist church permitted the proliferation of new congregations and buildings. Still, the Methodists built new churches and increased their membership. In Cincinnati, for example, membership in Allen Temple and Bethel AME churches rose from 227 in 1865 to 512 in the 1890s. Between 1906 and 1914, Cincinnati Methodists opened new migrant-based AME Zion and Colored Methodist Episcopal churches. By World War I, black Catholics had also formed their own churches: St. Benedict the Moor in Pittsburgh, St. Anne's in Cincinnati, and St. Augustine in Louisville.[18]

Supplementing black churches was a growing range of mutual aid and benefit societies, fraternal orders, and social clubs. The most important fraternal orders were local chapters of national organizations: the Masons, Knights of Pythias, Elks, Moose, and Odd Fellows, among others. In addition to serving the social, cultural, and leisure needs of members, these organizations provided significant aid to sick, disabled, and unemployed members. They also offered burial funds and assisted widows and their children. Reinforcing the work of the fraternal orders were a variety of social clubs, especially women's clubs. Such clubs not only addressed the social and cultural concerns of members, but issues of poverty, social welfare, and justice. Under the impetus of the National Association of Colored Women (NACW), formed in 1896, Ohio Valley women consolidated their efforts with those of black women elsewhere. Under their famous motto, "Lifting as we Climb," black women strengthened their role in the affairs of the black community at the local, regional, and national levels.[19]

The black press facilitated the cross-class and cultural integration of the black district. By 1910, the black *Indianapolis Freeman* described Cincinnati's black district as both a business "Mecca" and "Bronzeville"; i.e., a cultural center for black people. By reporting on the day-to-day doings of African Americans, particularly its business, professional, religious, civic, and political leaders, black newspapers reinforced efforts to build "a city within a city." In Evansville, despite its small size, African Americans published the biweekly *Transcript* in 1904-05 and the *Clarion* by 1914-15. In 1907, journalist Wendell Phillips Dabney initiated his *Cincinnati Union*. Between Reconstruction and the beginning of World War I, Louisville blacks published some eight newspapers, including William H. Steward's *American Baptist* and physician Henry Fitzbutler's *Ohio Falls Express*.[20] The most successful black newspaper, the *Pittsburgh Courier*, emerged in western Pennsylvania. A security guard at the H.J. Heinz Company, Edwin Nathaniel Harleson founded the paper at the turn of the century, but the paper thrived under the leadership of Robert L. Vann, who became editor and part owner by 1910. Originally from North Carolina, Vann attended the University of Pittsburgh Law School and became its first African American graduate in 1909. Like other black newspapers, the *Courier* repeatedly urged blacks to "concentrate" their earnings, "make capital," and hire, produce, and sell for themselves. In Vann's view, capital accumulation, businesses, and professional enterprises represented the keystones of African American institutional, intellectual, cultural, and community development.[21]

Wendell P. Dabney and his wife the former Nellie Foster Jackson. Dabney was born in Richmond, Virginia, and edited the *Cincinnati Union* for twenty years. From W.P. Dabney, *Cincinnati's Colored Citizens* (1926)

Even as African Americans constructed their own urban community, they advocated participation in the larger life of the city. Indeed, they used their expanding network of institutions as springboards for the formation of political clubs and civil rights organizations. Like blacks elsewhere in America, Ohio Valley blacks formed numerous Republican clubs, and supported the Republican Party as the party of emancipation and citizenship. Despite risk of bodily harm, black Republicans often defied their white Democratic opponents. During the 1880s, for example, a Cincinnati black challenged the illegal voting practices of the Democratic Party. "There upon," as one writer put it, "a gang of older hoodlums pounced upon the challenger, dragged him into the streets and beat him savagely." Other blacks also faced harassment and even incarceration when they resolved to vote for the candidate of their choice.[22]

Although black Republican organizations allied with the white-dominated Republican Party, they were not merely tools of white Republicans. African American political leaders used their organizations to wage demands for greater representation, influence, and patronage for black voters. In some cases, independent black Republican organizations openly challenged their white counterparts. In 1894, Louisville blacks formed the R.B. Elliott Club. Formed under the leadership of Dr. Henry Fitzbutler, the Elliott Club (named after the black South Carolina legislator) aimed "to elect men to office in the Republican party who are willing to accord to colored Republicans every political right as citizens, to the end that the general condition of the race might be bettered and the good of the community enhanced." In the same year, Evansville blacks formed the Bruce Club (named after the recently elected governor of the state). They soon met with white party officials to address the issue of patronage "that the colored people themselves [are] entitled to by reason of their fight for the success of the Grand Old Party."[23] Pittsburgh and Cincinnati blacks also pressed the party for more jobs and representation as a result of their loyalty. In order to improve their access to city jobs, under the leadership of William Parham, Cincinnati blacks threatened "a political revolution among colored voters."[24] As such, they challenged the political machine of boss George B. Cox.

As a result of their efforts, African Americans gradually increased their access to patronage positions. In Cincinnati, the number of black appointees rose from negligible numbers in 1880 to 164 in 1891. Together, black employees earned an estimated $120,000 for work in municipal and county positions, mainly as laborers and domestic servants, but they also gradually gained access to jobs as deputy sheriffs and clerks. The Bruce Club of Evansville had specified that "all of the janitorships at the court house should go to colored men since they can secure no clerkships or other positions higher than janitor." Under Democrats and Republicans, Evansville blacks received a few janitorial, police, and fireman positions. Blacks in Louisville achieved more patronage positions than their counterparts elsewhere in the Ohio Valley, but worked mainly as porters, janitors, and sanitation workers. While such workers also received assistance in the form of food and coal during periods of unemployment and hard times, few blacks gained jobs in skilled, professional, and clerical categories.[25]

Although African Americans occupied the bottom rung of the patronage ladder, their growing political mobilization kept them from slipping off altogether. In each city, Republicans also responded to blacks with a modicum of patronage concessions, partly because some blacks gradually turned toward the Democratic Party. Moreover, in Cincinnati, some blacks like teacher Peter Clark supported the Socialist Party. As historian

Peter Clark, the Cincinnati high school teacher and early black convert to the Socialist party. From W.P. Dabney, *Cincinnati's Colored Citizens* (19296)

David Gerber notes, following Clark's emergence as a socialist in 1877, such challenges "forced Republicans to take extraordinary measures." It was during this period that the Republican Party nominated and helped to ensure the election of George Washington Williams as the state's first black legislator. From Williams's election in 1877 to 1916, Cincinnati intermittently sent a black to the Ohio legislature. Four years after Williams's election, African Americans in Pittsburgh elected one of their own to the city council. Lemuel Googins, the renowned pre-war barber, became the first black to serve on the Pittsburgh city council. In Cincinnati and Louisville, blacks also gradually received prestigious appointments to state boards or directorships of state institutions like the Ohio Institution for the Education of the Blind and to black divisions of state prison, agriculture, and education bureaucracies.[26]

African Americans not only used their vote, formed political clubs, and influenced the electoral system, they also organized civil rights organizations and pushed for the enforcement of civil rights laws. In the Civil Rights Act of 1875, federal law prohibited racial discrimination in public accommodations, including public transportation, places of amusement, restaurants, hotels, barbershops, and theaters. White resistance, however, resulted in the civil rights cases of 1883, in which the U.S. Supreme Court pronounced the civil rights act unconstitutional. As a result, African Americans met in conventions, formed civil rights leagues, and pushed for the enactment of state civil rights laws designed to end racial discrimination in public accommodations. Following a national convention of blacks in Louisville, the movement for passage of state civil rights laws gained momentum. Along with blacks in other northern states, Ohio Valley blacks achieved victory when state legislatures passed new civil rights laws prohibiting racial discrimination in public accommodations: Ohio, 1884; Indiana, 1885; and Pennsylvania, 1887. Although the movement had gained momentum in Louisville, the state of Kentucky failed to pass such a law.[27]

As state civil rights laws went into effect, civil rights leagues declined but did not disappear. In 1890, under the leadership of T. Thomas Fortune, Ohio Valley delegates joined over one hundred African Americans in Chicago and launched the Afro-American League of the United States. The league aimed to end all vestiges of racial discrimination. In 1893, following a convention in Cincinnati, African Americans rejected Booker T. Washington's narrow emphasis on economic endeavors over political and civil rights struggles. The convention also rejected AME Bishop Henry McNeal Turner's call for a return to Africa. Instead, the convention voted to form a National Equal Rights Council and push for full citizenship rights. The Equal Rights League soon protested the enforcement of Kentucky's Jim Crow laws on Indiana and Ohio soil. In Cincinnati and Evansville, trains bound for Kentucky were out-fitted with "white only" signs before leaving the station. In a lawsuit filed to end the practice, a U.S. circuit court ruled on behalf of blacks. In 1896, African Americans won another victory when the Ohio legislature passed an anti-lynching law, declaring mob violence and the taking of life without due process of law a "crime." The law held the county responsible for mob violence and permitted victims (in cases of injury) or their families (in cases of death) to recover up to $5,000 in damages.[28]

After Ohio blacks gained an anti-lynching law, Louisville blacks formed the Negro Outlook Committee and pledged to protect blacks from police brutality. Although the organization disappeared within less than a decade, it did gather evidence on police brutality and filed complaints with city officials, who invariably ignored the evidence and dismissed charges against offending officers. By the eve of World War I, Ohio Valley blacks turned increasingly toward the new National Association for the Advancement of Colored People (NAACP). Formed in 1909, the NAACP reinforced the struggle against racial discrimination in all facets of American life. Indeed, the new organization would later build upon the achievements of earlier civil rights efforts, especially the campaign for a federal anti-lynching law modeled on the Ohio version.[29]

Even as Ohio Valley blacks resisted mob violence and pushed for equal access to public accommodations, they also pushed for black public schools. More specifically, African Americans demanded the formation and equal funding of black schools. This movement was most successful in Louisville, where the state of Kentucky mandated the equal funding of black and white schools from the early postbellum years (1882); least successful in Pittsburgh, where the state imposed integration and closed black schools (1881); and somewhat more successful in Evansville, where the state permitted local option, and in Cincinnati, where the state mandated integration but responded to black demands for their own schools. Unlike Pittsburgh, when the state mandated integration without local option, blacks in Cincinnati launched vigorous protests for the maintenance of all-black schools and won.[30]

In Cincinnati's Walnut Hills area, a separate black school persisted from the antebellum years. During the first decade of the new century, however, African Americans launched a movement to strengthen the institution. They changed its name to Frederick Douglass School and requested new educational programs and necessary repairs to the physical plant. In 1908, over two thousand blacks signed a petition to the school board, asking for construction of a new building on the same site. The board assented and allocated $160,000 for a new school, which opened in 1911. Under the leadership of the new principal Francis Russell, who was recruited from a neighboring Kentucky school, the new facility became a center of learning for young people and a social and cultural center for the entire black community. While some blacks reconciled the Douglass School with their integrationist values, others saw a return to

Jennie D. Porter, the black educator and founder of the Cincinnati's Harriet Beecher Stowe School and the first black woman to receive the Ph.D. degree from the University of Cincinnati. From W.P. Dabney, *Cincinnati's Colored Citizens* (1926)

segregation as a way station for expanding the opportunities for black teachers in Cincinnati.

By the eve of World War I, Cincinnati blacks escalated their campaign for black public schools. Under the leadership of black educator Jennie D. Porter, a graduate of the University of Cincinnati, African Americans gained a new school on West Fifth Street in the West End. Later known as the Harriet Beecher Stowe School, the facility would eventually become the "largest public school in Cincinnati, irrespective of race." Although the push for separate schools generated little dissent in Cincinnati, writer William Dabney offered a minor objection to the opening of one black school: "The 'Colored' school . . . is next door to a 'white' school in which the same grades are taught . . . There is no excuse for its establishment." Yet, when, upon her death, white philanthropist Sallie Peters McCall left $140,000 for the creation of a black industrial school in Cincinnati,

Dabney served on the board of trustees of the all-black facility, which opened with eighty-five students in 1914.[31]

As suggested by McCall's will, some whites continued their support of the African American cause. In Pittsburgh, as late as 1893, black attorney William H. Stanton launched his career in the law office of white attorney Charles F. McKeena. In Louisville, influential whites like lawyer Bennett Young, newspaper editor Henry W. Watterson, and businessman Basil Duke all supported the development of separate black institutions, both before and following the ascension of Booker T. Washington and the intensification of racial hostilities. By the onset of World War I, for example, Ohio Valley African Americans and their white supporters had raised sufficient funds to open black YMCAs and YWCAs. White philanthropists like James Gamble of the Procter and Gamble Company and businessman Joseph Schmidlapp contributed sufficient funds to open such institutions in Cincinnati.[32]

Although African Americans retained a small roster of white allies, interracial cooperation remained a weak affair. By the first decade of the new century, African Americans relied increasingly on their own resources. As discussed above, they pooled their resources and built new churches, fraternal orders, social clubs, and business and professional enterprises. Yet, based primarily upon the earnings of the expanding black working class, institution-building involved substantial friction along class and cultural lines. Although the shade-of-color factor persisted as a divisive force in African American life, class gradually supplanted the emphasis on pigmentation.

Black workers not only formed the economic foundation for the institutional development of the African American community, but for the slow emergence of middle class enclaves within both black and white residential areas. In Pittsburgh, as early as the 1880s and 1890s, Homewood became home for a small number of African American business people and skilled workers, supplemented by the persistence of well-to-do butlers and waiters who served a white clientele. In 1890, for example, the waiter and butler Isaac Watson and his wife, Carrie, purchased a house on Tioga Street. During the mid-1890s, another black man named John T. Writt opened a catering business in downtown Pittsburgh, but lived in his own home on Susquehanna Street in Homewood. Conversely, few blacks owned homes in the predominantly working-class Hill District.[33] In Cincinnati, some well-to-do blacks bought or rented commodious structures on the periphery of the East and West End, while others of the upper class moved farther out to parts of hilltop neighborhoods like Cumminsville and Avondale. In Louisville, the most affluent blacks lived in the Chestnut Street area. In 1910, a reporter for the *Indianapolis Freeman* visited Louisville and noted that some seventy-five of these homes were not only well-built but lavishly furnished, some with imported furniture.[34]

African American institutions and civil rights struggles also reflected the impact of class formation. By the late nineteenth and early twentieth centuries, established AME and Baptist churches gradually moved into relatively imposing edifices, while the newer, smaller, and struggling working-class congregations took up residence in homes and low-rent storefronts. Although this process of differentiation proceeded further among the AME—Bethel in Pittsburgh, Allen Temple in Cincinnati, Quinn Chapel in Louisville, and Alexander Chapel in Evansville—than the Baptists, the latter also exhibited growing differentiation by class. Black- middle-class-oriented Baptist churches emerged in each city: Cincinnati's Union Baptist (formerly First Baptist), Fifth Street Baptist in Louisville, Liberty Baptist in Evansville, and Ebenezer Baptist in Pittsburgh. Old established elite churches not only erected new edifices and expanded their social and religious programs, but employed relatively well-educated ministers whom they paid a substantial salary. Members of Pittsburgh's Ebenezer Baptist Church paid their pastor, Rev. George Howard, an annual salary of $4,000 and contributed $16,000 per year toward maintenance of the edifice. In Cincinnati, Allen Temple purchased an edifice replete with expensive carpets, several chandeliers (worth $1,000 each), pipe organs, and frescoes. Formerly owned by Sephardic Jews, the value of the property increased from $40,000 at the time of purchase in 1870 to $80,000 in the 1890s. The formal services, language, dress, and decor of the AME and elite Baptist churches contrasted with the informal modes of worship at the predominantly working-class churches.[35]

As elsewhere, educated business and professional people spearheaded efforts to reshape the behavior of the black working class. Doctors, lawyers, teachers, and ministers mediated the gradual transformation of black working-class culture and values in Ohio Valley cities. They regularly railed against dancing, drinking, prostitution, gambling, and other "sins." Such behavior, they believed, undercut the "morals, mind, and manners" of black workers and made them less productive and law-abiding citizens than they could be. The pulpit, school, and newspaper preached a regimen of hard work, sobriety, temperance, racial solidarity, and self-help. In October 1911, for example, the *Pittsburgh Courier* asked: "Do you buy everything you can from the Race's Enterprises? Where do you get your clothes, your groceries and soft drinks, if you please? Who's your doctor, dentist and lawyer? It is very inconsistent for any church, institution or individual to patronize elsewhere." In some cases, the efforts to regulate the behavior of the black workers' class and the poor became quite hostile. In 1914, Cincinnati blacks formed the National Negro Reform League and Criminal Elimination Society. In its statement of purpose, the organization defined old residents as the "better class" and newcomers as the "criminal class." More specifically, the organization aimed "to assist in the protection of the commonwealth from the criminal class of Negroes, to help the better class of Negroes distinguish itself from the bad citizens; to insure the arrest and conviction of lawbreakers and assist the innocent; and to protect young colored women."[36] In Louisville, the elite designated themselves "The Four Hundred," and "boasted that their education, close contact with whites, occupations, indeed their entire life-style, elevated them above other Negroes." Even in Evansville, a small elite articulated its belief that the "race problem" would be solved by teaching working class children "proper virtues."[37]

African American workers and the poor were by no means passive receptacles of such middle-class preachments. As noted above, they developed a variety of strategies for gaining a foothold in the urban economy. They not only responded to racial discrimination in the labor movement by adopting a strong work ethic and gaining industrial jobs through strike-breaking; they also addressed the racial practices of employers by forming their own unions and striking for better treatment and higher pay. Their activities revealed the extent of their willingness to work hard, effectively, and consistently in the interest of their employers. They were also highly class- as well as race-conscious participants in black business and professional enterprises. They sometimes withheld their patronage from black business and professional people who failed to satisfy their needs. Recognizing this fact, in one editorial, the *Pittsburgh Courier* queried and admonished black business and professional people: "Are you attending strictly to business? Are you on the job early and late giving your patrons full value for their money. If not, do so at once, as it is most essential and the road to success. . . . If you are not giving your customers their money's worth, get out of business. Don't complain about not getting the patronage and support of your people, if you are not giving full value and doing your part to deserve it."[38]

The African American community was not only influenced by changing class relations, it was also shaped by gender constraints. As suggested by the aims of Cincinnati's Reform League, contemporaries frequently commented on the lives of young, unattached women and the dangers that they faced in the urban environment. Whether single or married, established or migrant, however, black working women shouldered the chief burdens of gender, class, and race discrimination. While middle-class and educated black women gradually gained positions as teachers, nurses, and social workers, black women with less education remained disproportionately confined to domestic service jobs. Even so, black women from different class backgrounds faced significant constraints on their lives as women as well as blacks. In the legal and medical professions, for example, black men gradually gained positions as physicians and lawyers, while black women only slowly entered the nursing and clerical fields within the black community.[39]

Additionally, along with white women, black women endured disfranchisement and even greater limits on their quest for citizenship than black men. Consequently, some African American women would turn toward the suffrage movement. The pre–World War I career of Daisy Lampkin illustrates this point. Born in Washington, D.C., in 1883, Lampkin moved to Pittsburgh in 1909. She married restaurant proprietor William Lampkin and soon became active in local politics. By 1912, she had launched her political career as part of the suffrage movement. Lampkin played a key role in street-corner campaigns designed to organize black women into political clubs; and, by 1915, she became the third president of the Negro Women's Equal Franchise Federation, founded in 1911.[40]

Despite their keen gender consciousness, African American women represented the mainstay of cross-class institution-building activities. They outnumbered black men among church members, built energetic auxiliaries of black fraternal orders, and formed a plethora of social clubs that helped them to define key issues and fashion responses thereto, which affected the entire black community. Local chapters of the National Association of Colored Women symbolized their growing activism on behalf of the race. In other words, despite immense obstacles, as elsewhere, black women in the Ohio Valley region defined their gender and class interests in racial terms. As such, they supported efforts to build strong African American communities as springboards for broader political struggles for social justice.

Between the Civil War and World War I, Ohio Valley blacks made the transition from a disfranchised proletariat to new enfranchised workers and citizens. Under the growing impact of emancipation, citizenship rights, and especially industrial capitalism, African Americans voted, petitioned their government, filed lawsuits, and expanded their footing in the urban political economy. Unfortunately, before they could realize the full fruits of their freedom, a new era of segregation, class, and racial inequality emerged. Consequently, like their counterparts elsewhere in industrial America, Ohio Valley blacks repeatedly defined their class, cultural, and political interests in racial terms and struggled to build unified black urban communities. These developments would gain even greater articulation during the era of the Great Migration.

PART THREE

African Americans in the Industrial Age 1915-1945

5

Expansion of the Black Urban-Industrial Working Class

World War I disrupted immigration from overseas and stimulated the search for national sources of labor. Along with the rural-to-urban migration of northern and southern whites, blacks entered Ohio Valley cities in growing numbers. Moreover, during the 1920s, the enactment of federal immigration restriction legislation reinforced industrial opportunities for African Americans. For the first time in their history, African Americans moved from domestic and general labor jobs into industrial occupations in large proportions. Yet, compared to American-born whites, immigrants, and their children, African Americans continued to occupy the bottom rungs of the industrial ladder. As earlier, African American life was not only shaped by the attitudes, policies, and practices of white Ohio Valley industrialists, workers, and the state; it was also influenced by the political activities, culture, and consciousness of African American workers and their communities.

Expansion of the African American Urban-Industrial Working Class

Under the impact of World War I and immigration restriction legislation during the 1920s, Ohio Valley cities attracted increasing numbers of blacks from Southern farms and small towns. An estimated five hundred thousand blacks left the South between 1916 and 1920. By 1930, another eight hundred thousand to 1 million southern blacks moved to Ohio Valley and other northern cities. Unlike the pre-war migration, however, most of the new migrants came from the boll weevil–infested cotton regions of the Deep South. Between about 1915 and 1930, the number of black farmworkers in Georgia dropped by nearly 30 percent, from over

122,500 to less than 87,000. South Carolina, Alabama, and Mississippi experienced similar declines.[1]

Although cities like Chicago, Cleveland, and Detroit attracted the largest numbers of black migrants, Cincinnati and Pittsburgh also became important targets of black population movement. In 1917, *Iron Age*, a key journal in the steel industry, reported trains "filled with Negroes bound from the South to Pittsburgh."[2] According to one contemporary scholar, over 18,000 blacks arrived in Pittsburgh between 1915 and 1917. Pittsburgh's black population increased from 25,600 in 1910 to 37,700 in 1920, an increase from 4.8 to 6.4 percent of the total. The black population in the mill towns of Homestead, Rankin, Braddock, and others nearly doubled. By war's end, the black population in the major steel towns of western Pennsylvania had increased from 29,470 to nearly 50,000, an increase of about 70 percent. By 1930, over 78,000 African Americans lived in western Pennsylvania, about 7 percent of the total. Over 50 percent of these blacks continued to live in the city of Pittsburgh. At the same time, Cincinnati's African American population rose from 19,337 in 1910 to 30,079 in 1920 and to 47,818 in 1930, making up about 7.5 percent of the total in 1920 and 10.0 percent in 1930. Unlike Cincinnati and Pittsburgh, however, Evansville and Louisville gained few blacks through migration. Indeed, Louisville's black population declined during the war years (see Table 3).

African Americans earned from $3.50 to over $5.00 per eight-hour day in the steel industry. In the South, they made no more than $2.50 per twelve-hour day in cities. In southern agriculture, as farm laborers, African Americans made no more than $1.00 per day. According to one recent study, even after accounting for higher rents, life in the Pittsburgh region was better for most blacks than it was in their southern homes. In 1917, according to the Cincinnati Council of Social Agencies (CSA), out of forty recent black newcomers to the city, twenty-seven reported that they came to Cincinnati for better wages. Others cited opportunities to obtain "better privileges," "better conditions," and "better treatment." In a letter to the Pittsburgh Urban League, one man wrote for himself and seven other black men, "We Southern Negroes want to come to the north . . . they ain't giving a man nothing for what he do . . . they [white southerners] is trying to keep us down." Another black man from Savannah, Georgia, wrote, "I want to find a good job where I can make a living as I cannot do it here." From South Carolina, a black woman wrote to

Table 3. African American Population in Ohio Valley Cities, 1910-1930

	1910		1920		1930	
	No.	%	No.	%	No.	%
Pittsburgh	25,623	4.8	37,72	6.4	54,983	8.2
Cincinnati	19,639	5.4	30,079	7.5	47,818	10.6
Louisville	40,522	18.1	40,087	17.1	47,354	15.4
Evansville	6,266	9.0	6.394	7.5	6,514	6.4

Source: *Thirteenth Census of U.S.*, vol. 1: Population, 1910 (Washington: Government Printing Office, 1914), pp. 556-609; *Fourteenth Census of U.S.*, vol. 3: Population, 1920 (Washington: Government Printing Office, 1922), pp. 305-857; *Fifteenth Census of U.S.*, vol. 3, pt. 2, 1930 (Washington, Government Printing Office, 1932), pp. 525-744.

the Pittsburgh Urban League for her two sons: "[I have] two grown son[s] ... we want to settle down somewhere north ... wages are so cheap down here we can hardly live." A Georgia man wanted to come to Pittsburgh to "make a livelihood, and to educate my children."[3]

Labor recruiters from railroads, steel companies, and defense industries facilitated black migration to the region. In the summer of 1916, for example, the Pennsylvania and Erie Railroad launched a major campaign to recruit black labor for northern industries, including its own far-flung operations. Railroad companies provided free transportation passes to black workers, who authorized the deduction of travel expenses from their paychecks. By 1918, in western Pennsylvania, black steelworkers had increased from less than 3 percent of the total workforce to 13 percent. Over 50 percent of these employees worked at Carnegie steel plants in Allegheny county and at Jones and Laughlin in Pittsburgh.[4] One black migrant recalled, "One thing [that] impressed me very much was to look at the steel, the iron. All that I had seen in previous years was all finished and hard and everything. To come [to Pittsburgh] and see it running like water—it was amazing."[5] In a letter to his pastor back home, one migrant wrote, "Some places look like torment [hell] or how they say it look."[6]

Labor agents from Cincinnati also traveled south to recruit black workers. According to black social worker James Hathaway Robinson, such agents offered "wages of which he [the black worker] had never dreamed, and privileges of which he had only read in the constitution."[7]

Most blacks entered Cincinnati on four major rail lines: the Louisville and Nashville, the Southern, the Baltimore and Ohio, and the Chesapeake and Ohio. In his portrait of black Cincinnati, journalist William P. Dabney described recruiting activities of Joseph L. Jones and Melvin J. Chisum. During the war years, Jones and Chisum helped to transport southern blacks to industries throughout the North as well as to Cincinnati. Dabney noted the dangers faced by recruiters in the South, as well as the tactics that they sometimes employed to escape harassment:

Upon Chisum devolved "the dirty work," that is, the job of going South to get the "goods." No better character could have been selected. A product of Texas, a life-long newspaper man, short in stature, dark in complexion, aldermanic abdomen, a typical old-time Methodist preacher in appearance, but with a fluency of speech, a lightning rapidity of thought that would do honor to a 33rd Chicago lawyer, and the cheek, brass, nerve that would have made a reputation for a cowboy or a king. In addition, he was a Southern Negro, and who knows the white man better? He did an enormous business, ran a thousand risks. A price was set upon his life and liberty, but when cornered he would simulate a sweet simplicity, a servility that savored of the "good old days," as he talked with an unction and dialect that Uncle Tom would have envied. Thousands of Negroes were brought up by Chisum. That versatile genius is now located in Chicago, the representative of the Negro Press Association. He does business with the leading corporations and political interests of America, and has discarded forever the disguises and manner that enabled him so successfully to run the gauntlet in the cotton fields of the Sunny South.[8]

Northern black newspapers applauded the Great Migration to Ohio Valley cities and elsewhere in urban America. Some southern black newspapers reinforced the process. As one southern West Virginia editor stated, "Let millions of Negroes leave the South. It will make conditions better for those who remain." The black weekly *Chicago Defender* emerged as the most vigorous promoter of black population movement. The *Defender* repeatedly portrayed the South as the land of lynchings, disfranchisement, and economic exploitation. At the same time, the paper appealed to important elements in southern black religious culture. The *Defender* portrayed the North as the "promised land," "flight from Egypt," and "Crossing over Jordan." When one trainload of blacks crossed the Ohio River headed north, they knelt to pray and sang the hymn, "I done Come Out of the Land of Egypt with the Good News."[9]

Although African Americans often expressed their views of the Great

Migration in biblical terms and received encouragement from northern black newspapers, railroad companies, social service organizations, and industrial labor agents, they also organized elaborate kin and friendship networks and facilitated their own movement into the urban Ohio Valley. Southern black men and women formed migration clubs. They pooled their money, bought tickets at reduced rates, and often moved in groups. Before they moved, African Americans gathered information and debated the pros and cons of the process.[10]

As recent scholarship suggests, black women played a major role in migration networks. According to historian Peter Gottlieb, black women sometimes chose Pittsburgh over other places and thereby shaped patterns of black migration to the region. In 1919, one black woman recalled her response and the final result: "I wrote him a letter back. My older sister had come to Pittsburgh, and I took her as a mother because I had lost my mother. And I wrote him back, and said, 'I don't want to stay in Cincinnati. I want to go to Pittsburgh.' Next letter I got, he had got a job in Pittsburgh and sent for me."[11]

Unlike Pittsburgh and Cincinnati, Louisville and especially Evansville offered few attractions to blacks during the era of the Great Migration. During the war years, black men increased their numbers in the mining industry of Vanderburgh County, but lost about 50 percent of such jobs during the postwar era. Employment in the manufacturing sector failed to offset such losses. Evansville's black population increased only slightly, from 6,300 in 1910 to 6,400 in 1920 and to about 6,500 in 1930; indeed, the black proportion of the total dropped from 9.0 percent in 1910 to 6.3 percent in 1930.[12]

Likewise, despite the increased demand for workers during World War I, Louisville's black population declined by 1.1 percent during the war years, dropping from 40,500 to just over 40,000. During the economic expansion of the mid-1920s, however, the city's black population increased by 18.1 percent, rising to about 47,350 in 1930.[13] Still, only a handful of blacks worked in the city's steel mills and foundries, where wages averaged an estimated $15 to $25 per week. Black men and women workers remained overrepresented in the most difficult, low-paying, and dirty sectors of the tobacco industry. Moreover, Louisville employers paid blacks lower wages than whites for identical jobs. According to the Louisville Urban League (LUL), formed in 1920, black workers made between $4 to $10 per week less than their white counterparts for the same work.

As the LUL put it, "It is the low wage scale for colored workmen in Louisville that constitutes the basis for most of our industrial troubles."[14]

Unfortunately, in Cincinnati and Pittsburgh, too, as blacks entered the region in larger numbers during the 1920s, racism intensified and blocked their mobility. Between 1920 and 1930, an estimated 70 to 80 percent of Ohio Valley men and women worked in jobs defined as "unskilled labor." American-born white and immigrant men and women took the higher skilled and better-paying jobs. Unlike black women, however, black men entered such jobs within the manufacturing, transportation, and trade sectors rather than household or domestic service sectors of the economy. In Cincinnati, black men not only gained access to the building and metal trades, but to clothing, agricultural processing, soap, and leather-tanning industries, among others. In some areas blacks made up a disproportionately large percentage of the labor force. In the building trades, for example, black men made up 19 percent of the total, although 85 percent of these men worked in jobs classified as unskilled.[15]

In Pittsburgh, compared to their prewar counterparts, few black steelworkers gained skilled jobs in the wake of the Great Migration. Employers placed over 90 and sometimes 100 percent of the new workers in jobs classified as unskilled. This pattern prevailed at Carnegie Steel (all plants), Jones and Laughlin (all plants), National Tube (all plants), Crucible Steel, and others. African Americans worked in the most difficult, low- paying, and dirty categories of industrial labor. They fed the blast furnaces, poured molten steel, and worked on the coke ovens. Black workers repeatedly complained that their jobs were characterized by disproportionate exposure to debilitating heat, deadly fumes, and disabling and serious injuries. In 1919, blacks made up 4.6 percent of all the state's iron, steel, and manufacturing employees, but registered 8.5 percent of all victims of accidents. While 26 percent of blacks in metal industries suffered severe injuries or death, the figures were 24 and 22 percent, respectively, for immigrants and American-born whites.[16]

In addition, African Americans experienced disproportionate bouts of unemployment. They averaged about two to four months of unemployment per year, resulting in a working year of forty weeks or less and actual weekly earnings of about $18.00 per week. As a result of frequent periods of unemployment, one Hill District black, Harry Latimer, recalled, "You didn't worry about being promoted or getting a raise; you worried about keeping the job you had."[17] As a result of such instability in Ohio

Valley industries, some blacks contemplated returning south. In a letter to his old employer, one Pittsburgh migrant wrote, "I want you to save me my same place for me, for I am coming back home next year, and I want my same farm if you havent nobody on it. . . . When I get home no one will never get me away any more."[18] Some actually returned, but most stayed. In Pittsburgh during the war years, according to historical geographer Joe T. Darden, the war had "a positive effect on reducing occupational segregation between black and white men but the effect appears to have been very small and, heretofore, grossly exaggerated," particularly for black women.[19]

Although black women remained disproportionately concentrated in domestic service jobs, their experiences were by no means uniform from city to city. Before the war, for example, the Pittsburgh Survey reported the exclusion of black women from jobs in department stores as well as in the steel industry. In 1918, however, the city's department stores hired black women in their packing rooms and the Lockhart Iron and Steel Company hired a half-dozen black women. According to one contemporary report, black department store workers "had proved far more satisfactory than white girls in similar positions."[20] In Cincinnati, black women gained jobs in the production of men and women's clothing, while some of Evansville's black women found jobs in cigar factories.[21] In Louisville, black women continued to make up the majority of women workers in the tobacco industry. While some black female tobacco workers earned according to the quantity that they produced, others received a set wage and earned 25 to 30 percent less than their white counterparts doing the same work. Despite wage discrimination, industrial jobs offered better pay than domestic service. Indeed, black women used openings in industrial jobs to demand higher pay in domestic service. In Pittsburgh, for example, prospective employers complained that black women wanted $3.50 to $5.00 per day: "Hundred of jobs go begging at $15 per week." Still, as white women gained increasing access to jobs as teachers, social workers, telephone operators, typists, receptionists, and office secretaries, few black women found alternatives to domestic service.[22]

Whether employers hired or excluded blacks, they offered stereotypical and racist reasons for their choices. In Cincinnati, the Chamber of Commerce surveyed the conditions of black workers for the period 1925-1930. Employers who refused to employ black workers offered four major reasons: "1. Unable or unwilling to mix white and Negro workers. 2.

Skilled help required and Negroes lacked the proper training. 3. White workers preferred. 4. 'Nature of business' no further reason." The next four commonly cited reasons included: "5. Lack of separate facilities for white and Negro workers. 6. Union restrictions. 7. No consideration ever given to use of Negro labor. 8. Fear of public opinion if Negroes were introduced. 9. Fear of disturbance from white workers."[23] Conversely, employers who employed black workers expressed a range of stereotypes about the pliability of African Americans compared to white union or immigrant workers. "1. Loyalty and amiability. 2. Willingness to do types of work white workers refuse to do or at less price. 3. Better suited for hard and disagreeable work. 4. Quick adaptability. 5. Honesty." Although few companies employed blacks as foremen, some hired blacks as "straw bosses" over black crews at lower pay than regular foremen.[24]

As in the pre–World War I years, the membership policies and practices of labor unions reinforced the subordinate position of blacks in the industrial economy. In the Great Steel Strike of 1919, for example, the strike committee itself represented several decidedly hostile and racially exclusionary unions. The machinists and electrical workers barred African Americans altogether, while the blacksmiths relegated blacks to auxiliary lodges under the control of white locals.[25] Although African American strikebreaking activities would decline during the 1920s, few African American steelworkers walked out with their white brothers. In the city of Pittsburgh, less than two dozen blacks joined twenty-five thousand white workers on the picket line. In other plants along the Monongahela River, the response was little better. At the huge Homestead, Duquesne, Clairton, and Braddock works, only a handful of blacks walked out with their white counterparts.[26] Even more than blacks who stayed on the job, the huge importation of new black workers helped to defeat the strike. Along with a few white strikebreakers, the steel industry employed an estimated thirty to forty thousand African Americans nationwide. In Pittsburgh, Annie Morgan later recalled how her husband continued to work during the strike: "They would go in the mill and stay in there sometimes two or three days. They could go in from the Port Perry end because ... the railroad from Port Perry ran right into the mill, you know."[27] Black workers were often shifted from plant to plant, smuggled in at night and mixed with small groups of white strikebreakers.

Despite very difficult times and the disappointing record of labor unions, African Americans were by no means uniformly hostile to organized labor. From the outset of the Great Steel Strike, for example, the Pittsburgh Urban League urged William Z. Foster and the National Committee for Organizing Iron and Steel Workers to employ black organizers. Moreover, when some blacks discovered that white workers were on strike, they refused to work. Eugene Steward, a black worker from Charleston, South Carolina, described the coercive measures that the Pittsburgh Steel Products Company used to secure black strikebreakers: "We were not told that a strike was in progress. . . . When we took the train a guard locked the doors so that we were unable to get out." Additionally, as Steward put it, "When I found that there was a strike on I got out. . . . I told them that I would not go to work if they kept me there two years." In the Hod Carriers Union in Pittsburgh, blacks joined with American-born white workers and strengthened their hand against immigrants. In the cement finishers union, they joined immigrants and strengthened their hand against American-born whites. In most cases, however, they formed all-black organizations and resisted unions as well as the personnel departments of industrial firms.[28] They also frequently quit jobs and moved around in search of better pay, better treatment, and better working conditions. At the A.M. Byers Company, for example, the company had to hire 1,408 black employees in 1923 to maintain a regular workforce of 223 blacks.[29] In Cincinnati, black social worker Theodore Berry noted, "Labor turnover, generally, was not a cause of complaint, except in certain industries where the disagreeable nature of the work and low pay combined to make jobs less attractive, and caused workers to leave at the first opportunity."[30] Although employers, social welfare officials, and municipal authorities treated black turnover as evidence of unreliability, inconsistency, and dearth of a solid work ethic, such behavior also revealed black workers' efforts to improve their status.

Black workers linked their struggle at the workplace to a broader movement to transform the African American community. Although the region escaped the level of racial violence that erupted in Chicago, East St. Louis, and other northern cities during the period, African Americans nonetheless faced increasing restrictions on their access to housing, social services, public accommodations, and places of leisure and entertainment. Although Louisville and the state of Kentucky rejected legislation requiring racially segregated streetcars, they strengthened "informal seg-regation" of blacks on public transportation and systematically excluded blacks from hotels, restaurants, and places of leisure and entertainment. Moreover, unlike the prewar years, in 1924 the city excluded blacks from use of city parks.[31] The resolution declared that it was "not desirable or safe for whites and Negroes to use the same parks and swimming pools." Professional schools, hospitals, and clinics also barred African Americans from professional training except on a segregated and unequal basis. In Cincinnati, Pittsburgh, and Evansville, blacks also faced an expanding pattern of de facto racial segregation. In his wartime survey of black Cincinnati, sociologist James Hathaway Robinson reported, "Not only do hotels, restaurants, and soda fountains refuse to serve him [black people] . . . but moving picture houses and private parks refuse to admit him; theaters segregate and often embarrass him."[32] In Pittsburgh, downtown restaurants routinely excluded black customers, while theaters confined black patrons to the balcony. Ohio Valley theaters not only subjected African Americans to segregated sections, but to racist films like "The Nigger" and "Birth of a Nation." In Evansville, both films premiered in 1915, while Louisville theaters showed "Birth of a Nation" in 1915 and again in 1918.[33]

Despite their small population percentage in northern Ohio Valley cities, African Americans experienced disproportionately high rates of arrest and incarceration. In Cincinnati during the war years, blacks accounted for 23 percent of recorded crimes, although they made up an estimated 7 percent of the population.[34] In Evansville, blacks also made up about 7 percent of the total population, but accounted for over 20 percent of persons arrested for petty theft, vagrancy, and drunkenness.[35] In Pittsburgh, according to historian Laurence Glasco, "crime rates reached scandalous levels." In the Pittsburgh district, when white citizens of Duquesne complained, police raided a boardinghouse, arrested black workers, and fined them for shooting "craps." The local *Duquesne Times Observer* inflamed racial animosities by suggesting that "white citizens should physically retaliate against the colored visitors and their offensive acts."[36] In 1923, one of the most destructive racial conflicts emerged in the Pittsburgh district. In Johnstown, when authorities charged a black migrant in a shooting incident with police, the mayor, chief of police, and other officials blamed black newcomers for stirring up trouble and ordered them "to pack up" and "go back from where you came." An estimated five hundred black steelworkers and their families were forced to leave the area.[37]

During the mid-1920s, the city of Louisville launched a "drive on crime." Police raids on the black community resulted in wholesale arrests, especially for gambling and prostitution; white participants, however, were left unmolested. Although Louisville whites continued to reject mob violence, police brutality increased. During the 1920s, according to one contemporary observer, Louisville police murdered no fewer than seventeen blacks, usually black men who were unarmed and suspected or charged with petty crimes. Compounding such deaths were recurring cases of physical injury inflicted on blacks while in police custody.[38] In Ohio Valley cities, as elsewhere, discriminatory arrest policies and practices inflated black criminal statistics. As black Cincinnatian James Hathaway Robinson put it, "A noticeable factor in this rate is prejudice. . . . The presumption . . . is invariable against the Negro and he is often arrested and sentenced where others would be excused."[39]

The rapid growth of the Ku Klux Klan reflected as well as heightened the spread of racial conflict. Before its demise during the mid-1920s, the organization had enrolled 3,000 members in Louisville, nearly 4,000 in Evansville, nearly 12,200 in Cincinnati, and an estimated 125,000 in western Pennsylvania, where branches opened in Pittsburgh, Homestead, Johnstown, and other towns along the three rivers.[40] The Klan's impact on the Ohio Valley varied from city to city. In the Pittsburgh region it faced strong resistance from immigrant Catholics and their children. Following the shooting death of a Klansman in Carnegie, the organization withdrew and, according to historian Kenneth Jackson, "never again challenged authority in the Pittsburgh area."[41] In Louisville, the capital of "polite racism" and police brutality, public officials denounced the Klan and pledged to use "every lawful means to prevent and suppress its growth in our community."[42] Indeed, the mayor barred the organization from distributing literature on city streets and restricted its ability to hold public meetings. In Cincinnati, the Klan sponsored a fifty-piece band and held numerous public initiation ceremonies and displays of its influence at the city's Carthage Fairgrounds and Mount Healthy.[43] In Evansville, the Klan captured the mayor's office in 1924 and controlled the local Republican Party through 1929. According to historian Darrel Bigham, the Klan directed most of its antagonism toward German Catholics.[44] More importantly, however, although the Klan's influence on race relations varied from city to city, everywhere members of the "Invisible Empire" articulated their belief that the enemies of the republic were "non-Christians and colored people."[45] Such beliefs reinforced social policies and behavior that discriminated against blacks and created a highly volatile racial climate.[46]

As the Ohio Valley Klan, police harassment, and discrimination in public accommodations increased, so did residential segregation. Ohio Valley real estate firms, company officials, and homeowners collaborated in the rise of all-black areas. During the 1920s, the Cincinnati Real Estate Board instructed its employees that "no agent shall rent or sell property to colored people in an established white section or neighborhood and this inhibition shall be particularly applicable to the hill tops and suburban property."[47] In Cincinnati, the West End absorbed the bulk of newcomers. The black population rose to 17,209, nearly double the 1910 figure. As the black population increased, the white basin population dropped from 137,518 in 1910 to 98,776 in 1920 to 59,033 in 1930. The total black basin population increased from fewer than 13,000 in 1910 to 32,728 in 1930. While the city's index of dissimilarity stood at 40.5 percent in 1910, it now climbed to nearly 66.0.[48]

In western Pennsylvania, African Americans also found housing in carefully designated "colored areas": Port Perry in Braddock, Castle Garden in Duquesne, Rosedale in Johnstown, and the historic Hill District in Pittsburgh. During the war years, the black population in Pittsburgh's Third and Fifth wards increased by 13,814; at the same time, the immigrant population dropped by 7,613. In his study of the impact of World War I on African American housing in Pittsburgh, Darden concluded: "A segregation pattern remained despite the opportunity after the war for some blacks to engage in higher paid occupations. Blacks, regardless of income, had great difficulty either renting or buying good houses in nonsegregated areas." According to a visitor from the national office of the YWCA, "Poor housing conditions are universal, congestion is very great and the whole situation is critical."[49] In Evansville, residential segregation also increased. Whereas 62 percent of blacks lived in the downtown area north and east of Canal Street in 1914, by 1929 the figure increased to nearly 70 percent.[50]

Blacks in Louisville faced the most virulent effort to limit their space. From the outset of the period, Louisville officials moved to enforce its new residential segregation ordinance. In August 1915, police arrested two blacks for residing in white areas. State and local courts found the men guilty as charged, levied fines, and ordered them to move from white areas. Although the U.S. Supreme Court ruled the Louisville law unconstitutional in 1917, this ruling did little to halt the customary segregation of blacks in the city's housing market. Following the court's decision, Louisville whites changed the names of several streets that housed black and white residents. They made certain that blacks knew where their neighborhood ended and the white began. Thirtieth Street represented the West End dividing line. Walnut Street changed to Michigan, Chestnut to River Park, Madison to Vermont, and Jefferson to Lockwood. At a West Side homeowners association meeting, one speaker urged whites to make "a Negro living on the West End . . . as comfortable as if he was living in Hell."[51] Likewise, few blacks moved into the East End. Those who did lived in a segregated "Smoketown."[52]

Residential segregation entailed overcrowded, dilapidated, unsanitary, and overpriced housing for African Americans. During the early postwar years, the Cincinnati Better Housing League reported cases of extreme overcrowding: twenty blacks inhabited one three-room flat, while another twelve-room tenement housed ninety-four blacks. As housing and health conditions deteriorated for the city's black population, one public official lamented, "You could not produce a prize hog to show at the fair under conditions that you allow Negroes to live in this city."[53] Contemporary surveys and observations described Evansville's black housing as "undesirable or uninhabitable."[54] Pittsburgh realtors converted railroad cars, basements, boathouses, and warehouses into living quarters for black workers and their families. In 1917, Abraham Epstein reported, "In many instances, houses . . . are dilapidated dwellings with the paper torn off, the plaster sagging from the naked lath, the windows broken, the ceiling low and damp, and the whole room dark, stuffy and unsanitary."[55] Moreover, steel companies housed single men in bunkhouses or segregated camps, where they often occupied rooms with two, three, or four men to a bed on double shifts at the height of the migration.[56]

Although many blacks had grown up in rural poverty, they often expressed shock at the sight of Pittsburgh mill towns. One migrant recalled, "Man, it was ugly, dirty." He went on: "The streets were nothing but dirt streets." While the hills made walking and travel difficult, clouds of smoke and soot blanketed the city during peak work hours. From the vantage point of the South, some blacks saw a real contrast with their new environment: "The South is clean. Everything is white, beautiful. . . . Everything was black and smoky here."[57] In his contemporary study of housing in black Pittsburgh, social analyst Abraham Epstein emphasized the overcrowding of prewar black areas and the spread of blacks to new locations: "The sections designated as Negro quarters, have been long since congested beyond capacity by the influx of newcomers, and a score of new colonies have sprung up in hollows and ravines, on hill slopes and along river banks, by railroad tracks and in mill-yards." Consequently, labor turnovers, as discussed above, was not merely a change of jobs but a shift in housing. According to the Pittsburgh Urban League, in 1920 the Second Avenue section of the black community experienced "a complete family turnover on an average of every two months."[58]

As elsewhere, Ohio Valley landlords took advantage of the desperate housing needs of black migrants. African Americans invariably paid higher rents for housing of substantially less quality than their white counterparts. In Cincinnati, philanthropist Jacob G. Schmidlapp initiated low-income model homes for blacks on the eve of World War I. In 1915, a four-room flat rented for $11 per month in the Washington Terrace Complex. By 1923, the same space rented for $35 per month, well beyond the reach of most African Americans. Real estate speculators took over the large West End mansions and subdivided them into small tenement apartments, charged high rents, and forced tenants to take in large numbers of boarders to meet rent payments. In the West End, over 160 black families housed as many as three or four lodgers each night. In the meantime, white investors bought rural land adjacent to Lincoln Heights, an expanding black area to the north of the city. They sold the plots to blacks who sought alternatives to life in the most congested areas of the city and effectively reinforced patterns of racial segregation in the housing market.[59]

City zoning legislation reinforced residential segregation and housing exploitation. In 1924, Cincinnati passed a new comprehensive zoning law. The new legislation encouraged the building of single-family homes outside the basin, while limiting new residential construction within the area.[60] By 1930, African Americans accounted for only about 2.5 percent of the city's homeowners. Moreover, they occupied housing with a median value of $4,496 compared to $8,000 for American-born whites and over $7,460 for immigrants. As historian Henry Louis Taylor puts it, "No physical wall encircled the ghetto but a wall of high rent did isolate blacks from their ambivalent white neighbors. Building codes, zoning laws, the 1925 city plan, and sub-division regulations reinforced this wall."[61]

As the wall of segregation and racial discrimination increased in Ohio Valley cities, African Americans intensified their own struggle to dismantle it. Even more so than the pre–World War I years, African Americans responded to racial and class inequality by deepening their community-building activities. Despite the narrow opportunity structure available to African American workers, their numbers, income, and growing spatial concentration established the bedrock for the socioeconomic, political, and cultural transformation of black urban communities in the Ohio Valley. African American business, professional, religious, civil rights, and political organizations proliferated. These developments not only reflected the imperatives of racial solidarity, they also revealed the dramatic expansion of the black middle class and the emergence of new forms of unity and disunity within the African American community. When asked why they moved to the region, some southern black business and professional people replied simply that they were following their "practice."[62]

As elsewhere, Ohio Valley blacks expanded the range of prewar black business and professional services while adding new ones. Black barbers, undertakers, tailors, cobblers, beauticians, pharmacists, grocers, editors, and real estate agents all gained increasing opportunities along with doctors, lawyers, dentists, ministers, teachers, and social workers. In Evansville, such changes were modest. The number of black businesses increased from forty-seven on the eve of World War I to only fifty-one by 1920.[63] Unfortunately, some of these failed to survive the decade.[64]

In Louisville, Cincinnati and Pittsburgh, African American business and professional people were more successful. Under the editorship of Robert Vann, the *Pittsburgh Courier* continued to expand as an organ of national circulation. In Pittsburgh, blacks also initiated new, highly successful professional baseball teams that offered entertainment for black communities and employment for black athletes. Cumberland "Cum" Posey Jr. and W. A. "Gus" Greenlee spearheaded the growth of black baseball in Pittsburgh. Posey was born in Homestead in 1891, the son of a Maryland-born migrant who owned both a steamboat and a coal company and apparently left young Posey some money upon his death. As a student and basketball player at both Duquesne University and Pennsylvania State, Posey became interested in athletics and later became a player, manager, and part-owner of the Homestead Grays (organized in 1900 as the Murdock Grays by black Homestead workers and renamed in 1912). Steelworkers often received time off from their jobs to play for the Grays. The Homestead Grays flourished during the 1920s and by 1930 signed star hitter Josh Gibson to its roster of players.[65] For his part, Gus Greenlee operated a numbers game and became wealthy during the 1920s. In 1930, he purchased the Crawford Colored Giants, a baseball team originally organized by a black social work professional in the Hill District. Greenlee soon built his own stadium, invested $100,000 of his own money, and raided players from other teams, including the acquisition of Josh Gibson and the pitcher Satchel Paige. Rivalries between the two super teams, the Grays and the Crawfords, became major leisure-time and cultural events in the lives of Pittsburgh's black steelworkers and their communities. As sports historian Rob Ruck notes, "These teams prospered within a black community that supported them with cheers and spare change and looked to them for recreation and a source of identity."[66]

Despite its failure to offer blacks expanded opportunities in the industrial sector, Louisville's large, segregated black population continued to exhibit the most dynamic black business and professional growth. In 1915, Memphis-born I. Willis Cole came to Louisville. A graduate of LeMoyne Junior College, by 1917 Cole had launched a new black newspaper, the *Leader*. In 1924, he reported on the progress of the black middle class. After reviewing the early pattern of restaurants, barbershops, and undertaking establishments, he noted the emergence of "two banks, four insurance companies, two hotels . . . two building and loan associations, six real estate companies, three drug stores, eight undertakers, two photographers, fifteen groceries, four newspapers, three architects . . . three movie houses and buildings for our business and professional men."[67] Insurance and financial institutions emerged at the forefront of new black business and professional developments in the city. White insurance companies defined blacks as high-risk clients and charged them higher rates than they charged their white policyholders. Despite stiff resistance from white companies and the discriminatory practices of state licensing agencies, African Americans opened the Mammoth Mutual Company in 1915. Under the leadership of Henry Hall, an agent of the black Atlanta Mutual and Standard Life Insurance Company, and lawyer-entrepreneur William H. Wright, the Mammoth Company issued eighty thousand policies within the first five years and built its own six-story building. By 1924, the company reported total assets of $223,255 and liabilities of $19,464.[68] Tied to the resources of the black working class, other black insurance companies and banking firms followed suit.[69]

Closely intertwined with the expansion of black enterprises was the intensification of black religious, fraternal, civil rights, and political activities. As southern black workers, and business and professional people increased their numbers in Ohio Valley cities, they stimulated the expansion of black religious institutions. Unlike the prewar years, however, Holiness bodies also gradually increased alongside Baptists and Methodists. In his interview with 218 migrants to Cincinnati during the war years, James Hathaway Robinson reported 146 belonged to a church: 87 Baptists, 56 Methodists, and 3 Holiness.[70] In Pittsburgh, the different Methodist churches—AME, AME Zion, and Colored Methodist—increased their membership by an estimated one thousand between 1916 and 1926. At the same time, the number of Baptist churches rose from thirty-two to forty-four, with membership increasing by nearly a third compared to a national increase of about one-tenth.[71] In Evansville, the number of black churches, including Holiness bodies, increased from an estimated dozen on the eve of World War I to eighteen by the mid-1920s[72]

African American religious activities represented substantial cooperation across class, cultural, and regional lines. In Pittsburgh, Ebenezer Baptist Church continued to attract large numbers of steelworkers and their families, as well as some of the most influential black business and professional people. Ebenezer's membership increased from fifteen hundred to three thousand during the war years. Under the pastorship of Rev. J.C. Austin, Ebenezer developed a variety of programs designed to aid southern black newcomers to the city, including the founding of Steel City Bank to assist with housing and financial needs.[73]

While African American churches attracted blacks from different regional, cultural and class backgrounds, social cleavages increased under the impact of the Great Migration and the expansion of the black industrial working class. While the Congregational, Episcopalian, and Presbyterian bodies continued to attract blacks from the upper class, including disproportionate numbers of light-skinned blacks, Methodist and Baptist churches also experienced growing class and cultural tensions.[74] Organized in the 1890s, Homestead's black Baptist Clark Memorial Church offers a potent example of these changes. Under the leadership of college- or seminary-trained black ministers, old residents dominated Clark

Memorial. Along with its own substantial contributions, funds from the Carnegie Steel Company enabled Clark to build a new church and a community center during the 1920s. Church officials also adopted the newest techniques in administering the religious, social, and business affairs of the church.[75]

As the black population in Homestead increased, some members of Clark Memorial articulated the need to open a place of worship in their own section of the city. Although Second Baptist Church opened in 1905 to meet these needs, the advent of the Great Migration increased its importance among newcomers. Unlike Clark Memorial, the ministers at Second Baptist were not seminary trained; the church did not have a community center and it adhered closely to matters of the spirit. While sermons at Clark Memorial stressed both spiritual and temporal issues, including "God's Idea of Segregation," those at Second Baptist talked about the church as a "Blessing in the World," a "New Heart," and the "Character of the Holy Spirit." While the line between the secular and spiritual was no doubt blurred for both churches, working-class congregations tended to foreground matters of the spirit as a means of dealing with the realities of their poor material existence.[76]

Migrant steelworker preachers played an important role in the new black churches. These preachers sometimes set the pace for forms of resistance at work and at home. When company officials asked one steelworker preacher from Albany, Georgia, to work on Sunday, he refused on more than one occasion. Migrant lay preachers also formed a union to provide aid to ministers seeking their own churches. Black migrants repeatedly shared stories about the cold treatment that they received in established churches. Only in the churches with "down home" preaching and ways of greeting newcomers did they feel comfortable or at home. As one woman migrant put it, "The women, especially the older women—they were so friendly—they put their arms around me and made me feel so welcome." Another said that he liked "the way they do, talk, and everything—so I joined."[77]

A variety of social clubs, fraternal orders, and social welfare organizations also mirrored as well as bridged the gap between migrants, old residents, and the new middle class. In addition to fraternal orders such as the Masons, Elks, and Knights of Pythias, such professional social work organizations as the Urban League played important roles in the lives of

Cincinnati sociologist James Hathaway Robinson, his wife Neola E. Woodson, and their two children, James Jr. and Jeanne Cassie. A graduate of Fisk and Yale Universities, Robinson headed the city's Negro Civic Welfare Association. From W.P. Dabney, *Cincinnati's Colored Citizens* (1926)

black workers. In Cincinnati, under the leadership of James Hathaway Robinson, African Americans formed the Negro Civic Welfare Association during the war years.[78] Born in Sharpsburg, Kentucky, Robinson attended Fisk and received an M.A. from Yale University, where he also completed the residency requirement of the Ph.D. in sociology. In 1915, he migrated to Cincinnati and took a job at the black Douglass School in the Walnut Hills area. Under Robinson's leadership, the NCWA set the framework of black middle-class professional social service through the 1920s. By decade's end, the organization had played a key role in expanding the range of social services available to black workers and their communities. According to historian Andrea Tuttle Kornbluh, Robinson and black social welfare activists pursued two interrelated goals: "organizing the black community internally and then making that community, as a group, an equal participant in the larger metropolitan community."[79]

Formed in 1918, the Pittsburgh Urban League (PUL) took the lead in helping black workers adjust to life in the city. John T. Clark and Alonzo Thayer directed the PUL between 1918 and 1930. Before taking the job as head of the PUL (1918-1926), Clark had earned his B.A. degree from Ohio State University, taught high school in Louisville, Kentucky, and headed the housing department at the National Urban League headquarters in New York City. For his part, Alonzo Thayer, who served as director from 1927 to 1930, received degrees from Avery Normal Institute in Charleston, South Carolina, and Fisk University in Tennessee. Before coming to Pittsburgh, he also served as director of the Atlanta Urban League. Guided by Clark and Thayer, the League, as elsewhere, initiated crucial employment, housing, health, and social services for black workers and their families. The PUL not only aided workers in their jobs, homes, and a variety of social services, but played a mediating role in the black workers'relations with employers, landlords, and law enforcement officials. Under the leadership of the PUL, for example, the court sometimes employed League staffers to investigate cases of criminal misconduct among southern newcomers and helped to reduce the number of African Americans incarcerated for certain crimes.[80]

African Americans also used their community-based institutions to assault racial discrimination in the larger community and political life of the city and region. These efforts gained potent expression in the work of the NAACP, the Garvey Movement, and the growing participation of blacks in electoral politics. Louisville's NAACP branch emerged in 1914 to fight the city's residential segregation ordinance, while the Pittsburgh, Cincinnati, and Evansville branches developed in 1915 to protest the racist film "Birth of a Nation."[81] The NAACP branches linked Ohio Valley blacks to the national struggle for equal rights, while fighting discrimination at the local level. Their achievements were substantial. In 1917, the U.S. Supreme Court struck down Louisville's residential law.[82] While Louisville blacks failed to halt showing of "Birth of a Nation" in 1915, they closed it down after two days of showing in 1918.[83] In 1920, the Louisville branch spearheaded passage of Kentucky's anti-lynching law. The state's anti-lynching law provided for punishment of persons violating the provisions of the act and for the removal of officers permitting a prisoner to be in-

The Rev. Junius Caesar
Austin of Pittsburgh's
Ebenezer Baptist Church,
who was also a firm
supporter of the Garvery
Movement. Courtesy
historian Randall K.
Burkett

jured or lynched by a mob. And, during the mid-1920s, the Louisville
branch initiated the movement that led to municipal restrictions on Klan
activities.[84]

In addition to joining the national campaign against "Birth of a Nation" and mob rule, NAACP branches in Pittsburgh and Cincinnati also
waged local struggles against racial injustice. In1921, Rev. J.C. Austin, pastor of Ebenezer Baptist Church, became president of the Pittsburgh
branch. Under Austin's leadership, the Pittsburgh NAACP pushed for the
employment of black teachers, the admission of black students to previously all-white schools, passage of a state civil rights law, an end to labor
union discrimination, and termination of police harassment of black
workers. The branch complained that police arrested migrants as vagrants
for the purpose of forcing them "back to the flames of the torturing
South."[85] The Cincinnati branch was also active, especially during the war
and early postwar years. Editor W.P. Dabney described it as one of the
"Big Movements" of the period.[86] When the Ohio legislature proposed a

racist intermarriage bill in 1925, the Cincinnati branch of the NAACP helped to kill the measure.[87]

Interconnected with the expansion of civil rights activities was the growing participation of blacks in electoral politics. As the black population expanded and residential segregation increased, African Americans increasingly used their votes to influence municipal politics in their own behalf. In 1919, Pittsburgh blacks elected Robert H. Logan to city council. While Logan served only one term, his victory symbolized efforts of urban blacks to transform segregation into a base of political influence.[88]

As elsewhere in pre-Depression black America, Ohio Valley blacks supported the "Party of Lincoln." They not only pressed for more patronage positions, but organized to elect their own numbers to municipal offices. Unlike blacks in other southern cities, African Americans in Louisville retained the franchise and continued to participate in municipal politics. In 1921, nearly 100 percent of the twenty-five thousand registered black voters were Republicans, a pattern that prevailed in Louisville and elsewhere until the 1930s. Still, African Americans expressed increasing dissatisfaction with their low percentage of patronage jobs, failure to gain white endorsement of black candidates, and efforts of some Republicans to expand the segregationist system.[89] Under the leadership of funeral director Arthur D. Porter, banker Wilson Lovett, and journalist William Warley, a new generation of black leaders established the Lincoln Independent Party and challenged the Republican Party during the early postwar years. Although the party faced harassment and defeat at the hands of the established black and white leadership of the party, it served notice that African Americans in Louisville were dissatisfied with their lot. Shortly thereafter, Republican officials increased the number of blacks hired in clerical positions at city hall, and, for the first time, African Americans gained employment as policemen and firemen, a struggle that they had waged since the late nineteenth century.[90]

In Cincinnati, although African Americans continued to support the Republican Party, municipal politics changed with the adoption of the reform city charter of 1924. The new charter abolished the ward-based system and instituted a city manager and a nine-member city council. The city adopted a complicated "proportional representation" approach to voting, which proponents argued would end "corrupt Republican" or "one party" domination of municipal government. Theoretically, any group, including African Americans, could obtain election to city council by garnering one tenth of the total votes plus one vote. Following the charter victory in 1924, the local black *Cincinnati Union* enthusiastically reported: "The Citizens Charter Wins! . . . All races, creeds and colors now have a chance: God still lives." Under the new charter, African Americans mobilized behind the candidacy of Frank A.B. Hall, a retired detective. It was not until the early years of the Depression, however, that blacks succeeded in electing Hall to city council.[91]

For its part, Evansville's black population also allied with the Republican Party and pushed for more benefits. According to historian Darrel Bigham, ironically, African Americans gained more patronage under the Klan-dominated Republican regimes of the mid- to late 1920s than before. Black political leaders like funeral director W. Gaines and attorney Ernest Tidrington supported the mayoralty of Herbert Males, a Republican who joined the Klan and used that organization to secure his election. According to the black *Indianapolis Recorder*, by 1926 Males had appointed 100 blacks to city posts; these jobs included appointments to the police and fire departments and represented eighty more jobs for blacks than under the previous mayor.[92] Unfortunately, available evidence makes this black Klan-linked phenomenon difficult to assess. At any rate, we cannot conclude, as Bigham does, that: "Klan-dominated government, in a word, provided more political reward and gave black leaders more autonomy than ever."[93]

Even more so than in the pre–World War I era, black women facilitated the political struggles of Ohio Valley African Americans. From the outset of the period, as president of the Negro Women's Franchise Federation, Daisy Lampkin played a key role in the political life of black Pittsburgh. After participating in the campaign to gain woman suffrage, Lampkin held positions as local chair of the Allegheny County Negro Women's Republican League, vice-chair of the Negro Voters League, and vice-chair of the Colored Voters Division of the Republican National Committee. Lampkin soon gained a prominent place within the national Republican Party. As historian Edna McKenzie notes, "Only six years after American women gained the vote, she was elected as an alternate delegate at large to the national Republican Party convention, a stellar achievement for any black or woman of that era." Black women's political activities, like those of the black community, were deeply embedded in their support of churches, fraternal orders, and social clubs. In early 1925, for example, Cincinnati's City Federation of Colored Women's

Building of Cincinnati's City Federation of Colored Women's Clubs, purchased in 1925 on Chapel Street, near Gilbert. From W.P. Dabney, *Cincinnati's Colored Citizens* (1926)

Clubs purchased an imposing brick building on Chapel Street, near Gilbert Avenue. In his report on the building, Dabney proclaimed: "It is an imperishable monument to the women whose brains and energy transformed their dreams into a building of such magnificence."[94]

Despite substantial racial solidarity in their civil rights and political activities, African Americans faced significant conflicts along class and cultural lines. More so than the NAACP or conventional electoral politics, for example, the Garvey Movement appealed to the expanding black industrial working class. Under the leadership of Marcus Garvey, the Universal Negro Improvement Association (UNIA) was formed in Jamaica in 1914. It moved to New York City two years later and by the early 1920s claimed a membership of some 6 to 11 million African peoples world-

William Ware was not only a member of Cincinnati's chapter of the Universal Negro Improvement Association but founder of the city's Welfare Association for the Colored People in 1917. From W.P. Dabney, *Cincinnati's Colored Citizens* (1926)

wide. Even conservative estimates of less than a half million members acknowledge the national and international influence of the Garvey Movement. By the mid-1920s, the movement not only faced close surveillance and repression by the federal government, but determined opposition from black civil rights, social service, and labor organizations such as the NAACP, Urban League, and Brotherhood of Sleeping Car Porters. Still, before its demise, with the possible exception of Evansville, the Garvey Movement played an important role in the lives of Ohio Valley blacks.[95]

In 1920, William Ware of Cincinnati attended the first international convention of the Negro Peoples of the World in New York. Ware invited representatives of the UNIA to visit Cincinnati and form a chapter. The Garvey organization, Ware heralded, "would mean a new birth to the Negroes of Cincinnati."[96] Garvey visited Cincinnati in February 1921. In his Cincinnati speech, Garvey expounded his message of race pride: "To you colored men of Cincinnati and of the world[,] the Universal Negro Improvement Association says get ready to build yourselves in Africa great cities and set up a great nation. When you do[,] no man can tell you you cannot have a job in another nation. Otherwise you are going to ask him the reason why."[97] The UNIA soon reported a membership of eight thousand in Cincinnati.[98] In Louisville, despite strong opposition from the NAACP, black newspaper editor I. Willis Cole and minister Rev. Andrew W. Thompson supported the Garvey Movement.[99] In western Pennsylvania, more than twenty industrial communities witnessed the formation of UNIA chapters and the outpouring of financial support for the organization's economic, social, and financial programs, including the Black Cross Navigation and Trading Company, the Colonization Fund, and the Black Star Line. When white workers attacked blacks in the city of Johnstown, Garvey criticized the city's public officials—the mayor, police, and white workers.[100]

African American workers perceived the UNIA as an appropriate response to the rising tide of Klan terror in the region. With its emphasis on race pride and independence for people of African descent, the UNIA struck an exceedingly responsive chord in the hearts and minds of black workers. After hearing speeches by Marcus Garvey in Pittsburgh, unemployed steelworker Matthew Dempsey organized a UNIA chapter in Aliquippa, where the Klan had brazenly burned crosses, held marches, and delivered inflammatory speeches against blacks and immigrants. But Dempsey also hoped to use the UNIA to combat discriminatory hiring and lay-off practices in the steel industry.[101] On one occasion, two steel company officials attended Garvey's talk at the Gospel Tabernacle auditorium. Garvey spoke on the "fundamentals and principles of the UNIA" and "confined his talk to the social equality rights of the negro." When Jones and Laughlin officials discovered the Garvey activities of steelworkers Matthew Dempsey and Joe Williams, they fired the two men and threatened to terminate others. Surveillance of Garveyites in Pittsburgh was part of the FBI's larger effort to kill the organization nationwide.[102]

While some black clergymen actively discouraged their members from participating in the UNIA, some boldly supported the Garvey Movement. Reverend J.C. Austin of Ebenezer Baptist Church became the most prominent clergyman supporting the Garvey cause. He not only allowed members to use his church for meetings, but invited UNIA leaders to speak from his pulpit. In 1923, Austin delivered the opening address at the International Convention of the organization. According to the *Negro World*, the official organ of the UNIA, Austin "received a loud and enthusiastic greeting" when he addressed the audience as "my beloved yoke fellows in tribulation and co-partners in this struggle for freedom and justice."[103] The Rev. John Gibbs St. Clair Drake, originally from Barbados and pastor of Bethany Baptist Church in Pittsburgh, became an international organizer for the organization. Also supporting the UNIA in Pittsburgh was Rev. E.R. Bryant, pastor of the Braddock Park African Methodist Episcopal Zion Church. Despite advice from some of his fellow black clergymen to bar Garveyites, the minister at John Wesley AME Zion Church supported the activities of the UNIA and explained that, "if radicalism meant telling the truth, he was glad to have Garvey with him."[104] Although the Garvey Movement would decline by the mid-1920s, it offered African American workers an alternative to the cross-class and interracial, but elite-dominated organizations like the Urban League, NAACP, and Republican Party.

Although the Garvey Movement symbolized increasing social stratification within the African American community, a variety of factors reinforced cross-class alliances. Under the impact of wartime production, immigration-restriction legislation, and economic expansion, African Americans moved into Ohio Valley cities in growing numbers. Black men took new jobs in the industrial sector, supplemented by increasing numbers of black women in domestic and personal service work. Despite strong demands for their labor during World War I and the mid-1920s, however, African Americans faced stiff constraints on their lives at work and in the larger community life of Ohio Valley cities. Discriminatory employment and managerial, social welfare, and government policies limited their access to housing, public accommodations, and places of leisure and culture. As a result, African Americans from different class backgrounds perceived racial inequality as evidence that blacks shared a common fate and that their class interests were closely intertwined with the imperatives of racial solidarity. The early years of the Great Depression and New Deal would confirm their judgment.

6

African Americans, Depression, and World War II

The Depression and World War II highlighted the tenuous economic foundation of African American communities in the Ohio Valley region. As elsewhere in urban America, black unemployment and suffering increased and greatly exceeded that of whites. The discriminatory lay-off and hiring policies of industrial firms ensured that African Americans would enter the unemployment lines earlier and remain there longer than their white counterparts. Franklin D. Roosevelt's New Deal would usher in greater protection for labor unions, relief for unemployed workers, and housing subsidies, but such programs were insufficient to erase disparities between blacks and whites. In varying degrees, the discriminatory policies and practices of white employers, organized labor (particularly the AFL), and the state undermined the position of African American workers and their communities.

Only during the labor shortages of World War II would Ohio Valley African Americans regain and expand their industrial foothold in the urban economy. Whereas industrialists hired blacks primarily in general labor and custodial positions during World War I, they would now employ blacks on skilled and semiskilled production jobs. Still, despite the labor demands of World War II serving as a catalyst for expanding opportunities for black workers, only the mass mobilization of African Americans in the March on Washington Movement (MOWM) made such jobs a reality. As part of the MOWM, Ohio Valley blacks joined forces with African Americans from across the country and established the foundations for the rise of the Modern Civil Rights Movement.

Unemployment, Relief, and the Limits of the
Early New Deal, 1929-35

The Great Depression gripped the entire nation. It brought mass suffering to large sectors of the white as well as black population. By 1933, unemployment rose to about 25 percent of the labor force nationwide. The nation's income dropped by nearly 50 percent, forcing an estimated 20 million Americans to seek public and private relief.[1] Despite the onset of hard times, however, southern blacks continued their trek from the rural South to American cities, where the African American unemployment rate rose to over 50 percent, substantially above that of their white counterparts and over two times the national average. The percentage of blacks living in urban areas increased from just under 45 percent in 1930 to nearly 50 percent in 1940.[2]

Ohio Valley cities absorbed a substantial proportion of Depression and World War II era black migration. Pittsburgh's black population increased from about 55,000 in 1930 to over 82,000 by war's end. Blacks increased their percentage of the city's total from 8.2 in 1930 to 9.3 in 1940 and to over 12 percent during the war and early postwar years. Similarly, Cincinnati's African American population rose from nearly 48,000 at the onset of the Depression to over 78,000 during World War II and its early aftermath; blacks also increased from about 11 to over 15 percent of the city's total. While Louisville's black population declined in absolute numbers and percent of the total during the Depression years, it experienced a revival in both numbers and proportion of the total during World War II. As during the 1920s, however, few blacks migrated to Evansville during the inter–World War years (see table 4).

The persistence of black migration during the Great Depression intensified the impact of hard times on Ohio Valley blacks. As unemployment escalated for Ohio Valley whites, it rose even higher for blacks. African Americans in Pittsburgh faced perhaps the most difficult time partly because of their extraordinary dependence on the heavy metal industry. As early as 1928-29, the Pittsburgh Urban League had discouraged black migration to the city, emphasizing "how difficult it is to find work in Pittsburgh today." By 1931, while black men accounted for only 7 percent of Allegheny County's male population, they made up 22 percent of the men seeking employment at the county's Emergency Asso-

Table 4. African American Population in Ohio Valley Cities, 1930-1950

| | 1930 | | 1940 | | 1950 | |
	No.	%	No.	%	No.	%
Pittsburgh	54,983	8.2	62,215	9.3	82,453	12.2
Cincinnati	47,818	10.6	55,593	12.2	78,196	15.5
Louisville	47,354	15.4	47,158	14.8	57,657	15.6
Evansville	6,514	6.4	6,862	7.1	8,483	6.6

Source: *Fifteenth Census of U.S.,* vol. 3, pt. 2, 1930 (Washington, D.C.: Government Printing Office, 1932); *Sixteenth Census of the U.S.,* vol. 2, pt. 2, 3, 5, and 6, 1940 (Washington, D.C.: Government Printing Office, 1952)

ciation. In February 1934, African Americans made up 40 percent of the county's unemployed workers. Blacks also had over 43 percent of their numbers on relief compared to 15.7 percent for whites.[3]

As the Depression spread, blacks who retained their jobs faced increasing racial discrimination, speed-ups, and insults on the job. In 1934, the Allegheny Steel Company in Brackenridge replaced its black workers with whites, arguing that black workers' gambling, bootlegging, and disturbances justified the decision. A Duquesne worker declared, "The colored has a hard way to go. They . . . bawl you out and make you work fast."[4] Black women continued to work mainly as maids, cooks, and laundresses, but the Depression weakened their access to these jobs, as employers expressed a growing preference for white women. In a report to the national office, the Metropolitan YMCA of Pittsburgh acknowledged that: "The [black] girls from Centre Avenue (in the Hill District) felt the full brunt of the depression. Low pay, long hours, discrimination and the ever present formula 'last to be hired, first to be fired.'"[5]

If black steelworkers and their families faced the brunt of economic discrimination, their black Ohio Valley counterparts also faced disproportionate hardships. Although Cincinnati's diversified economic base and an aggressive public works program cushioned the early impact of the Depression on its workers, the city's unemployment rate rose to 19 percent by May 1931, up from about 6 percent two years earlier. Over the next three years, the city's unemployment rose to 30 percent, with another 18 percent of the labor force holding part-time positions. For Cincinnati blacks, unemployment was much higher, about 54 percent in 1933.[6] According to an unemployment census of 12,000 unemployed workers in the city, blacks made up 25 percent of the total, although they constituted no more than about 10 percent of the population in 1930. Moreover, as in Pittsburgh, when white men lost their jobs and white women sought domestic service employment, this increased the difficulties of black women. In their "want ads," Cincinnati employers repeatedly expressed a preference for white women. By 1930, when asked if they would hire competent blacks if they could be found, 90 percent of Cincinnati employers said "no" or "refused to answer." Black social worker Theodore Berry concluded that: "Employers were . . . not interested in employment problems of the Negro. . . . there was not much desire to have Negro workers advance above a certain low level of occupations."[7]

Black men and women faced similar conditions in Evansville and Louisville. In 1934, an estimated one-third of Evansville's black families received relief, and African Americans made up over 10 percent of the city's total unemployment rate.[8] In Louisville, many black men and women retained jobs in the domestic and personal service sectors at significantly less pay for the same work than their white counterparts. Moreover, white workers often received vacations and time off for special occasions, but blacks were compelled to work without such considerations. When they complained of these inequities, they lost their jobs and faced even greater difficulties making ends meet. While some black men and women retained jobs in the city's clothing and tobacco industries, most Louisville industrialists excluded blacks from the higher-paying production jobs with better working conditions and shorter hours.[9]

As elsewhere, from the early Depression years through the mid-1930s, Ohio Valley blacks justly complained that they received a "raw deal" rather than a "new deal" from their government, fellow citizens, and workers. After his election, FDR did little to build confidence among African Americans. The new president depended on southern segregationists to pass and implement his "New Deal" programs. Roosevelt opposed federal anti-lynching legislation, prevented black delegations from visiting the White House, and refused to make civil rights and racial equity a priority. He justified his actions on the grounds that he needed southern white support for his economic relief and recovery programs: the National

Recovery Administration (NRA), the Federal Emergency Relief Administration (FERA), and the Civilian Conservation Corps (CCC), among others.[10]

Federal officials rejected proposals from African Americans and
their white allies to make racial discrimination in New Deal social programs illegal. Federal legislation permitted state, county, and municipal
authorities a great deal of autonomy in the implementation of New Deal
measures. Thus, African Americans in the Ohio Valley and elsewhere confronted stiff racial barriers at the local level, where white employers and
agency officials controlled the distribution of resources. African Americans repeatedly complained of their inability to secure relief. In Pittsburgh,
when a father of six lost his job and sought relief in the city of Pittsburgh,
relief officials denied his request. Only when he deserted his family, his
wife reported, did she and the children receive aid. According to the
woman's testimony, "He told me once that if he wasn't living at home
the welfare people would help me and the kids, and maybe he just went
away on that account."[11]

African Americans not only faced discrimination in their efforts to
obtain federal relief benefits, they also confronted racial bias in youth,
housing, social security, and federal work programs as well. The CCC developed along segregationist and unequal lines, the Federal Housing
Administration refused to guarantee mortgages in racially integrated
neighborhoods, and social security and NRA programs excluded general
laborers and domestic service employees from its benefits.[12] Since the
majority of blacks worked in jobs defined as unskilled, the minimum wage
and hour codes had little meaning, especially for African American
women. When lower hour and higher wage provisions did cover jobs occupied by blacks, some employers paid whites the higher wage, while re-
taining blacks at the old lower wage scale. In Cincinnati, as Raymond
Wolters notes, one of the city's major chain drugstores "refused to increase
the wages of colored girls doing the same work as white girls whose wages
were increased."[13]

On the other hand, Section 7a of the NRA gave labor the right to organize and bargain collectively with employers. When the U.S. Supreme
Court declared NRA unconstitutional in 1935, Congress quickly passed
the Wagner Labor Relations Act and set up the National Labor Relations
Board to protect the collective bargaining rights of workers. Such New

Deal labor legislation enabled organized white workers to strengthen their hand in the struggle with employers. At the same time, it also buttressed their efforts to exclude blacks. African American workers, the NAACP, and the National Urban League protested the exclusion of unskilled and semiskilled workers and proposed a nondiscriminatory clause in the new Wagner Labor Relations Act, but white labor leaders defeated the measure. According to Wagner's assistant, Leon Keyserling, "The American Federation of Labor fought bitterly to eliminate this clause and much against his will Senator Wagner had to consent to elimination in order to prevent scuttling of the entire bill."[14]

Thus, New Deal labor laws reinforced racial restrictions on black workers, including the all-black Brotherhood of Sleeping Car Porters. AFL Unions continued to use a variety of formal and informal procedures to exclude, segregate, and/or subordinate African Americans within the labor movement. At the 1934 national convention of the AFL, black workers escalated their fight against such discriminatory practices, including pickets and banners reading "Labor Cannot Be Free While Black Labor Is Enslaved."[15] Given their uphill struggle during the early New Deal years, it is not surprising that some blacks dubbed the NRA, the "Negro Run Around," "Negroes Ruined Again," and "Negro Rarely Allowed."[16]

As in previous years, Ohio Valley blacks devised a variety of strategies for dealing with hard times. Almost from the outset, when lay-offs started and some companies cut wages, some black workers joined Unemployment Councils, sometimes spearheaded by the Communist Party (CP), to gain necessary relief. Under the pressure of such councils, some companies issued food baskets, but insisted that workers sign forms promising to repay upon the return of good times. Along with such company assistance, black workers also depended on the earnings of their wives and children; cultivated gardens, hunted, and fished; took in boarders and held "rent parties"; and, as alluded to above, turned to private social welfare agencies as well as to their own community institutions— churches, fraternal orders, and mutual benefit societies. Some blacks relied exclusively on the underground economy. In their interviews with steelworkers in Homestead, historians John Hinshaw and Judith Modell discovered that one black worker, Jim, "did not get a job in the mill -he did not indicate how hard or if he tried—but instead survived on a variety of legal, semi-legal, and illegal activities which rose and declined along with the fortunes of the mill."[17] Unlike the pre-Depression years, however, federally funded public welfare programs would now play a key role in African American strategies for making ends meet.

Toward a New Deal for Blacks, 1935-39

Despite the significance of such family and community strategies, only the gradual extension of New Deal work and social welfare programs brought substantial relief to Ohio Valley blacks. From the mid-1930s through 1939, African Americans gained increasing access to the benefits of New Deal programs and gradually shifted their assessment of FDR and the Democratic Party. In Evansville, the WPA became the principal employer of black workers and offered important social services—a nursery school, adult education classes, vocational training, school lunch programs, and a low-income public housing project, Lincoln Gardens, which opened in 1938. In Pittsburgh, unemployed black steelworkers gained increasing access to employment in CCC camps and on WPA projects. By 1937, Pittsburgh blacks made up less than 10 percent of the population, but accounted for 23 percent of all emergency workers. At the same time, in Allegheny County, black males made up 6 percent of the male population, but 20 percent of workers on WPA.[18]

As suggested by Evansville's Lincoln Gardens, Ohio Valley blacks also gradually gained access to federally-funded low-income housing. African Americans gained access to Lincoln Court in Cincinnati and Bedford Dwellings, Addison Terrace, Allequippa Terrace, and Wadsworth Terrace in Pittsburgh. For its part, the city of Louisville also constructed low-income housing projects, officially segregated by race. As historian George Blakey put it, public housing projects in Louisville and other Kentucky cities "were segregated by race and income, sequestered in blighted areas, stigmatized by purpose and appearance, the apartments were nonetheless more desirable than what applicants had been accustomed to."[19]

The growing participation of Ohio Valley blacks in New Deal social programs was part of a larger national process. As the federal government took responsibility for the social welfare of American citizens, it helped to change the terms of the African American struggle for social justice. By 1939, African Americans nationwide had increased their share of New Deal social programs and improved their socioeconomic conditions. Income from various New Deal work and relief programs nearly equaled

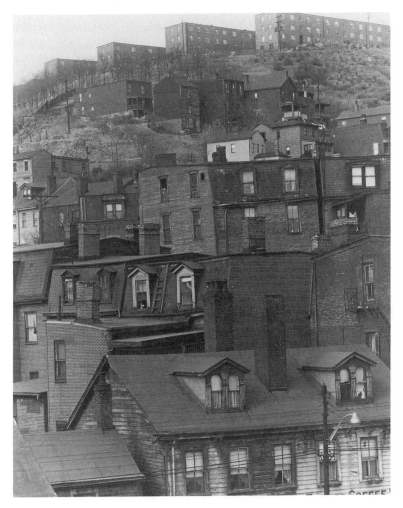

A 1951 view of Pittsburgh's low-income public housing, Terrace Village, in the background on the hill. Carnegie Library, Pittsburgh, Pennsylvania

the income that African Americans received from private employment. Between 1935 and 1938, for example, African Americans increased their percentage on CCC projects from less than 6 to 11 percent. African Americans also occupied about one-third of all low-income Public Works Administration (PWA) housing units, and benefited from a growing share of WPA educational and cultural programs. African Americans in the Ohio Valley could now join blacks in Chicago and elsewhere who praised the New Deal as "a godsend."[20]

The shifting relationship between blacks and the New Deal was not simply a matter of the government's changing attitude toward the social welfare of "all Americans." It also responded to the escalating activities of the Communist and Socialist parties, the rise of a new mass-based labor movement, and the growing political organization and consciousness of blacks themselves. As an unpopular minority, the Communist Party was especially eager to attract black members. Its activities on behalf of African Americans, particularly southern blacks, attracted the growing and favorable attention of blacks across the country. The influence of the Communist Party was most apparent in its defense of the Scottsboro Boys of Alabama, nine young black men unjustly accused of raping a white woman and summarily sentenced to death.[21]

Only after World War II was the last defendant released, but the Communist Party (CP) had demonstrated its willingness to confront racial and class injustice and received substantial support among African Americans. In the early phases of the case, when the NAACP and the *Pittsburgh Courier,* one of the organization's staunchest supporters, refused to cooperate with the CP, local and national readers of the paper "showed a noticeable lack of both confidence and patience."[22] The *Chicago Defender,* the nation's largest black weekly, the *Atlanta World,* the *Amsterdam News,* the *Baltimore Afro-American,* and other black weeklies endorsed the party's national and international campaign to free the young men, urging organs of black public opinion and the NAACP to do the same.[23]

Although few Ohio Valley blacks actually joined the CP, those who did made a lasting impression on their white comrades. During the early Depression years, Ernest McKinney, the grandson of an active member of the United Mine Workers of America (UMW), joined a splinter group of the CP and participated in demonstrations on behalf of unemployed workers in Pittsburgh. Originally from Chattanooga, Tennessee, Ben Careathers, another black communist, had migrated to Pittsburgh before

World War I. In succession he worked as a janitor and helper on the railroads, opened an upholstery shop, and joined the Socialist and then the Communist Party by the early 1930s. He also participated in the CP's unemployed councils. Black pullman porter William Scarville also joined the party in Pittsburgh and became well known in the circle of white communists in western Pennsylvania. As the Croatian immigrant communist Steve Nelson recalled:

One of the things about the Pittsburgh Party that impressed me most was the small group of black Communists there. The most popular figure was William Scarville, a well-known activist in the Pullman Porters Union and a veteran Socialist and IWW organizer. His friend and constant companion was a white worker by the name of Smith, another former Socialist, with whom he shared an apartment. It was the first time I had seen comradeship across racial lines. Scarville was a striking figure—he was over six feet tall, had shining gray hair, and always wore an immaculate suit, white shirt, tie, and polished shoes. He had a quiet sort of dignity that inspired admiration in you the first time you met him. He was a favorite at Party and YWL educationals not only because he knew how to pepper his presentations with anecdotes about what went on during the night on the train but also because of his remarkable facility for demonstrating complicated concepts with living examples. . . . It was out of respect for workers like Scarville that young Communists in Pittsburgh developed a fuller understanding of racism.[24]

As suggested by the experiences of William Scarville, Ben Careathers, and Ernest McKinney, the Communist and Socialist parties facilitated the emergence of closer and more cooperative relations between black and white workers. Under the impact of New Deal labor legislation, the labor movement escalated but soon split over the efficacy of industrial versus craft unionism. When national black labor and civil rights leaders failed to persuade the AFL to drop racial barriers in constituent unions, they supported the insurgent movement of John L. Lewis's Committee for Industrial Organization (later named the Congress of Industrial Organizations in 1936).[25]

Impatient with the exclusionary policies of the AFL, the Committee for Industrial Organization (CIO) broke from the AFL at the 1935 convention. Under the leadership of John L. Lewis, head of the United Mine Workers of America, the CIO embarked upon an aggressive organizing drive. The CIO criticized both the craft and racial exclusiveness of the AFL and pushed for a multiracial movement that cut across craft and skill lines, bringing blacks and whites, skilled and unskilled, together in one huge industrial organization. The CIO immediately targeted large mass production industries like transportation, steel, auto, rubber, meatpacking, and others that the AFL showed little interest in organizing. Learning from its experience in interracial organizing in the coalfields of the South, the UMW made a firm commitment to organize black and white workers. Following the "UMW Formula," the CIO soon launched the Steel Workers Organizing Committee (SWOC), the Packinghouse Workers Organizing Committee (PWOC), and the United Automobile Workers (UAW). In each case, the union appealed to black organizations like the NAACP and the National Urban League, employed black organizers, placed African Americans in key union offices, and advocated an end to racially biased pay scales.[26]

Moreover, under the prodding of black labor leaders like A. Philip Randolph, competition from the emerging CIO, and company resistance to Section 7a, AFL unions also recognized the growing importance of recruiting black workers into their ranks. Even before the emergence of the CIO, the AFL's Amalgamated Association of Iron and Steel Workers (AAISW) had responded to steel companies' union-breaking efforts by gradually accepting blacks into the union. These efforts helped to establish a foundation for the organizing drives of the CIO during the mid- to late 1930s.[27]

The CIO soon spread into all Ohio Valley cities. A strong UAW-CIO union emerged at the Chrysler plant in Evansville, where blacks became members and officers in the organization.[28] In 1937, the CIO opened an office in Louisville and made plans to intensify its southern campaign. The CIO also gradually gained a footing in Cincinnati, where the UAW fought bitter battles with the entrenched AFL.[29] Although blacks became members and even officers of CIO locals in these cities, rank-and-file white resistance persisted as a major obstacle to their advancement. In Evansville, as Darrel Bigham concludes: "Rank-and-file members of Local No. 705, many of whom were Kentuckians, were generally hostile to blacks." Similarly, in a visit to Louisville in September 1937, journalist George S. Schuyler of the *Pittsburgh Courier* reported that Louisville was "a typical anti-CIO town, where union labor has never had much of a foothold." Schuyler also talked to Peter Campell, the former AFL official who now headed the Louisville office of the CIO. He described Campell as, "the first big CIO official I've met who seemed to be completely steeped in the traditions of the Old South so far as Negroes are concerned." For its part, Cincinnati also developed and retained a reputation as a strong anti-union city. It was in Cincinnati that "Hate Strikes" against black workers would erupt during World War II.[30]

The new labor movement gained its strongest support in the Pittsburgh region. Steel Workers Organizing Committee (SWOC) leaders welcomed socialists and communist organizers, who promised to separate their "politics" from CIO activities. As noted above, the socialists and communists had already demonstrated their commitment to organizing the mass production industries. By the early 1930s, for example, the communists had formed the Steel and Metal Workers Industrial Union and the socialists had initiated the National Unemployed League. When SWOC turned to these parties for organizers, it recruited two black organizers from the Pittsburgh district, Careathers and McKinney.[31]

In addition to black communists like Careathers and McKinney, black coal miners like Milford Peter Jackson also played an important role in early organizing efforts among black steelworkers, but rank-and-file black steelworkers soon played the major part in organizing their own numbers. The four Taylor brothers at McKees Rocks, Rev. Fletcher Williamson and Rev. John McLaurin at Duquesne, John Thornton in the Beaver Valley, and Jim Downing, Jeff Phelps, Frank Senson, Sam Jackson, and Bartow Tipper at Aliquippa all helped to organize their fellow black steelworkers. Black steelworkers also acquired positions as first vice president and sometimes as president of steelworker unions. In 1937, for example, black and white unionists elected a black puddler, Hunter Horvell, president at Penn Iron and Steel Company in Tarentum.[32]

Black organizers not only encountered substantial resistance from steel companies, including violent attacks by mill police and hired hands; they faced entrenched and justified skepticism from many black workers, who often responded to organizers with statements like: "I've never seen a union mean anything to a Negro yet." One steelworker retorted, "The CIO wants black employees to join a union where we would be compelled to pay monthly dues and get absolutely nothing in return." Some blacks believed that a closed CIO shop would mean "our race closed out." Others came close to perceiving the CIO in the same terms as the company union: it "doesn't mean us any good."[33]

Despite justified skepticism toward the labor movement, under the leadership of black organizers, growing numbers of black workers entered the "house of labor." In NLRB elections, most black workers supported the new unions and helped to inaugurate a new era of interracial unionism. On 17 March 1937, for example, Carnegie Illinois Steel signed a contract with SWOC. Jones and Laughlin and Crucible Steel soon followed. The new agreements increased wages and established an eight-hour day, forty-hour week, and a week of paid vacation for black and white workers with five years' employment with the firm. In addition to establishing grievance procedures to address issues of unfair firing and other mistreatment, the contract stipulated that seniority rather than color would govern promotions and lay-offs. By 1939, significant numbers of black steelworkers believed that the union would curb the abuses of foremen and give them "the same job as the white man if they are qualified to do the work."[34]

As black workers developed stronger ties to organized labor, they cemented even stronger links with middle-class black business and professional people. As the Depression undercut the position of black workers, the black middle class also suffered. More so than in the 1920s, however, the African American middle class and elites now supported the participation of black workers in the labor movement as consistent with their own interests. As early as 1933, attorney Homer Brown served as president of the Pittsburgh NAACP and increased the organization's support of black workers and labor issues. By 1934, the National Urban League (NUL) had not only endorsed the industrial union movement, but established workers' councils to facilitate movement of blacks into unions. In Pittsburgh, the Urban League's Workers Council endorsed the Amalgamated Association, when it shifted toward a nondiscriminatory policy toward black workers. With the emergence of the CIO, the NUL soon assisted the organizing campaigns of SWOC.[35]

The National Negro Congress (NNC) symbolized growing cross-class African American support for the labor movement. A confederation of organizations seeking equal treatment for blacks in New Deal programs, the NNC emerged following a conference at Howard University in 1935. Under the leadership of A. Philip Randolph, who became president of the organization; Ralph Bunche, a political scientist at Howard; and John P. Davis, head of the Joint Committee on National Recovery; the NNC adopted unionization of black workers as a major objective. It offered detailed recommendations to the SWOC leadership on ways to reach black workers including the use of black as well as white organizers and educational campaigns in black newspapers, churches, and other community organizations.[36]

In 1936, the Pittsburgh NNC and CIO sponsored a conference that not only included national leaders like T. Arnold Hill of the Urban League and A. Philip Randolph of the Brotherhood of Sleeping Car Porters, but Robert L. Vann, editor of the *Pittsburgh Courier*; Bishop William J. Walls of the Allegheny Annual Conference of the AME Zion Church; and Rev. T. J. King, pastor of Ebenezer Baptist Church. Black religious leaders offered their churches as a base for organizing black workers and promoting their movement into unions. For his part, Robert L. Vann "pledged the full support of the *Pittsburgh Courier* to the steel drive and declared that it would expose in its pages those Negroes who betrayed the best interests of their people by supporting the bosses."[37]

Participation in the labor movement reinforced the political mobilization of the black community and strengthened its role in the New Deal coalition. Ohio Valley blacks participated in the gradual reorientation of African American politics from the Republican to the Democratic Party. As early as 1932, Robert Vann urged blacks to abandon the party of Lincoln. His editorial words are now staples in historical accounts of black politics during the period. "My friends," he said, "go turn Lincoln's picture to the wall. That debt is paid in full."[38] David Lawrence, state chairman of the Democratic Party and leader of the Pittsburgh political organization, soon echoed Vann's words. In a 1933 speech to a black audience, Lawrence complained that every year the Republican Party "collected its reward from the colored people for the Emancipation Proclamation," but offered little in return. In 1933, according to the City County Colored Democratic Committee, African Americans made up 16 percent of the popular vote, but received only 180 patronage jobs, compared to 600 for the Italians and 720 for the Jews, who, respectively, made up 9 and 10 percent of the city's popular vote. Vann became an active supporter of the Democratic Party and played an important role in the party's national effort to attract black voters. His growing support of the labor movement was also closely interconnected with his new alliance with the Democratic Party.[39] By the mid-1930s, nearly forty-five blacks held appointments in various New Deal agencies and cabinet departments, including Robert L. Vann in the office of the Attorney General. The "Black Cabinet," as these black advisers were called, enabled African Americans to improve their position in a variety of New Deal programs.[40]

Daisy Lampkin would remain active through the Second World War and its aftermath. Here she is shown delivering a speech at the 1947 meeting of the National Council of Negro Women. Courtesy Mary McLeod Bethune Council House, National Park Service, Washington, D.C.

Mary McLeod Bethune became the most influential of the New Deal black advisors. Founder of Bethune-Cookman College in Florida, she headed the Negro Division of the National Youth Administration. Bethune's role in the New Deal coalition suggests that black women as well as men helped to shape Depression-era black politics. In Pittsburgh, Daisy Lampkin increased her role as a stellar example of black female participation in the political life of the Ohio Valley. Lampkin served as vice president of the Pittsburgh Courier Publishing Company and was also on the staff of the Pittsburgh Urban League and the NAACP. She also served as regional and national field secretaries of the NAACP during the period. As historian Edna McKenzie notes, "Daisy Lampkin's role as a social and political activist, though frequently overlooked, was a fundamental part of the black struggle for full citizenship." Other black women also played a heretofore little-acknowledged role in the political life of the region. In 1930, for example, Evansville educator and club woman Sallie Wyatt Stewart became president of the National Association of Colored Women and soon received an invitation to attend the White House Conference on Children.[41]

As elsewhere, however, only gradually did Ohio Valley blacks make

Sallie Wyatt Stewart, educator and founder of Evansville's City Federation of Colored Women's Clubs, who, in 1930, became president of the National Association of Colored Women. Courtesy Special Collections, University of Southern Indiana, Evansville

the transition to the Democratic Party. Attorney and civil rights activist Homer S. Brown symbolized the shift of Pittsburgh's black community to the Democratic Party and the New Deal coalition. In the election of 1934, Brown became the first black nominated on both the Republican and Democratic tickets for the state legislature. A graduate of the University of Pittsburgh Law School, Brown won the election and became one of five black legislators in the state as well as the second black to be elected by the city's black electorate in the Third and Fifth Wards. Although Brown ran as an independent and won, a new state law required that he declare his party. He soon declared himself a Democrat and joined forces with the New Deal coalition in the state. As a representative of the city's Hill District, Brown allied with Democratic Governor George Earle and pushed for a "Little New Deal for Pennsylvania" and its black citizens, particularly black workers.[42] When the state legislature passed the McGinnis Labor Relations bill, which sanctioned the provisions of the Wagner Act at the state level, Brown did what national leaders had failed to do: he obtained an amendment that penalized unions that excluded members on the basis of color or race. Although the AFL put up a vigorous fight to defeat the amendment, the Brown provision gained support from the CIO and passed into law in May 1937. Brown's tenure in the state legislature not only reinforced the struggle for black workers' rights at the workplace, but also in the larger community. In 1935, Pennsylvania passed and enacted a Civil Rights law, strengthening the ban on racial segregation in public accommodations.[43]

C. Eubanks Tucker, a lawyer and bishop in the African Methodist Episcopal Church, spearheaded the black transition to the Democratic Party in Louisville. He joined Louisville's Democratic Party in 1933 and helped Democrats gain control of municipal government for the first time since their ouster in the aftermath of World War I. Although Tucker ran for the state legislature on the Democratic ticket in the predominantly black 58th District, he lost to a black Republican, attorney Charles W. Anderson. Still, the black Democrat's challenge to the party of Lincoln encouraged white Republicans to endorse a black for elective office for the first time in the city's history.[44] In the presidential election of 1936, Cincinnati blacks, concentrated mainly in Ward 16, returned 65 percent of their vote to FDR compared to only about 29 percent in 1932.[45] In 1935, Evansville blacks joined African Americans from across the state and formed the Indiana Negro Democratic Central Committee, and delivered 75 percent of their votes to FDR in the election of 1936.[46]

By 1939, African Americans had gained access to much-needed social welfare services. They had also strengthened their position in the house of labor and joined FDR's Democratic coalition. Additionally, the U.S. Supreme Court gradually shifted its position in cases involving race and issues of social justice. In a 1938 Kentucky case the court noted the systematic exclusion of blacks from jury service and overturned the conviction of a black man accused of murder. Over the next three years, the U.S. Supreme Court also strengthened the economic position of African Americans.[47] It upheld the right of African Americans to boycott businesses that discriminated in their employment practices. As such, it legitimated the emergence of black "Don't Buy Where You Can't Work" campaigns during the early years of the Depression.[48] It also upheld the elimination of unequal black and white teacher salaries in Norfolk, Virginia, which had profound implications for the large numbers of black teachers in the Louisville public schools and the gradual employment of black teachers in Pittsburgh, Cincinnati, and Evansville.[49] In short, by the

Charles W. Anderson, a
Republican and first
black to be elected to the
Kentucky legislature,
is shown here with his
mother. Courtesy
Kentucky Historical
Society, Frankfort

time of America's entrance into World War II, the U.S. Supreme Court
had responded to the increasing political activism of blacks and their
white allies and slowly undermined the historical *Plessy v Ferguson* (1896)
decision, which mandated a "separate but equal" society for blacks and
whites.[50]

Despite such achievements and benefits, Ohio Valley African Americans faced continuing constraints on their efforts to improve their position. By decade's end, they remained disproportionately unemployed and
on relief compared to their white counterparts. While CIO unions such
as SWOC had brought growing numbers of blacks into their ranks, the

AFL unions remained recalcitrant and resisted efforts to improve the position of black workers.[51]

Moreover, although African Americans gained access to much-needed low-income housing projects, such housing came at a tremendous cost. Under the "neighborhood composition rule," federal housing authorities mandated racial segregation and reinforced the residential segregation of blacks and whites in the urban environment. Federal housing programs also required the demolition of old structures, predominantly dwellings occupied by black families, without adequate provisions for replacement units. Thus, federal housing authorities now joined state and local real estate agencies, financial institutions, and white home-owners in relegating African Americans to the bottom of the urban housing market.

For example, under the leadership of the Better Housing League, Cincinnati acquired federal aid, demolished old buildings, and constructed new low-income housing units. By late 1934, the city had demolished more than 1,169 residential structures. Although the demolished units had sheltered over 3,514 families, disproportionately African Americans, the city's redevelopment plan omitted the lower West End, which included census tract 5, which was over 95 percent black and the locale of the worst housing, health, and sanitary conditions in the city. Authorities classified West End housing as unfit for human occupancy, very bad, bad, and only occasionally fair.[52]

When Cincinnati finally constructed its public housing under the PWA, it allocated fourteen hundred units for white families and only six hundred for black families. Making matters worse, when the city sought land to build black units, white resistance led to the redesignation of the proposed units as "all-white." Only black protests secured a portion of the units for African Americans on a segregated basis. When the city finally established Lincoln Court under the Housing Act of 1937, the project was insufficient to meet the needs of the city's poorest blacks; it provided a net increase of thirty-eight units for the displacement of 1,030 black families.

At the same time, Cincinnati's small coterie of black homeowners, particularly those in the Lincoln Heights area, complained of neglect. Their areas lacked sufficient city services, including fire and police protection, paved streets, lighting, plumbing, and sewage disposal. By 1939, black homeowners in Lincoln Heights petitioned the county to become an independent municipality. Before black homeowners could improve their housing and before displaced black families could occupy new low-income housing units, Ohio Valley blacks and the nation faced the labor demands of World War II. Priority now shifted to the recruitment of war workers.[53]

World War II, 1940-45

Only the advent of World War II returned blacks to full employment in the Ohio Valley region. The production demands of World War II not only brought about reemployment of unemployed blacks, but the recruitment of new southern blacks. Under the impact of wartime labor demands and the labor recruitment activities of the U.S. Employment Service, the War Production Board, and the War Manpower Commission, African Americans migrated from southern farms and small towns to the industrial centers in increasing numbers. The acceleration of technological changes in southern agriculture and New Deal agricultural programs also fueled the process. As southern farmers turned toward the use of mechanical cotton pickers and tractors, and federal aid was used to drive cotton prices up, black agricultural workers found it even more difficult to make a living. Nearly 1.6 million blacks left the South during the 1940s. As their numbers increased, so did racial violence in the major industrial centers of the nation.[54]

Even more so than during World War I, African Americans resolved to fight white violence and social injustice. Their determination received potent reinforcement and inspiration from the *Pittsburgh Courier*'s "Double V" campaign for victory at home and abroad.[55] In a survey of black wartime opinion in Cincinnati and Baltimore, the Office of War Information reported growing dissatisfaction and militancy among black workers. African Americans in the two cities highlighted police brutality as a major grievance that they hoped to rectify: "One thing they could stop—the white cops from arresting colored people and beating them with their guns. You could just turn around and chop their heads off . . . the other day they run a black boy in here—they knew that they had him. After they had him they took their guns and beat him. . . . If I'd had a bomb I would have tried my best to blow them to hell." Police brutality underlay an increasing demand for black policemen who could arrest whites as well as blacks.[56]

The "Fighters," a wartime baseball team at the Chrysler Corporation in Evansville, part of the "Double V" struggle of African Americans for "Victory" at home and abroad. Courtesy Special Collections, University of Southern Indiana, Evansville

The treatment of blacks in the military also fueled African American anger and resolve to combat social injustice at home as well as abroad. One black mill worker pinpointed a galling contradiction in the nation's war against Fascism: "You would think that when you get in the Army and show that you want to help fight this war they would treat you all right, but they don't. The officers will call you nigger and treat you any kind of way and in some of these southern towns the white people will beat you up." When Ernest E. Trimble, an FEPC investigator, arrived in Cincinnati in September 1943, he heard rumors that "Negroes had organized what were called 'pusher clubs,' designed to push whites off the trolleys and buses." Although Trimble found little corroboration of the "pusher clubs," many employers feared that "a race riot might easily develop." An NAACP official warned: "White people are sitting on a powder keg ... blind to what is developing. I expect to see race riots flare up all over the country unless something is done to give the Negro a real opportunity in this war effort."[57]

Although largescale race riots did not erupt in Ohio Valley cities as they did in Detroit, Harlem, and elsewhere during the period, racial tensions, discrimination, and segregation nonetheless escalated. In a letter to the *Homestead Daily Messenger*, a black soldier from Pittsburgh complained of on- and off-base discrimination at a southern military installation. The black soldier not only faced harassment from local whites, but confronted racial segregation on public transportation facilities as well as in hotels, theaters, restaurants, and other places of amusement and business. The editor of the *Daily Messenger* articulated the black soldier's frustration: "These boys, whether white or black, are Americans. They are willing and eager to take up arms so that freedom and democracy may come through victoriously against our enemies. Yet, how much freedom and how democratic are southern states when they tell these boys they must not do this or that for if they will be fined." A subsequent letter to the editor suggested that racial conflict also "steamed" up and down "in the city's schools of Pittsburgh and on the streets of Homestead." African Americans lodged increasing complaints of police brutality, intimidation, and segregation in the residential, social, and institutional life of the region.[58]

Racial conflict gained potent manifestation in the wartime housing market. In June 1944, when two black families occupied a home in the Mt. Adams area of Cincinnati, a mob of some fifty to one hundred men and boys stoned the home, destroying all the doors and windows. Described as the "first Negro residents" on the street, the family had to vacate their home and flee for their lives. When a white female neighbor publicly criticized whites for their actions, several hundred whites marched to her home and hung an effigy of the woman. In Pittsburgh, while the Hill District (particularly the Third and Fifth Wards) would continue its trajectory toward a predominantly black community, most black newcomers crowded into the Beltzhoover area on the city's Southside, where housing was poor for whites and even more so for blacks. By the end of World War II, the percentage of Pittsburgh housing described as substandard stood at 30 percent for all black units compared to 12.3 percent for white ones. At about the same time, nearly 98 percent of Lower Hill residents rented their homes compared to about 75 percent in the Polish Hill area and just over 50 percent for Italians in Bloomfield. These discrepancies were also apparent in the surrounding steel towns.[59]

Mill expansion projects aggravated the housing problems of African Americans. In Homestead, most blacks lived in the path of company plans to add several openhearth furnaces, a plate mill, and a forge and machine shop to its operations. In January 1942, the company demolished more than 60 percent of the twelve hundred homes in the area and only about 10 percent of the ten thousand residents of the area remained. Similarly, in Duquesne, African Americans in the town's Castle Garden community stood in the path of plans to add three electric furnaces, a conditioning plant, and a heat-treating mill. An estimated 2,900 people lost their homes to make room for plant expansion. The displacement of black workers from these areas placed tremendous pressure on the existing housing market. Although the emergence of federally funded public housing projects, discussed above, alleviated some of the housing problems of blacks in Pittsburgh and other Ohio Valley cities, they also reinforced racial segregation and inequality in the housing market.[60]

Ohio Valley blacks responded to wartime injustices by joining African Americans in the national March on Washington Movement (MOWM). They perceived national organization as not only the key to fighting economic injustice, but the key to social justice in the larger community life of the region and nation.[61] Under the leadership of A. Philip Randolph of the Brotherhood of Sleeping Car Porters(BSCP), the MOWM emerged in 1941 following a meeting of civil rights groups in Chicago. The critical moment came when a black woman angrily addressed the chair: "Mr. Chairman . . . we ought to throw 50,000 Negroes around the White House, bring them from all over the country, in jalopies, in trains and any way they can get there, and throw them around the White House and keep them there until we can get some action from the White House."[62] A. Philip Randolph not only seconded the proposal but offered himself and the BSCP as leaders: "I agree with the sister. I will be very happy to throw [in] my organization's resources and offer myself as a leader of such a movement."[63]

By early June, the MOWM had established march headquarters in Harlem, Brooklyn, Washington, D. C., Pittsburgh, Detroit, Chicago, St. Louis, and San Francisco. The movement spread through the major rail centers and soon joined forces with local NAACP and Urban League chapters, churches, and fraternal orders. *The Black Worker*, the official organ of the BSCP became the official newspaper of the MOWM. The paper's May issue reprinted the official call to march: "We call upon you to fight for jobs in National Defense. We call upon you to struggle for the integration of Negroes in the armed forces . . . of the Nation. . . . We call upon you to demonstrate for the abolition of Jim Crowism in all Government departments and defense employment. . . . The Federal Government cannot with clear conscience call upon private industry and labor unions to abolish discrimination based upon race and color so long as it practices discrimination itself against Negro Americans."[64]

The MOWM helped to mobilize the masses of black working people as well as the middle and upper classes. According to Randolph, "The March on Washington Movement is essentially a movement of the people. It is all Negro and pro-Negro, but not for that reason anti-white or anti-Semitic, or anti-Catholic, or anti-foreign, or anti-labor. Its major weapon is the non-violent demonstration of Negro mass power."[65] Randolph further stated: "It was apparent . . . that some unusual, bold and gigantic effort must be made to awaken the American people and the President of the Nation to the realization that the Negroes were the victims of sharp and unbearable oppression, and that the fires of resentment were flaming higher and higher." Though the MOWM welcomed liberal white support, Randolph insisted that African Americans lead the movement. Randolph was wary of the labor movement, the major political parties, and the growing communist influence in black organizations like the National Negro Congress (NNC). When the Communist Party gained control of the NNC in early 1940, Randolph resigned from the presidency and soon left the organization.[66]

Although Roosevelt resisted the movement as long as he could, the MOWM finally produced results. Roosevelt met with black leaders A. Philip Randolph and Walter White of the NAACP on 18 June 1941. A week later, 24 June 1941, FDR issued Executive Order 8802, banning racial discrimination in government employment, defense industries, and training programs. The order also established the Fair Employment Practices Committee (FEPC) to implement its provisions. The government empowered FEPC to receive, investigate, and address complaints of racial discrimination in the defense program.[67]

Executive Order 8802 proved to be a turning point in African American history. It linked blacks in the Ohio Valley and elsewhere even more closely to the Democratic Party and helped to transform the federal government into a significant ally. It also helped to strengthen the bond between black workers and organized labor. While the AFL unions and the railroad brotherhoods did much to hamper this process, the unions of the Congress of Industrial Organizations often supported the FEPC claims of black workers and helped them to break the job ceiling. At its annual convention in 1941, for example, the CIO denounced racial discrimination as a "direct attack against our nation's policy to build democracy in our fight against Hitlerism." A year later, the organization established its own Committee to Abolish Racial Discrimination and urged its affiliates to support national policy against discrimination: "When a decision to employ minority group workers is made, the union must be prepared to stand behind it."[68]

Ohio Valley African Americans used the FEPC to broaden their participation in the war effort, but it was a slow process. Although the government trained an estimated 118,000 blacks in industrial, professional, and clerical jobs in 1941, by the end of 1942 only a small percentage had obtained employment in defense industries. Industrial firms in the North and South dragged their feet on the implementation of fair employment practices. In 1942, according to the report of the Pennsylvania Temporary Commission on the Urban Conditions among Negroes, 50 percent of Pittsburgh firms barred blacks from employment or relegated them to the lowest rungs of their employment ladder. By war's end, nearly 40 percent of all Allegheny County employers continued to bar black applicants. Some of the firms included metal industries. After Superior, Columbia, Bethlehem, and other area steel plants turned down black applicants in 1942, the Pittsburgh Urban League lamented that "there are still plants in this area which refuse to hire Negroes even at common labor."[69] In Cincinnati, FEPC investigators cited the Crosley Radio Corporation, the Formica Insulation Company, the American Can Company (which produced machine gun shells during the war), Victor Electronics, the Baldwin Company, and the Streitmann Biscuit Company (which packed food for the military), among others, for racial discrimination in their employment practices. Upon completing his survey of Cincinnati firms in 1943, investigator Ernest E. Trimble concluded, "On the whole, it seems clear that the defense industries in the Cincinnati area have rather generally refused to employ colored people equally with whites."[70] Other Ohio Valley firms hired blacks but denied them opportunities for skilled work. In Louisville, the Urban League reported that the city's industrialists made "little or no effort to comply with the President's Executive Order." When black workers applied for jobs in predominantly skilled labor departments, foremen invariably remarked, "There is no point in referring Negroes to those departments as they would not be accepted because of race."[71]

Black women faced even greater constraints on employment opportunities than black men. Black women complained that white women received work, while they remained unemployed. "When there is so much defense work," one Cincinnati woman asked, "how is it I cannot have a chance to work?" When they did gain jobs, they occupied the least desirable slots. In a letter to P.T. Fagan, area director of the Labor Manpower Commission, George E. Denmar, secretary of the Pittsburgh Urban League, complained of discrimination against black women at the American Bridge Company:

White women by the hundreds have entered training and the employ of the company, as welders and burners. They have been employed in the plate shop, also in the clean-up gangs of the ways and docks. But in all, only five Negro women have been hired to clean the lavatories. . . These Negro women have come to realize that advertisements for help, the need for skilled workers, the need for training, the need for American citizens to push the war effort as proclaimed over the radio and through the press does not mean Negroes, particularly women.[72]

Similarly, in a letter to FDR, a Pittsburgh woman wrote: "There are two plants close by. . . . They will hire the white girls but when the colored girls go there they always refuse them." In Cincinnati, one light-skinned woman advanced further along in the interview process before she was stopped cold:

Well, after I filled out the application, the young man came to the door of the office and asked me what I wanted, so I told him that I was sent there by the United States Employment Service Center for the job of inspector training. I asked him if he had such a job and he said yes. So then he asked me to come into the office. I handed him my application back that was filled out. So he told me that the job would require two weeks training period and I said, "That is quite alright," In speaking he glanced down at my application and he said, "Oh, you are a Negro," I said, "Yes." At this point, the interview stopped.[73]

Black women received the most labor-intensive jobs, while white women secured the less arduous positions. At Carnegie-Illinois Steel in Clairton, the plant manager promised three black women work as jamb cutters for four hours out of each eight-hour shift, but reneged on the promises and kept them there the entire shift. When they protested after six days of continuous labor as jamb cutters, they were fired. Although it is unclear whether the FEPC helped these women get their jobs back, other black women received FEPC aid in getting transfers to "less arduous toil."[74]

As during the 1920s, employers offered a variety of excuses for excluding African Americans: absence of "separate toilet facilities"; seeking skilled not unskilled workers; and no "qualified" blacks had applied. Some company spokespersons admitted that they barred black men and women from employment, but justified their practices by arguing that white employees would not work with blacks. Indeed, rank-and-file white workers as well as AFL and some CIO unions reinforced job discrimination during World War II. When asked if white workers would strike if the company hired blacks, a white worker at Cincinnati's Victor Electronics, which barred blacks entirely, retorted: "They certainly would . . . just send one [black] out there and the whole place would empty in five minutes. No union, no guards, no management will hold them." Fred Ross, president of the International Brotherhood of Electrical Workers (IBEW), corroborated the claim. According to historian Andrew Kersten, Ross not only confirmed that white workers would strike to bar blacks, but expressed the view that the war aimed "to preserve the American way of life" and to keep black people "in their places."[75]

Cincinnati's white workers conducted a series of "hate strikes" against the employment of black workers. An estimated fifteen thousand white workers walked off the job at the city's Wright Aeronautical Corporation when managers sought to hire blacks in the machine shop in June 1944. As late as 1945, white workers at Delco Products and the Lunkenheimer Company also walked out to protest the employment of black workers. When the Lodge and Shipley Company hired blacks under pressure from the FEPC, it did so on a segregated basis—employing blacks in Plant #2 but barring them from Plant #1. As one personnel manager put it, "The sudden influx might cause considerable troubles in our plant, so that we have gone on the slow, sure method of doing it gradually, getting the other employees used to seeing them around."[76] Complaints of racial discrimination became so numerous near war's end that federal officials opened a subregional FEPC office in Cincinnati and made plans to open one in Pittsburgh.[77] Every year, at the annual meetings of the AFL, A. Philip Randolph repeatedly exhorted white workers to end racial bias. He repeatedly stated that: "It won't do for the trade union movement, which ought to be the bulwark of democracy and which ought to maintain the tradition of democracy, to say 'no, you cannot participate in our organization, because you are not competent, because you are not worthwhile, because you are colored, because you are not white."[78]

Despite the persistence of discrimination, as the wartime labor shortages increased, the FEPC facilitated the movement of black workers into defense plants. Black industrial workers also took a direct hand in facilitating their own advancement into production jobs. Some black workers walked out to protest discrimination in promotion and violations of seniority rules. In Clairton, over six hundred black steelworkers struck the company on 25 February 1944. Similar walk-outs occurred throughout the war years. Partly as a result of similar actions nationwide, blacks in war production increased from less than 3 percent in March 1942 to over 8 percent in 1944. Even in Cincinnati, where white resistance was perhaps most intense, three companies—Kirk and Blum Manufacturing, Cambridge Tile, and the Schaible Company—settled with the FEPC and agreed to hire and upgrade black workers. By 1943, in Evansville, the Chrysler plant, which had located there during the mid-1930s, initiated the training of black workers as machinists. By war's end, black steelworkers in the Pittsburgh region had recovered their previous footing, rising to a peak of about 14 percent of the labor force.[79]

During World War II, African American activism not only manifested itself in the March on Washington Movement, but in the formation of new civil rights organizations. The new organizations staged mass demonstrations and protests against discrimination in places of public amusement and leisure. In Cincinnati, for example, blacks and their white allies formed the Citizens Committee for Human Rights (CCHR), which later became an affiliate of the Congress of Racial Equality (CORE).[80] As elsewhere, the Cincinnati branch staged interracial sit-ins at downtown restaurants. By December 1945, the organization had targeted more than ten restaurants for regular protests. Although some establishments resisted the protesters, others relented and served African Americans on a nonsegregated basis as required by law. Along with the emergence of the MOWM, their actions not only reinforced the wartime political mobilization of African Americans, but planted the seeds of the Modern Civil Rights Movement.

While the depression ushered in a long period of unemployment, public service work, and suffering for Ohio Valley blacks, World War II created new opportunities for socioeconomic, political, and community development. Under the impact of wartime labor demands, African Americans regained and strengthened their foothold in the urban-political economy. Yet, the wartime emergency and the need for workers were not enough to ensure the reemployment of African Americans and the protection of their civil rights. On the contrary, despite the emergence of the new CIO unions, the New Deal coalition, and labor shortages, African Americans faced stiff barriers in jobs, housing, and institutional life of Ohio Valley cities. In varying degrees, white workers, employers, and the state reinforced racial inequality and made it more difficult for the region and the nation to address the persistence of inequality along class lines. Consequently, only the organizational and political activities of African Americans in their own behalf ensured them access to industrial jobs, somewhat better housing, and new forms of political empowerment. As elsewhere in wartime America, Ohio Valley blacks learned that "closing ranks" in support of the nation's war effort did not preclude the continuation of their own struggle for social justice. The "Double-V" campaign for victory at home and abroad, the March on Washington Movement, and the growing use of the federal government to secure their aims, all helped to write a new chapter in Ohio Valley history and set the stage for a new and more intense struggle for social change in the postwar years.

Epilogue

As Ohio Valley African Americans faced the postwar years, they grew increasingly dissatisfied with the persistence of class and racial inequality. Building upon the successes of the March on Washington Movement, they would launch new offensives against racial discrimination and segregation in the social, economic, and political life of the region and nation. Their actions would also help to fuel the rise of the Modern Civil Rights Movement. As in the years between World Wars I and II, however, their efforts were deeply rooted in the continuing transformation of rural southern blacks into new urban workers. Along with the persistence of racial segregation and discrimination in the rural South, the expansion of New Deal economic programs for farmers and the intensification of technological changes in agriculture heightened the movement of blacks off the land.

Based partly upon federal assistance, large landowners gained increasing control of southern agriculture and applied new laborsaving technology. The growing use of tractors, flamethrowers, herbicides, and mechanical cotton pickers undercut the demand for black workers, who moved into cities in even greater numbers than before. The percentage of all blacks living in urban areas increased from about 62 percent in 1950 to over 80 percent by 1970. At the same time, the proportion of blacks living in the South dropped from almost 70 percent to a little over 50 percent.

Ohio Valley cities continued to absorb a substantial part of the black population movement. With the exception of Evansville, the black population of Ohio Valley cities not only increased, but made up a larger percentage of the total. Between 1950 and 1970, Pittsburgh's black population increased from 12 to over 20 percent of the total; Cincinnati's from 15 to over 27 percent; and Louisville's from less than 16 to nearly 24 percent (see Table 5). In short, the Ohio Valley played an important part in the transition of African Americans from a southern regional to a new na-

Table 5. African American Population in Ohio Valley Cities, 1950-1980

	1950		1960		1970		1980	
	No.	%	No.	%	No.	%	No.	%
Pittsburgh	82,453	12.2	100,692	16.7	104,904	20.2	101,549	24.0
Cincinnati	78,196	15.5	108,754	21.6	125,070	27.6	130,490	33.9
Louisville	57,657	15.6	70,075	17.9	86,040	23.8	84,254	28.2
Evansville	8,483	6.6	9,307	6.6	9,180	6.5	11,522	8.8

Source: *Seventeenth Census of U.S.*, vol. 2, pt 14, 17, 35, and 38 (Washington, D.C.: Government Printing Office, 1952); *Eighteenth Census of U.S.*, vol. 1, pt 16, 19, 37, and 40 (Washington, D.C.: Government Printing Office, 1961); *1970 Census of Population*, vol. 1, pt 16, 19, 37, and 40 (Washington, D.C.: U.S. Department of Commerce, 1973); *1980 Census of Population*, vol. 1, pt 16, 19, 37, and 40 (Washington, D.C.: U.S. Department of Commerce, 1983)

tional population, with its numbers spread across the north, west, and south.[1]

As blacks moved off the land in growing numbers, they continued to gain employment in the mass production industries of the Ohio Valley and elsewhere. Building upon their gains of the war years, African Americans not only entered the older steel, rubber, meatpacking, and automobile plants, but slowly gained jobs in new aircraft, electronics, and chemical industries and improved their footing in the industrial sector. For their part, black women gradually gained access to clerical and sales jobs in offices and department stores. Between 1947 and the early 1950s, the unemployment rate of black men and women reached a postwar low of 4.4 and 3.7 percent, respectively. At the same time, the number of African Americans in middle-class occupations also increased, as reflected in the gradual reduction of the gap in the wages and salaries of black and white employees.[2]

Unfortunately, before African Americans could consolidate their gains in the industrial sector and take a proportionate share of skilled, technical, professional, and managerial positions, they faced the brunt of deindustrialization. As the nation made the gradual transition from a goods-producing to a new service-producing economy, manufacturers adopted new laborsaving technology, relocated to low-priced suburban land, or took up residence in the low-wage sunbelt states of the South and Southwest. Consequently, as the black urban population increased between 1947 and the late 1960s, manufacturing in the nation's central cities declined from about 66 percent to about 40 percent of the total. These postwar technological and economic changes intersected with the persistence of racial discrimination and nearly canceled out the postwar progress of black Americans. From the early 1950s through the 1960s, the unemployment rate of African Americans was nearly double the rate of whites, while the unemployment rate of black youth was nearly triple.[3]

Despite a significant core of blacks with seniority and union membership, seniority provisions proved to be a mixed blessing. Black workers could not claim seniority beyond their own, often segregated, general labor departments. Thus, when mechanization eliminated their jobs they could not turn to jobs in other departments, where numerous younger white employees had less seniority than veteran black workers and union men. Whites sometimes acknowledged this form of discrimination. On one occasion, the white recording secretary of one United Steelworkers of America (USW) local bluntly reported: "I wish to express with regret that the range of jobs now open to minority groups has not changed one bit since our plant organized. In fact, the negroes are worse off now, in some respects, than they were before the plant was organized."[4] Moreover, although black women gradually improved their position during the period, they faced increasing competition from white women who entered the labor force in the postwar years. While the percentage of black women in the labor force remained relatively stable at about 44 percent, the number of white women in the labor force increased from 30 percent in 1948 to nearly 40 percent during the 1960s.[5]

In the postwar years, the alliance between African Americans, the federal government, and the labor movement also deteriorated. Following World War II, the federal government refused to renew the Fair Employment Practices Committee and left blacks vulnerable to the resurgence of racial discrimination in industrial jobs. It also enacted the repressive Taft-Hartley Act (which limited the ability of unions to organize and encouraged the enactment of right-to-work laws in southern states) and launched a vigorous campaign to eliminate communists from civil rights and labor organizations. Under pressure from the House Un-American Activities Committee, the NAACP, the AFL, and the CIO purged communists from their ranks. In Pittsburgh, steelworker Ben Careathers, Steve

A postwar photo of Pittsburgh Communist party members Ben Careathers and Steve Nelson. The photo was taken during the Smith Act trial on un-American activities. Courtesy University of Pittsburgh Press

Nelson, and other co-defendants in the Smith Act trials were found guilty and sentenced to a maximum of five years' imprisonment and $10,000 fines for conspiring to overthrow the government. Fortunately, the Pittsburgh party members were released on bail and three years later exonerated.[6] The removal of communists weakened the alliance for social change. As early as 1948, at the Atlantic City meeting of the USW, black workers exhibited growing impatience with the insensitivity of white labor to the ongoing needs of blacks as a group. At that meeting white international officers took accommodations in a hotel that displayed the sign: "No Negroes, No Jews, and No Dogs"! Black local and district officer Carl Dickerson and several other black steelworkers picketed the hotel and forced their white officers to move elsewhere.[7]

The postwar decline of labor militancy set the stage for the merger of the AFL and CIO in 1955. As the new AFL-CIO got underway, some African Americans hoped that the merger would strengthen their hand. Two black labor leaders, A. Philip Randolph and Willard Townsend, received

Carl O'Neal Dickerson, pictured here at the blast furnace of the Duquesne Works of the United States Steel Corporation near Pittsburgh. A union loyalist, Dickerson served as recording secretary of his local and regularly joined fellow workers on the picket lines. Courtesy Mrs. Oswanna Dickerson, Philadelphia, Pennsylvania

leadership positions in the new union. Although they used their positions to articulate the grievances of black workers, their presence did little to allay the disappointment of black workers. From the outset, the new union admitted the Brotherhood of Locomotive Firemen and the Brotherhood of Railroad Trainmen, which barred blacks from membership by constitutional provisions. Although the AFL exhibited little interest in the welfare of black workers, it received over 75 percent of the executive council positions in the new union. When African Americans filed discrimination suits against constituent unions, the new AFL-CIO opposed their claims in court. The black press, the NAACP, and black labor leaders repeatedly complained of racial discrimination in the postwar labor movement.[8]

Racial discrimination in the postwar labor movement reinforced discrimination in the housing market. Although the U.S. Supreme Court ruled restrictive covenants unconstitutional in 1948, federal housing policies, exclusionary zoning laws, and discriminatory real estate and lending agencies all helped to reinforce residential segregation, which in turn separated blacks from jobs in the expanding industrial suburbs.[9] Also, white homeowners employed informal covenants, intimidation, and violence to bar blacks from their neighborhoods. In 1954, for example, only the services of a white friend enabled black businessman Andrew Wade and his wife to purchase a house in the Louisville suburb of Shively. When white neighbors learned that a black couple occupied the house, they resorted to violence and intimidation to force the couple out. Within a month's time, the Wades' home became the target of ten gunshots and finally a bomb that severely damaged the structure.[10]

Federal housing policies also undermined the African American search for neighborhood improvement and community development. In the Housing Act of 1949, the federal government provided funds for the twin processes of urban redevelopment and public housing. Although African Americans applauded the construction of new housing for the working class and poor, the social costs of such programs remained high. In Pittsburgh, the city's urban renewal project resulted in the destruction of the Lower Hill District, where large numbers of the city's black population resided. Under the rubric of Renaissance I, urban renewal displaced some fifteen hundred black families to make room for the new Civic Arena and luxury apartments. Displaced families crowded into available public housing projects and into emerging black neighborhoods in other parts of the city, including the Upper Hill, the Homewood-Brushton area, and East Liberty. By the late 1960s, African Americans lived in seven widely dispersed but segregated neighborhoods, supplemented by smaller pockets of black settlement elsewhere in the city.[11]

Cincinnati's urban redevelopment plans unfolded more gradually than those of Pittsburgh, but with similar results. The urban policies of both cities reinforced the residential segregation of blacks and whites. Cincinnati's Comprehensive Plan of 1948 revealed the persistence of racial discrimination in the housing market. In 1951, Charles Stamon, head of the Urban Redevelopment Division, reported, "The great majority of people living in the project area are colored, and are certain to be discriminated against in their efforts to relocate in other parts of the city."

According to one report, any effort to build homes for blacks "automatically" eliminated some seventy sites from consideration. When the Cincinnati Metropolitan Housing Authority proposed a project for poor and black residents in one area, white residents formed homeowners' associations, asking their neighbors, "Do you want Niggers in your backyard?"[12]

Although such resistance frustrated efforts to find sites for black occupancy, passage of the Housing Act of 1954 allowed Cincinnati to redevelop the Avondale-Corryville section and demolish the West End. Located near the University of Cincinnati, the Avondale-Corryville area was key to the transformation of the CBD, riverfront, and lower West End. As the city destroyed the old West End, Avondale emerged as the so-called second ghetto. Between 1950 and 1960, Cincinnati's black population increased by 15 percent, but the West End black population dropped by fifteen thousand. Avondale's population increased to 56 percent black, about 18 percent of the city's total black community. By 1970, Avondale's black population reached 59,767, over 80 percent of all inhabitants in the area and nearly 50 percent of the city's total black population.[13]

Housing segregation also underscored the separation of blacks and whites in the public schools. In Louisville, blacks not only attended segregated schools, but faced barriers to training programs in higher education. Although the state's black colleges prepared African Americans for teaching in primary and secondary schools, they provided few opportunities for professional school and graduate training. In its de facto form, separate and unequal schooling also characterized black education in Evansville, Cincinnati, and Pittsburgh. In 1952, Cincinnati's Springmeyer school district not only refused to admit three black children, but rejected the NAACP's appeal for city-funded transportation to another area. As a result, the children missed a year of schooling because "school bus facilities could not be arranged for them."[14]

As Ohio Valley blacks faced the persistence of racial discrimination in the social, economic, and political life of the city, they escalated their civil rights activities and helped to transform the Modern Civil Rights Movement from a local and regional development into a national phenomenon. In Ohio Valley cities, as elsewhere, the combined and, at times, rival forces of the NAACP, Urban League, and CORE spearheaded the desegregation movement. In early 1952, for example, the Cincinnati branches of the NAACP and CORE demanded desegregation of the city's

Coney Island amusement park. When park officials resisted, demonstrations and litigation continued over the next two years. As a result, in April
1955, park officials met with civil rights leaders and agreed to "a quiet
opening" of the park, primarily under the leadership of the Cincinnati
Urban League (CUL). When CUL failed to orchestrate a "quiet opening"
of the swimming pool and dance hall to black patrons, the local CORE
and NAACP chapters took leadership of the movement and initiated new
demonstrations in May 1961. On one occasion, police arrested twenty-
seven black and white demonstrators for "trespassing and disorderly conduct." On another occasion, when activists "blocked the turnstiles at the
pool," police arrested six people. As the demonstrations escalated, park
officials met with leaders of CORE and the NAACP and agreed to desegregate "all facilities" at Coney Island on 27 May 1961. Similar movements
to desegregate public facilities took place in Pittsburgh and Evansville.[15]

Whereas Cincinnati, Pittsburgh, and Evansville blacks resisted informal patterns of segregation and exclusion, African Americans assaulted
the legal bastions of racial separation and inequality in Louisville, the
capital of "polite racism." In 1949, Lyman L. Johnson, a Louisville history teacher and civil rights activist, demanded entrance to the all-white
University of Kentucky graduate school. When university officials rejected
his application on racial grounds, Lyman received the endorsement of
the NAACP and lodged a lawsuit against the institution. When a federal
court ordered his admission, the state legislature amended its university
laws and permitted the enrollment of blacks. Two years later, other Louisville institutions followed suit: Roman Catholic colleges, Southern Baptist and Presbyterian technological seminaries, the University of Louisville,
and the Louisville Public Library.[16] When the U.S. Supreme Court handed
down its *Brown v Board of Education* decision in 1954, the city of Louisville quickly established a voluntary and peaceful plan of desegregation.
As a *New York Times* article stated: "Yesterday as schools opened there
were no mobs, no pickets, no need for calling the Guard to put out fires."[17]

Although Louisville's legacy of "polite racism" manifested itself in the
postwar years, it failed to curb the strong currents of discontent within
the city's black community. As elsewhere during the late 1950s and early
1960s, the black community mobilized its forces and demanded the desegregation of "all" public accommodations. Under the leadership of
CORE, the NAACP, and black religious and fraternal orders, Louisville
blacks launched a series of economic boycotts, demonstrations, and non-

violent protests. Under the growing effectiveness of black mass action, Louisville's corporate, civic, and political leaders relented. On 14 May 1963, Louisville became the first southern city to enact a public accommodations ordinance, which prohibited any public establishment from denying "food, shelter, recreation, entertainment or amusement" to any person on the basis of race, color, religion, or national origin. A year later, the Civil Rights Act of 1964 barred such discrimination throughout the country.[18]

The Civil Rights Movement in the Ohio Valley witnessed the growing convergence of community and workplace struggles. As organized labor neglected the needs of black workers, African Americans formed their own labor organizations and closed ranks with broader civil rights and community-based organizations like the Urban League, NAACP and CORE. In 1951, under the leadership of William R. Hood, black workers formed the National Negro Labor Council (NNLC) and initiated strikes, boycotts, and job training programs to assist in the upgrading of black workers. The organization also demanded black representation in a broad range of leadership positions in the labor movement. Although the organization declined under the twin opposition of organized white labor and the House UnAmerican Activities Committee (HUAC), black unionists soon regrouped and formed the American Negro Labor Council (ANLC).[19] Under the leadership of A. Philip Randolph, the ANLC demanded an end to racial discrimination in skilled apprenticeship programs, a ban on segregated and unequal black and white locals, and the expulsion of racist unions like the railroad brotherhoods. Their activities culminated in the mass March on Washington in 1963. As Randolph put it, "Demonstrations are the hallmark of every revolution since the birth of civilization.... And there is no way ... to stem these demonstrations until the cause is removed; and the cause is racial bias, the cause is exploitation and oppression, the cause is second-class citizenship in a first-class nation."[20]

The March on Washington not only symbolized the maturation of the Modern Civil Rights Movement, but accented its ties to black workers and its deep roots in the struggles of the Great Depression and World War II. Ohio Valley blacks were part of this important social movement, which resulted in Martin Luther King's "I Have a Dream" speech, the Civil Rights Act of 1964, and the rise of what some historians call the Second Reconstruction.[21] The Civil Rights Movement demolished the legal foundations of the segregationist system and mandated an end to employment discrimination. As such, it ushered in a new era of hope for African Americans.

In the wake of Martin Luther King's assassination in 1968, the Civil Rights Movement would give way to the Black Power Movement and an intensification of the struggle for social justice. Before the goals of these important movements could be fully realized, however, Ohio Valley African Americans and the nation would face a new era of global economic change, inequality, and violent social conflict along class and racial lines. The late twentieth century would again reveal the African American search for the elusive "River Jordan." Yet, while the achievements of the postwar years would fall far short of their promise in the Ohio Valley and elsewhere, they demonstrate how our current struggles are deeply rooted in the past and remind us that a historical perspective is crucial to our contemporary quest for social change.

Notes

Preface

1. Goings and Mohl, *Urban History;* Kusmer, "Black Urban Experience"; Trotter, "African Americans in the City," pp. 438-57.

2. Lynwood Montell and Rita Cohn, "Ohio Valley Series" announcement, Univ. of Kentucky Press, 1993.

1. African Americans, Work, and the "Urban Frontier"

1. Baldwin, *Pittsburgh,* p. 15.

2. Quoted in Wade, *Urban Frontier,* p. 10.

3. See Trotter and Bickley, *Honoring Our Past,* p. 4.

4. Ibid.

5. Quote in Baldwin, *Pittsburgh,* p. 159.

6. C.M. Green, *American Cities,* p. 41. Under the influence of the Society of the Cincinnati, an association of veteran Revolutionary War officers and residents changed the name of the settlement to Cincinnati.

7. Wade, "Negro in Cincinnati," pp. 43-57; Bigham, *We Ask,* pp. 1-7.

8. Share, *Cities in the Commonwealth,* p. 3.

9. Ibid.

10. Quoted in Wade, *Urban Frontier,* p. 64.

11. Ibid.; Share, *Cities in the Commonwealth,* pp. 1-22; Bigham, "River of Opportunity," especially pp. 130-37; Allen, *Western Rivermen,* pp. 27-40.

12. Baldwin, *Pittsburgh,* pp. 102-16; Wade, *Urban Frontier,* pp. 22-30; Tarr, "Infrastructure," pp. 216-18; Toker, *Pittsburgh,* pp. 7-10.

13. C.M. Green, *American Cities,* pp. 39-41; Wade, *Urban Frontier,* pp. 22-25; Ross, *Workers on the Edge,* p. 18; Z.L. Miller, *Boss Cox's Cincinnati,* p. 33.

14. Wade, *Urban Frontier,* pp. 15-16; Larsen, *Urban South,* p. 30; Share, *Cities in the Commonwealth,* pp. 2-8.

15. Bigham, "River of Opportunity," p. 136. Also see Bigham, *We Ask,* pp. 1-7.

16. Bigham, "River of Opportunity," pp. 134-39; Wade, *Urban Frontier,* pp. 39-71; C.M. Green, *American Cities,* pp. 39-56; Share, *Cities in the Commonwealth,* pp. 5-7; Muller, "Metropolis and Region," pp. 181-91; Faires, "Immigrants and Industry," pp. 3-32; and Oestreicher, "Working-Class Formation," pp. 111-50.

17. See n. 16, especially essays by Muller, Faires, and Oestreicher.

18. See Allen, *Western Rivermen*, pp. 70-72; Bigham, "River of Opportunity," pp. 139-40; C.M. Green, *American Cities*, pp. 44-49.

19. C.M. Green, *American Cities*, p. 49; Ross, *Workers on the Edge*, pp. 72-74; Z.L. Miller, *Boss Cox's Cincinnati*, p. 5; Levine, "Community Divided," p. 48.

20. C.M. Green, *American Cities*, p. 49.

21. Tarr, "Infrastructure," pp. 217-19; Muller, "Metropolis and Region," pp. 186-87; Tarr, *Sister Cities*, especially essay by Houston, "Capital Accumulation," pp. 29-70; Wade, *Urban Frontier*, pp. 39-49.

22. Share, *Cities in the Commonwealth*, pp. 33-43; Wade, *Urban Frontier*, pp. 64-66, 197-200; Bigham, "River of Opportunity," p. 144.

23. Share, *Cities in the Commonwealth*, pp. 33-43.

24. Bigham, "River of Opportunity," p. 151.

25. Ingham, "Steel City Aristocrats," p. 268.

26. Ross, *Workers on the Edge*, pp. 78-79.

27. Wade, *Urban Frontier*, p. 108.

28. Ibid., p. 126; Share, *Cities in the Commonwealth*, pp. 6-7, 33-43; Lucas, *Blacks in Kentucky*, pp. 104-05.

29. See U.S. Census Bureau, decennial population reports, 1820-1850; Bigham, "River of Opportunity," pp. 130-57; Hays, *City at the Point*, especially essays by Faires, Oestreicher, Greenwald, Muller, and Kleppner.

30. Faires, "Immigrants and Industry," pp. 3-32; C.M. Green, *American Cities*, pp. 54-55; Ross, *Workers on the Edge*, pp. 72-74; Larsen, *Urban South*, p. 45; Curry, *Free Black*, p. 29.

31. Oestreicher, "Working-Class Formation," pp. 111-50; Ross, *Workers on the Edge*, pp. 6, 32-33.

32. Ross, *Workers on the Edge*, pp. 33, 82 ff; Greenwald, "Women and Class," p. 35.

33. See Ross, *Workers on the Edge*, pp. 149, 163-67.

34. Oestreicher, "Working-Class Formation," pp. 111-50.

35. Ross, *Workers on the Edge*, p. 74.

36. See Oestreicher, "Working-Class Formation," pp. 124; Faires, "Immigrants and Industry," pp. 4-15.

37. Tarr, "Infrastructure and City-Building," pp. 226-29; Z.L. Miller, *Boss Cox's Cincinnati*, pp. 3, 6; Share, *Cities in the Commonwealth*, pp. 47-48.

38. See Z.L. Miller, *Boss Cox's Cincinnati*, pp. 4-5; Shapiro and Sarna, *Ethnic Diversity*, p. 132; Ross, *Workers on the Edge*, pp. 177-78; Wade, *Urban Frontier*, p. 133.

39. Faires, "Immigrants and Industry," pp. 3-31.

40. Ibid., "Immigrants and Industry," pp. 3-32; Shapiro and Sarna, *Ethnic Diversity*, especially essays by Bruce Levine and James Campbell; Wade, *Urban Frontier*, p. 133; Share, *Cities in the Commonwealth*, pp. 56-57; Kleppner, "Government, Parties, and Voters," pp. 151-80.

41. This and the following discussion of Republicanism is based mainly on

Ross, *Workers on the Edge,* pp. 23, 56-63; and Oestreicher, "Working-Class Formation," pp. 118-20. For the general notion of white Republicanism, see Roediger, *Wages of Whiteness.*

42. Ross, *Workers on the Edge,* p. 57.

43. Ibid.

2. Disfranchisement, Racial Inequality, and the Rise of Black Urban Communities

1. Lucas, *Blacks in Kentucky,* p. 108.

2. For this and the following quotes in the paragraph, see Berwanger, *Frontier against Slavery,* pp. 21, 32, and 52.

3. Ibid., p. 52.

4. Ibid., pp. 21-33.

5. Thornbrough, *Negro in Indiana,* p. 31. Also see Berwanger, *Frontier against Slavery,* pp. 21-33.

6. Ibid., p. 68, and Berwanger, *Frontier against Slavery,* p. 45.

7. Berlin, *Slaves without Masters,* pp. 92; Berwanger, *Frontier against Slavery,* p. 36, n. 17.

8. Berlin, *Slaves without Masters,* pp. 317-18; Berwanger, *Frontier against Slavery,* pp. 36-37, n. 18.

9. Berwanger, *Frontier against Slavery,* pp. 37-39.

10. Ibid., p. 34.

11. Wilmoth, "Pittsburgh and the Blacks", p. 123; Glasco, "Double Burden," pp. 69-109; Turner, *Negro in Pennsylvania;* R.R. Wright, *Negro in Pennsylvania;* Taylor, *Race and the City;* Bigham, *We Ask;* Curry, *Free Black.*

12. Curry, *Free Black,* pp. 252-53; Bigham, *We Ask,* p. 6; DeBow, *Statistical View,* p. 83.

13. Wilmoth, "Pittsburgh and the Blacks," pp. 9-11; Curry, *Free Black,* pp. 81-111, 245-58.

14. Berteaux, "Structural Economic Change," p. 133.

15. Ibid.

16. Ibid., pp. 134-35.

17. Horton and Flaherty, "Black Leadership," p. 87.

18. Berteaux, "Structural Economic Change," pp. 134-35.

19. Curry, *Free Black,* p. 260.

20. Berteaux, "Structural Economic Change," p. 135; Lucas, *Blacks in Kentucky,* p. 102; Curry, *Free Black,* pp. 15-36, 258-66; Bigham, *We Ask,* pp. 6-9.

21. Lucas, *Blacks in Kentucky,* p. 102.

22. Ibid., p. 103.

23. Quoted in Cheek and Cheek, "John Mercer Langston," p. 33.

24. Curry, *Free Black,* p. 87; Berwanger, *Frontier against Slavery,* pp. 7-59; and Gerber, *Black Ohio,* pp. 3-12.

25. Quillin, *Color Line*, pp. 38-43.

26. Wilmoth, "Pittsburgh and the Blacks, p. 123; Turner, *Negro in Pennsylvania*, pp. 169-70.

27. Lucas, *Blacks in Kentucky*, p. 109.

28. Curry, *Free Black*, p. 86; Taylor and Dula, "Black Residential Experience," pp. 90-125.

29. Curry, *Free Black*, p. 56; Wilmoth, "Pittsburgh and the Blacks," pp. 2, 24, 197.

30. Curry, *Free Black*, pp. 30-51.

31. Taylor and Dula, "Black Residential Experience," p. 102.

32. Ibid. Also see Curry, *Free Black*, p. 56.

33. Lucas, *Blacks in Kentucky*, p. 14; Curry, *Free Black*, p. 63; Bigham, *We Ask*, p. 6.

34. Taylor and Dula, "Black Residential Experience," p. 115.

35. Curry, *Free Black*, p. 91.

36. Wilmoth, "Pittsburgh and the Blacks," pp. 24-25, 150-59; Curry, *Free Black*, pp. 129-30; Turner, *Negro in Pennsylvania*, pp. 130-34.

37. Gerber, *Black Ohio*, p. 14; Quillin, *Color Line*, pp. 45-50; Curry, *Free Black*, pp. 162-69; Lucas, *Blacks in Kentucky*, pp. 140-41; Thornbrough, *Negro in Indiana*, pp. 160-81.

38. See Staudenrous, *African Colonization Movement*; and F.J. Miller, *Search for a Black Nationality*.

39. Wilmoth, "Pittsburgh and the Blacks," pp. 31-59.

40. Ibid.; Bigham, *We Ask*, pp. 14-15.

41. Lucas, *Blacks in Kentucky*, p. 116.

42. Bigham, *We Ask*, pp. 14-15; Thornbrough, *Negro in Indiana*, pp. 130-31.

43. Wade, "Negro in Cincinnati," p. 53.

44. Ibid., pp. 43-57; Woodson, "Negroes of Cincinnati," pp. 6-7; Curry, *Free Black*, pp. 105; and Cheek and Cheek, "John Mercer Langston," pp. 29-69.

45. Cheek and Cheek, "John Mercer Langston," p. 46.

46. Ibid., pp. 46-50.

47. Ibid.

48. See Turner, *Negro in Pennsylvania*, pp. 236-38; Wilmoth, "Pittsburgh and the Blacks," pp. 100-01.

49. Wilmoth, "Pittsburgh and the Blacks," p. 105., Bigham, *We Ask*, p. 14; Lucas, *Blacks in Kentucky*, p. xviiii[14]; Berteaux, "Structural Economic Change," p. 130; Curry, *Free Black*, pp. 245-57.

50. Wade, "Negro in Cincinnati," p. 53.

51. Wilmoth, "Pittsburgh and the Blacks," pp. 203-05.

52. Cheek and Cheek, "John Mercer Langston," p. 34; Curry, *Free Black*, pp. 42-43, 267-69; Bigham, *We Ask*, pp. 8-9.

53. Dabney, *Cincinnati's Colored Citizens*, p. 184.

54. Cheek and Cheek, "John Mercer Langston," p. 32.

55. Glasco, "Taking Care of Business," p. 178.

56. Lucas, *Blacks in Kentucky,* pp. 112-13; Dabney, *Cincinnati's Colored Citizens,* p. 183.

57. Cheek and Cheek, "John Mercer Langston," p. 51.

58. Wade, "Negro in Cincinnati," pp. 56-57.

59. Cheek and Cheek, "John Mercer Langston," pp. 44-45.

60. Ibid., p. 45.

61. Horton and Flaherty, "Black Leadership," p. 90.

62. Brown, *Historic Sites Survey,* p. 61.

63. Lucas, *Blacks in Kentucky,* p. 124.

64. Ibid., pp. 123-40.

65. Cheek and Cheek, "John Mercer Langston," p. 37.

66. Ibid., p. 38.

67. Bigham, *We Ask,* pp. 9-10.

68. Cheek and Cheek, "John Mercer Langston," p. 40.

69. Quoted in Cheek and Cheek, "John Mercer Langston," p. 39.

70. Ibid., p. 40.

71. Smith, "Pittsburgh Memorial." Also see Wilmoth, "Pittsburgh and the Blacks," pp. 123-24.

72. Blackett, "Freedom or the Martyr's Grave," pp. 117-34; Wilmoth, "Pittsburgh and the Blacks," pp. 98-124; and quote in Cheek and Cheek, "John Mercer Langston," pp. 43-44.

73. Blackett, "Freedom or the Martyr's Grave," pp. 117-34; Wilmoth, "Pittsburgh and the Blacks," pp. 47-48; and quote in Horton and Flaherty, "Black Leadership," p. 70.

74. Blackett, "Freedom or the Martyr's Grave," pp. 117-34; Wilmoth, "Pittsburgh and the Blacks," pp. 155-56; Curry, *Free Black,* pp. 159-60; Horton and Flaherty, "Black Leadership," pp. 76-77; Dabney, *Cincinnati's Colored Citizens,* pp. 103-04; Bigham, *We Ask,* p. 11; Lucas, *Blacks in Kentucky,* pp. 140-45.

75. Blackett, "Freedom or the Martyr's Grave," pp. 117-34; Wilmoth, "Pittsburgh and the Blacks," pp. 26-27, 48-49, 127-84, 251-75; Balfour, "Charles Avery," pp. 19-22; Dabney, *Cincinnati's Colored Citizens,* pp. 58-61, 65-68, 80-81; Curry, *Free Black,* pp. 151-52.

76. Wilmoth, "Pittsburgh and the Blacks," p. 22.

77. Cheek and Cheek, "John Mercer Langston," p. 44.

78. Curry, *Free Black,* pp. 104-05.

79. Horton and Flaherty, "Black Leadership," p. 83.

80. Ibid., pp. 70-80.

81. Ibid., p. 80.

82. Wade, "Negro in Cincinnati," p. 53.

83. Delany, *Condition, Elevation, Emigration, and Destiny.*

84. Ibid., p. 192.

85. Ibid., Blackett, "Freedom or the Martyr's Grave," pp. 117-34; Wilmoth, "Pittsburgh and the Blacks," pp. 19-21, 52-56.

86. Wilmoth, "Pittsburgh and the Blacks," pp. 93-95.

87. Ibid., pp. 50-51.

3. Occupational Change and the Emergence of a Free Black Proletariat

1. Gerber, *Black Ohio*, p. 42.

2. Ibid., pp. 28-34, quote, p. 34; Bigham, *We Ask*, pp. 15-16.

3. Wilmoth, "Pittsburgh and the Blacks," p. 134; Gerber, *Black Ohio*, pp. 33-34; Davis, "Pittsburgh's Negro Troops," pp. 101-13, quote, p. 103.

4. G.C. Wright, *Life*, p. 16.; Clark, *Black Brigade*; Gerber, *Black Ohio*, p. 33.

5. Quote from Sara Dunlap Jackson in Preface to Clark, *Black Brigade*.

6. Ibid.

7. See Litwack, *Been in the Storm*; E. Foner, *Reconstruction*; Du Bois, *Black Reconstruction*.

8. Wilmoth, "Pittsburgh and the Blacks," p. 137; Mitchell, *Beyond Adversity*, pp. 11-12; Bigham, *We Ask*, p. 17; Gerber, *Black Ohio*, p. 34.

9. G.C. Wright, *Life*, pp. 16-20.

10. R.L. Reid, *Always a River*, particularly Bigham, "River of Opportunity," pp. 130-79; Hays, *City at the Point*, especially essays by Muller and Ingham; Couvares, *Remaking of Pittsburgh*; Houston, "Capital Accumulation," pp. 29-70.

11. Bigham, "River of Opportunity," pp. 153-63; Temin, *Iron and Steel*; Warren, *American Steel Industry*, pp. 124-44; Chandler, *Visible Hand*; Muller, "Metropolis and Region," pp. 181-211; Ingham, "Steel City Aristocrats," pp. 265-94; McLaughlin, *Growth of American Manufacturing*.

12. Ross, *Workers on the Edge*, pp. 220-32; Z.L. Miller, *Boss Cox's Cincinnati*, pp. 3-56; Knepper, *Ohio and Its People*, pp. 286-312; Houston, "Capital Accumulation."

13. Larsen, *Urban South*, pp. 55-68; Share, *Cities in the Commonwealth*, pp. 66-87.

14. Quote in Larsen, *Urban South*, p. 62.

15. Ibid., pp. 55-68; Share, *Cities in the Commonwealth*, pp. 66-87.

16. Bigham, *We Ask*, pp. 21-23, 53-55, and 152-54; Bigham, "River of Opportunity," pp. 153-163; Thornbrough, *Negro in Indiana*, pp. 347-66.

17. See n. 10 above; U.S. Census Bureau, decennial reports, population, 1860-1910; and Klebanow, Jonas, and Leonard, *Urban Legacy*, pp. 40-41.

18. Quote in Share, *Cities in the Commonwealth*, p. 76.

19. See note 10 above and U.S. Census Bureau, decennial reports, population and occupations, 1860-1910.

20. Z.L. Miller, *Boss Cox's Cincinnati*, p. 14; Larsen, *Urban South*, pp. 76-77; Bigham, *We Ask*, pp. 22-23; G.C. Wright, *Life*, p. 46; Faires, "Immigrants and Industry," pp. 3-31; Bodnar, Simon, and Weber, *Lives of Their Own*, pp. 20, 30.

21. See U.S. Census Bureau, decennial reports of occupations, 1890-1910; Dickerson, *Out of the Crucible*, p. 22; Ross, *Workers on the Edge*; Bigham, *We Ask*, pp. 23-24, 53-63.

22. Chandler, *Visible Hand*, pp. 266-67; Oestreicher, "Working-Class Formation," pp. 111-50, especially pp. 116, 120; Warren, *American Steel Industry*, pp. 109-44; Houston, "Capital Accumulation," pp. 35-55; Temin, *Iron and Steel*, pp. 164-65; Brody, *Steelworkers in America*, pp. 2-26; Ross, *Workers on the Edge*, pp. 220-21.

23. Chandler, *Visible Hand*, pp. 265-67; Oestreicher, "Working-Class Formation," pp. 120-21; Warren, *American Steel Industry*, pp. 109-44; Temin, *Iron and Steel*, pp. 164-65.

24. Laurie, *Artisans*, pp. 141-210; J.R. Green, *World of the Worker*, pp. 32-99; Montgomery, *Fall of the House*; Fink, *Workingmen's Democracy*; Gutman, *Work, Culture, and Society*.

25. Oestreicher, "Working-Class Formation," pp. 126-34; Brody, *Steelworkers*, pp. 50-79; Krause, *Battle for Homestead*; Kleinberg, *Shadow of the Mills*.

26. Oestreicher, "Working-Class Formation," pp. 127-79; Ross, *Workers on the Edge*, pp. 246-95, quote p. 271.

27. See U.S. Census Bureau decennial reports, occupations 1890-1910. Also see Greenwald, "Women and Class," pp. 33-67; and Kleinberg, *Shadow of the Mills*, pp. 3-40.

28. Gerber, *Black Ohio*, p. 278; Bodnar, Simon, and Weber, *Lives of Their Own*, pp. 30-32; Dickerson, *Out of the Crucible*, pp. 18-19; Logan, *Betrayal of The Negro*, pp. 88-104; Williamson, *Crucible of Race*, pp. 111-224.

29. U.S. Census Bureau, decennial reports, 1890-1910.

30. Dickerson, *Out of the Crucible*, p. 18; Trotter, "Reflections," p. 153; Gerber, *Black Ohio*, pp. 277-79; Bigham, *We Ask*, p. 24; G.C. Wright, *Blacks in Kentucky*, pp. 1-3; Share, *Cities in the Commonwealth*, p. 79; Darden, "Effect of World War I," p. 301.

31. Harlan, *Booker T. Washington*, pp. 137-38, 290.

32. Trotter, "Reflections," p. 154; Glasco, "Taking Care of Business," pp. 177-85; Gerber, *Black Ohio*, p. 67; G.C. Wright, *Life*, pp. 84-85; Bigham, *We Ask*, pp. 108, 157.

33. Glasco, "Double Burden," pp. 73-74; Darden, "Effect of World War I," p. 301.

34. G.C. Wright, *Life*, p. 82.

35. Quote in Dabney, *Cincinnati's Colored Citizens*, pp. 184-85.

36. Berteaux, "Structural Economic Change," pp. 126-55; Gerber, *Black Ohio*, pp. 307-08; G.C. Wright, *Life*, p. 83. The process of displacement was by no means

uniform from city to city. Between 1890 to 1910, the number of black barbers dropped from 150 to 124 in Cincinnati. Despite white opposition in Louisville, however, the number of black barbers serving a predominantly white clientele stabilized rather than declined. According to historian George Wright, "In Louisville whites felt secure with blacks performing services for them, since they viewed this as part of the southern tradition."

37. Dickerson, *Out of the Crucible,* p. 15.

38. Spero and Harris, *Black Worker;* R.R. Wright, *Negro in Pennsylvania,* pp. 94-100; Dickerson, *Out of the Crucible,* pp. 13-17; Harris, *Harder We Run,* pp. 7-50; Gerber, *Black Ohio,* pp. 302-03; G.C. Wright, *Life,* pp. 88-91.

39. Spero and Harris, *Black Worker,* pp. 284-315; Gerber, *Black Ohio,* pp. 302-03.

40. Berteaux, "Structural Economic Change," p. 142; Gerber, *Black Ohio,* pp. 301-02; Dickerson, *Out of the Crucible,* p. 24.

41. Spero and Harris, *Black Worker,* pp. 246-55; quote, p. 250; *Iron Age* quote from Dickerson, *Out of the Crucible,* p. 17.

42. Trotter, "Reflections," p. 156.

43. For the literature on industrial slavery, see Trotter, "African-American Workers," pp. 504-07.

44. Dickerson, *Out of the Crucible,* pp. 8-10.

45. Trotter, "Reflections," pp. 152-53.

46. Dickerson, *Out of the Crucible,* pp. 20-21.

47. Ibid., pp. 11-13.

4. The Persistence of Racial and Class Inequality

1. Quoted in Z.L. Miller, *Boss Cox's Cincinnati,* p. 30.

2. Glasco, "Double Burden," pp. 69-110, quote, p. 73.

3. Gerber, *Black Ohio,* p. 53; Bigham, *We Ask,* pp. 51-52.

4. Gerber, *Black Ohio,* p. 330.

5. G.C. Wright, *Life,* pp. 41-76, especially pp. 4-5, 48-49, on the notion of "polite racism"; Gerber, *Black Ohio,* pp. 257-58; Bigham, *We Ask,* pp. 97-98.

6. G.C. Wright, *Life,* p. 75.

7. Ibid., pp. 103, 120; Bodnar, Simon, and Weber, *Lives of Their Own,* pp. 70, 177.

8. Bodnar, Simon, and Weber, *Lives of Their Own,* p. 24.

9. Taylor, "City-Building," pp. 156-91; Gerber, *Black Ohio,* pp. 100, 290; Z.L. Miller, *Boss Cox's Cincinnati,* pp. 13-16; Dabney, *Cincinnati's Colored Citizens,* pp. 161-63.

10. Bigham, *We Ask,* pp. 28-29, 109-10; G.C. Wright, *Life,* pp. 102-11.

11. See notes 7-10 above.

12. For insight into this process, see Tarr and Dupuy, *Technology;* Jackson, *Crabgrass Frontier;* Tarr, "Infrastructure," pp. 213-63; Bodnar, Simon, and We-

ber, *Lives of Their Own,* pp 22-23; Z.L. Miller, *Boss Cox's Cincinnati,* pp. 6-73; Bigham, *We Ask,* p. 32; Larsen, *Urban South,* p. 76.

13. Glasco, "Taking Care of Business," pp. 177-82; R.R. Wright, *Negro in Pennsylvania,* pp. 82-91; Bodnar, Simon, and Weber, *Lives of Their Own,* pp. 61, 78-80.

14. Bigham, *We Ask,* p. 163.

15. G.C. Wright, *Life,* pp. 7, 93-94, 98-99; Gerber, *Black Ohio,* pp. 379; Bigham, *We Ask,* p. 139; Bodnar, Simon, and Weber, *Lives of Their Own,* p. 79; Glasco, "Taking Care of Business," pp. 179-82.

16. Gerber, *Black Ohio,* pp. 90, 318-19; G.C. Wright, *Life,* pp. 99-101; Glasco, "Double Burden," p. 73; Proctor, "Racial Discrimination," pp. 37-44; Bigham, *We Ask,* p. 42; Thornbrough, *Negro in Indiana,* pp. 317-46.

17. Gerber, *Black Ohio,* pp. 140-58; 312, 433-45; Bodnar, Simon, and Weber, *Lives of Their Own,* pp. 74-80; G.C. Wright, *Life,* pp. 126-27; Bigham, *We Ask,* pp. 21, 74-78, 178-81.

18. Gerber, *Black Ohio,* p. 143; G.C. Wright, *Life,* p. 131; Bodnar, Simon, and Weber, *Lives of Their Own,* pp. 75, 77-78.

19. G.C. Wright, *Life,* pp. 131-36; Gerber, *Black Ohio,* p. 329; Glasco, "Double Burden," p. 75; Bigham, *We Ask,* pp. 186-87.

20. Gerber, *Black Ohio,* p. 310; Bigham, *We Ask,* p. 166; G.C. Wright, *Life,* pp. 171-72.

21. Buni, *Robert L. Vann,* pp. 42-53; Glasco, "Double Burden," p. 82; Daniel, *Black Journals;* Oak, *Negro Newspaper;* Wolseley, *Black Press.*

22. G.C. Wright, *Life,* pp. 178-180; Bigham, *We Ask,* pp. 87-100; Gerber, *Black Ohio,* pp. 214-44; Tucker, *Cincinnati's Citizen Crusaders,* pp. 13-15, quote, p. 13; Glasco, "Taking Care of Business," p. 178; Kleppner, "Government, Parties, and Voters," pp. 151-80; Holt, *Forging a Majority;* Stave, *New Deal,* pp. 27-28.

23. G.C. Wright, *Life,* p. 181; Bigham, *We Ask,* p. 93.

24. Glasco, "Taking Care of Business," p. 178; Gerber, *Black Ohio,* p. 334.

25. Gerber, *Black Ohio,* p. 229; Bigham, *We Ask,* pp. 93, 198; G.C. Wright, *Life,* p. 188; Tucker, "Cincinnati's Colored Crusaders," p. 30.

26. Gerber, *Black Ohio,* pp. 175, 225-29; G.C. Wright, *Life,* pp. 185-87; Glasco, "Taking Care of Business," p. 178.

27. Nieman, *Promises to Keep,* pp. 78-113; Thornbrough, *Negro in Indiana,* pp. 259-60; especially note 7 for list of states that passed civil rights laws.

28. Franklin and Moss, *From Slavery to Freedom,* p. 288; Bigham, *We Ask,* p. 97; Gerber, *Black Ohio,* pp. 58, 251-52.

29. G.C. Wright, *Life,* pp. 74-75.

30. G.C. Wright, *Life,* pp. 65-70; Proctor, "Racial Discrimination," pp. 37-44; Bigham, *We Ask,* pp. 42-48, 124-29.

31. Gerber, *Black Ohio,* pp. 397, 450-53; Dabney, *Cincinnati's Colored Citizens,* pp. 235-36. Porter later became the first black woman to earn the Ph.D. from the University of Cincinnati.

32. Glasco, "Taking Care of Business," p. 181; G.C. Wright, *Life*, pp. 158-75; Gerber, *Black Ohio*, pp. 90, 447-49.

33. Bodnar, Simon, and Weber, *Lives of Their Own*, pp. 177-78. A major exception was the janitor and laborer Samuel H. Golden. Upon his death in 1904, Golden owned four houses valued at a total of more than $25,000.

34. Gerber, *Black Ohio*, pp. 114-15, 126; G.C. Wright, *Life*, p. 111.

35. See notes 17 and 18, above.

36. Bodnar, Simon, and Weber, *Lives of Their Own*, pp. 74-75, 78-79, quote, p. 78; Gerber, *Black Ohio*, pp. 424-25.

37. Quotes in G.C. Wright, *Life*, p. 135; Bigham, *We Ask*, pp. 82-83.

38. Quoted in Bodnar, Simon, and Weber, *Lives of Their Own*, p. 79.

39. Consuelo, the daughter of Peter Clark of Cincinnati, became a physician, but she practiced in Youngstown rather than Cincinnati (Gerber, *Black Ohio*, p. 124). For insight into Ohio Valley black women and gender relations, also see Glasco, "Double Burden," pp. 74-75; Glasco, "Taking Care of Business," pp. 177-82; Berteaux, "Structural Economic Change," pp. 126-55; Kornbluh, "James Hathaway Robinson," pp. 209-31; and references in Gerber, *Black Ohio*; Bigham, *We Ask*; Wright, *Life*; and Bodnar, Simon, and Weber, *Lives of Their Own*.

40. McKenzie, "Daisy Lampkin," pp. 9-12.

5. Expansion of the Black Urban-Industrial Working Class

1. Trotter, *Great Migration*; Trotter and Lewis, *African Americans in the Industrial Age*.

2. Trotter, "Reflections," pp. 153-57. In this essay, I am especially indebted to Dickerson, *Out of the Crucible*; and Gottlieb, *Making Their Own Way*.

3. Ibid.; Kornbluh, "James Hathaway Robinson," pp. 209-31.

4. Trotter, "Reflections," p. 154; Dickerson, *Out of the Crucible*, p. 45.

5. Gottlieb, *Making Their Own Way*, pp. 122-23.

6. Ibid.

7. Kornbluh, "James Hathaway Robinson," pp. 216-17.

8. Dabney, *Cincinnati's Colored Citizens*, p. 197.

9. Trotter, *Coal, Class, and Color*, p. 79. For quote from *Chicago Defender* see Trotter, "Reflections," p. 154.

10. On the southern roots of black migration, see Grossman, *Land of Hope*; Bodnar, Simon, and Weber, *Lives of Their Own*, p. 33.

11. Gottlieb, *Making Their Own Way*, p. 49. On the general notion of black women as "primary kinkeepers," see E. Lewis, "Expectations"; and Hine, "Black Migration," pp. 46-67.

12. Bigham, *We Ask*, pp. 108-10, 154-73.

13. G.C. Wright, *Life*, pp. 45, 213-20; Carmichael and James, *Louisville Story*, p. 25.

14. Wright, *Life*, quote, p. 216.

15. Taylor, "City-Building," pp. 172-73; Berry, "Negro in Cincinnati Industries," pp. 361-81; and Kornbluh, "James Hathaway Robinson," pp. 216-17.

16. Dickerson, *Out of the Crucible*, pp. 61-62; Gottlieb, *Making Their Own Way*, pp. 99-100.

17. Proctor, "Racial Discrimination," p. 20.

18. Trotter and Lewis, *African Americans in the Industrial Age*, p. 19; I.A. Reid, "Negro in the Major Industries"; quoted in Gottlieb, *Making Their Own Way*, p. 102.

19. See Sherman, "Johnstown v. the Negro," pp. 454-64; Darden, "Effect of World War I," pp. 297-312, quote, p. 306.

20. Greenwald, "Women and Class," pp. 39-40; Spratt, "Unity within Diversity," quote, pp. 4-5.

21. Berry, "Negro in Cincinnati Industries," pp. 361-63; Bigham, *We Ask*, pp. 162-63.

22. G.C. Wright, *Life*, p. 214; Gottlieb, "Black Miners," pp. 102, 108.

23. Berry, "Negro in Cincinnati Industries," pp. 361-81.

24. Ibid.

25. Trotter, "Reflections," p. 156. Also see Brody, *Labor in Crisis;* Harris, *Harder We Run;* Spero and Harris, *Black Worker;* P.S. Foner, *Organized Labor.*

26. Trotter, "Reflections," p. 156; Dickerson, *Out of the Crucible*, pp. 85-100; Gottlieb, *Making Their Own Way*, pp. 156-64, 174-75.

27. David Demarest, interview with Annie Morgan, see introduction to re-print of Bell, *Out of This Furnace.*

28. "Monesson, November 23, 1919," Typescript courtesy of Pascale Tufau, copy in author's possession; Dickerson, *Out of the Crucible*, pp. 85-100; Trotter, "Reflections," p. 156; 150-51; G.C. Wright, *Life*, pp. 216-17; Bigham, *We Ask*, pp. 169-70.

29. Gottlieb, *Making Their Own Way*, pp. 126-27; also see pp. 135-38, 188.

30. Berry, "Negro in Cincinnati Industries," p. 362.

31. G.C. Wright, *Life*, pp. 238-43; Carmichael and James, *Louisville Story*, pp. 21-22.

32. Kornbluh, "James Hathaway Robinson," p. 220.

33. Bigham, *We Ask*, pp. 121-22; G.C. Wright, *Life*, pp. 238-39.

34. Kornbluh, "James Hathaway Robinson," p. 220.

35. Bigham, *We Ask*, p. 139.

36. Dickerson, *Out of the Crucible*, p. 63.

37. See Sherman, "Johnstown v. the Negro," pp. 454-64; Darden, "Effect of World War I," pp. 297-312, quote, p. 306.

38. G.C. Wright, *Life*, pp. 255-59.

39. Kornbluh, "James Hathaway Robinson," p. 220, Glasco, "Double Burden," p. 79.

40. Bigham, *We Ask*, p. 209; Trotter, "Reflections"; Jackson, *Ku Klux Klan*, pp. 170-73; G.C. Wright, *Life*, pp. 239-40.

41. Jackson, *Ku Klux Klan,* p. 171.

42. Ibid., p. 87.

43. Ibid., p. 164.

44. Bigham, *We Ask,* p. 209.

45. Ibid., p. 207.

46. Ibid., p. 209; Jackson, *Ku Klux Klan,* pp. 9-27.

47. Quote in Taylor, "City Building, Public Policy," p. 176.

48. Ibid., pp. 163-64.

49. Gottlieb, "Black Miners," pp. 68-69; Darden, "Effect of World War I," p. 309; Darden, *Afro-Americans in Pittsburgh;* Spratt, "Unity within Diversity," p. 4.

50. Bigham, *We Ask,* pp. 115-16.

51. Ibid., p. 237.

52. G.C. Wright, *Life,* pp. 231-37.

53. Fairbanks, "Cincinnati Blacks," pp. 193-208, quote, p. 197.

54. Bigham, *We Ask,* p. 118.

55. Gottlieb, *Making Their Own Way,* p. 69.

56. Ibid.

57. Ibid., pp. 74-75.

58. Epstein, *Negro Migrant,* p. 16; Gottlieb, *Making Their Own Way,* p. 76.

59. Fairbanks, "Cincinnati Blacks," p. 197; Taylor, "Building of a Black Industrial Suburb"; Koehler, *Cincinnati's Black Peoples.*

60. Taylor, "City Building, Public Policy," p. 171.

61. Ibid., pp. 173-75.

62. Kornbluh, "James Hathaway Robinson," p. 217.

63. Bigham, *We Ask,* pp. 163-65.

64. Ibid., p. 165.

65. Buni, *Robert L. Vann,* pp. 113-32; Dickerson, *Out of the Crucible,* p. 75; William Brashler, *Josh Gibson, A Life in the Negro Leagues* (New York: Harper & Row, 1978); Ruck, *Sandlot Seasons,* p. 136.

66. See Ruck, *Sandlot Seasons;* Banks, *Pittsburgh Crawfords.* In this section, I also benefited from interactions with my upper division undergraduate student, Richard Gilmore Jr., who wrote "A Historical Look at the Pittsburgh Crawfords and the Impact of Black Baseball on American Society," *Sloping Halls Review: Select Works by H & SS Undergraduates* 3 (1996), pp. 63-72. In Cincinnati, the number of black retail dealers increased from about 107 in 1910 to 160 in 1920 and to 200 in 1930. At the same time black insurance agents rose from fewer than a dozen to about thirty. See *U.S. Census of Occupations, 1910, 1920, and 1930,* respectively, Vol. 4, pp. 547-48; Vol. 5, pp. 1081-84; and Vol. 4, pp. 1281-84; Dabney, *Cincinnati's Colored Citizens,* sections 7 and 8.

67. G.C. Wright, *Life,* pp. 199, 221-22.

68. Ibid., pp. 222-24.

69. Ibid., pp. 224-28.

70. Kornbluh, "James Hathaway Robinson," p. 217.

71. Gottlieb, *Making Their Own Way*, pp. 198-99.

72. Bigham, *We Ask*, pp. 75-76, 179-82.

73. Dickerson, *Out of the Crucible*, p. 65.

74. Ibid.

75. Gottlieb, *Making Their Own Way*, p. 199.

76. Ibid., pp. 200-203.

77. Ibid.

78. Kornbluh, "James Hathaway Robinson," pp. 210-11.

79. Ibid., pp. 210-13.

80. Dickerson, *Out of the Crucible*, pp. 43-48, 101-18; Gottlieb, *Making Their Own Way*, pp. 52, 53, 107, 192-97.

81. Bigham, *We Ask*, p. 122; G.C. Wright, *Life*, p. 231; Gerber, *Black Ohio*, pp. 466-67; Dickerson, *Out of the Crucible*, p. 78.

82. Wright, *Life*, pp. 231-38.

83. Ibid., p. 239.

84. Ibid., pp. 239-41. Cf. the Committee for Interracial Cooperation in Louisville, which emerged during the early postwar years and later affiliated with the Southern Regional Council. Carmichael and James, *Louisville Story*, pp. 36-37.

85. Dickerson, *Out of the Crucible*, p. 78.

86. Dabney, *Cincinnati's Colored Citizens*, pp. 188-206.

87. Ibid.

88. Buni, *Robert L. Vann*, pp. 125-27; Glasco, "Double Burden," p. 85.

89. G.C. Wright, *Life*, pp. 247-48.

90. Ibid., p. 252.

91. Burnham, "Cincinnati Charter Revolt," pp. 202-24; Burnham, "Reform, Politics, and Race," pp. 131-63; Spencer, "Cincinnati Politics," pp. 68-69; Tucker, *Cincinnati's Citizen Crusaders*, p. 137, n. 16. I am indebted to my upper division undergraduate student Teresa Marx, originally from Cincinnati, for helping to broaden my understanding of black politics in the city.

92. Bigham, *We Ask*, pp. 165, 209-12.

93. Ibid., p. 211.

94. McKenzie, "Daisy Lampkin," pp. 9-12; Dabney, *Cincinnati's Colored Citizens*, p. 361.

95. R.A. Hill, *Garvey Papers*; Martin, *Race First*; Stein, *World of Marcus Garvey*.

96. See R.A. Hill, *Garvey Papers*, Vol. 2, pp. 512, 524 and Vol. 3, pp. 161-62; Dabney, *Cincinnati's Colored Citizens*, pp. 213-14.

97. Ibid., Vol. 3, p. 162.

98. Ibid., Vol. 2, p. 524.

99. Ibid., Vol. 3, p. 363.

100. Dickerson, *Out of the Crucible*, p. 80.

101. Ibid., p. 81.

102. Ibid.

103. Burkett, *Black Redemption*, pp. 113-120, quote p. 117.

104. Ibid., p. 81.

6. African Americans, Depression, and World War II

1. Watkins, *Great Depression*; Nash, *Crucial Era*; Kirby, *Roosevelt Era*; Leuchtenburg, *Franklin D. Roosevelt*; Harris, *Harder We Run*, pp. 95-122.

2. Trotter and Lewis, *African Americans in the Industrial Age*, pp. 169-247.

3. Gottlieb, *Making Their Own Way*, pp. 103-04; Dickerson, *Out of the Crucible*, pp. 119-20; Stave, *New Deal*, pp. 33-34.

4. Dickerson, *Out of the Crucible*, pp. 120-21, 124.

5. Moss, "Negro in Pittsburgh's Industries," pp. 40-42, 59; Edmonds, *Daybreakers*; Gottlieb, *Making Their Own Way*, pp. 103-06; Spratt, "Unity within Diversity," quote, p. 8.

6. Also see Fairbanks, "Cincinnati Blacks," pp. 193-208; Fairbanks, *Making Better Citizens*, p. 73.

7. Berry, "Negro in Cincinnati Industries," pp. 361-63.

8. Bigham, *We Ask*, pp. 173, 217.

9. G.C. Wright, *Blacks in Kentucky*, pp. 8-10, 15-16; Blakey, *Hard Times*, p. 11.

10. Wolters, *Negroes and the Great Depression*, pp. 83-213; Sitkoff, *New Deal for Blacks*, pp. 34-57; Sternsher, *Depression and War*, especially the essay by Fishel; Wright and Rosskam, *12 Million Black Voices*.

11. Quote from Meltzer, *In Their Own Words*, pp. 93-94.

12. Wolters, *Negroes and the Great Depression*, pp. 83-168; Sitkoff, *New Deal for Blacks*, pp. 47-48, 52-55, 104; Fishel, "Negro in the New Deal," pp. 7-28.

13. Wolters, *Negroes*, pp. 83-168, quote, p. 139.

14. Wolters, *Negroes and the Great Depression*, pp. 169-92; quote in Sitkoff, *New Deal for Blacks*, p. 52.

15. Anderson, *A. Philip Randolph*; Harris, *Keeping the Faith*; Sitkoff, *New Deal for Blacks*, pp. 54-55; Wolters, *Negroes and the Great Depression*, pp. 83-229; Dickerson, *Out of the Crucible*, p. 131.

16. Sitkoff, *New Deal for Blacks*, pp. 54-55.

17. Dickerson, *Out of the Crucible*, pp. 126-28; Bodnar, Simon, and Weber, *Lives of Their Own*, p. 217; Hinshaw and Modell, "Perceiving Racism," pp. 17-52, quote, p. 26.

18. Dickerson, *Out of the Crucible*, pp. 128-32; Kornbluh, "James Hathaway Robinson," p. 224; Bigham, *We Ask*, pp. 217-21; Lubove, *Twentieth-Century Pittsburgh*, pp. 83-86; Collins, "Cincinnati Negroes," pp. 258-63; Fairbanks, *Making*

Better Citizens, pp. 201-06; On the national level, see notes 10-12 above. Dickerson, *Out of the Crucible,* pp. 128-29.

19. Lubove, *Twentieth-Century Pittsburgh,* pp. 83-86; Collins, "Cincinnati Negroes," pp. 260-61; Blakey, *Hard Times,* pp. 36-103, quote p. 37; Fairbanks, *Making Better Citizens,* pp. 72-148; and Fairbanks, "Cincinnati Blacks," pp. 193-208.

20. Cf. Drake and Cayton, *Black Metropolis.*

21. During the 1930s the Socialist Party also campaigned against racial injustice. In 1929, the party established the United Colored Socialists of America (UCSA). Party head Norman Thomas appointed a special black organizer for the South and supported a resolution condemning racial discrimination by trade unions. By 1933, the Socialist Party endorsed federal anti-lynching and anti-poll tax legislation, organized sharecroppers' unions, and elevated blacks to leadership positions. Carter, *Scottsboro,* pp. 68-69; Painter, *Hosea Hudson;* Kelley, *Hammer and Hoe,* pp. 42-43, 78-92, 109-10; Naison, *Communists in Harlem,* pp. xvii, 57-89; Meltzer, *In Their Own Words,* pp. 101-13.

22. Carter, *Scottsboro,* quote p. 68.

23. Ibid., pp. 68-69.

24. Nelson, Barrett, and Ruck, *Steve Nelson,* p. 25; Bonosky, "Ben Careathers," pp. 34-44, reprinted in Foner and Lewis, *Black Worker,* pp. 46-48; P.S. Foner, *Organized Labor,* pp. 219-37.

25. See Harris, *Keeping the Faith,* pp. 208-16; Anderson, *A. Philip Randolph,* pp. 296-97; Cayton and Mitchell, *Black Workers,* pp. 111-22, 190-224.

26. Harris, *Harder We Run,* pp. 43-44, 95-114 ; Harris, *Keeping the Faith,* pp. 208-16; Anderson, *A. Philip Randolph,* pp. 296-97; Dickerson, *Out of the Crucible,* pp. 130-36, quote on p. 134; Cayton and Mitchell, *Black Workers,* pp. 111-22, 190-224; R.L. Lewis, *Black Coal Miners,* pp. 58-164; Trotter, *Coal, Class, and Color,* pp. 51-52, 111-15.

27. Harris, *Keeping the Faith,* pp. 43-44, 95-114; Anderson, *A. Philip Randolph,* pp. 296-97; P.S. Foner, *Organized Labor,* pp. 177-237; Dickerson, *Out of the Crucible,* pp. 132-34.

28. Bigham, *We Ask,* p. 219; P.S. Foner, *Organized Labor,* p. 233; Harris, *Harder We Run,* p. 125; Myrdal, *American Dilemma* pp. 1115-19.

29. Reed, *Seedtime,* pp. 217-22; Foner and Lewis, *Black Worker,* p. 89.

30. Foner and Lewis, *Black Worker,* p. 89;

31. J.R. Green, *World of the Worker,* p. 147; Sitkoff, *New Deal for Blacks,* pp. 152-53; Cayton and Mitchell, *Black Workers,* pp. 111-22, 190-224; Dickerson, *Out of the Crucible,* pp. 139-49.

32. Dickerson, *Out of the Crucible,* p. 142; Gottlieb, "Black Miners," pp. 233-41; R.L. Lewis, *Black Coal Miners,* pp. 99-164; Trotter, *Coal, Class, and Color,* pp. 64-122; P.S. Foner, *Organized Labor,* pp. 215-37.

33. Dickerson, *Out of the Crucible,* all quotes, p. 143.

34. Ibid., pp. 133, 147; Cayton and Mitchell, *Black Workers,* pp. 223-24.

35. Dickerson, *Out of the Crucible,* pp. 136-39, 146; Cunningham, "Homer S. Brown," pp. 304-17; Glasco, "Double Burden," pp. 75-88.

36. Sitkoff, *New Deal For Blacks,* pp. 258-60; Wolters, *Negroes and the Great Depression,* pp. 353-82; Streater, "National Negro Congress."

37. See Lapin, "Negro America," pp. 46-48.

38. Editorial, *Pittsburgh Courier,* 11 Sept. 1932.

39. Stave, *New Deal,* pp. 59-61; Buni, *Robert L. Vann,* pp. 174-221, 264-98.

40. Kirby, *Roosevelt Era,* pp. 106-51; Buni, *Robert L. Vann,* pp. 206-07; Sitkoff, *New Deal for Blacks,* pp. 77-79.

41. McKenzie, "Daisy Lampkin," pp. 9-12; Bigham, *We Ask,* p. 223.

42. Cunningham, "Homer S. Brown," pp. 304-17.

43. Ibid.

44. G.C. Wright, *Blacks in Kentucky,* pp. 158-61; Carmichael and James, *Louisville Story,* p. 27.

45. Collins, "Cincinnati Negroes," p. 260.

46. Bigham, *We Ask,* p. 224.

47. Nieman, *Promises to Keep,* pp. 114-47; Naison, *Communists in Harlem,* pp. xvii, 50-51, 100; Sitkoff, *New Deal for Blacks,* pp. 258, 263; G.C. Wright, *Blacks in Kentucky,* pp. 162-92.

48. Bigham, *We Ask,* p. 219; P.S. Foner, *Organized Labor,* p. 233; Harris, *Harder We Run,* p. 125; Myrdal, *American Dilemma,* pp. 1118-19.

49. Bigham, *We Ask,* p. 219; Hunter, "Public Education of Blacks"; Proctor, "Racial Discrimination."

50. Schuyler, "Union Drive Slows," pp. 87-92.

51. Reed, *Seedtime,* pp. 217-22.

52. Lubove, *Twentieth-Century Pittsburgh,* pp. 85-86, especially n. 84; Bigham, *We Ask,* p. 219; Fairbanks, "Cincinnati Blacks," pp. 202-03; Taylor, *Race and the City,* p. 177.

53. Fairbanks, "Cincinnati Blacks," p. 205; Taylor, "Building of a Black Industrial Suburb"; Koehler, *Cincinnati's Black Peoples,* pp. 174-75.

54. W.J. Wilson, *Declining Significance of Race,* p. 69; Shapiro, *White Violence,* pp. 301-48.

55. Buni, *Robert L. Vann,* p. 325; Dalfiume, "Forgotten Years,"[51] pp. 298-316.

56. Shapiro, *White Violence,* p. 339; Carmichael and James, *Louisville Story,* p. 28.

57. Shapiro, *White Violence,* pp. 339-40; Kersten, "Publicly Exposing Discrimination," pp. 9-22; quote, p. 12.

58. Quotes in Trotter and Lewis, *African Americans in the Industrial Age,* pp. 290-95. Cf. Shapiro, *White Violence,* pp. 301-48; Capeci and Wilkerson, *Layered Violence;* Greenberg, *Or Does It Explode?*

59. Burnham, "New Interracialism," pp. 53-64; Bodnar, Simon, and Weber, *Lives of Their Own,* p. 256; Bunzel, *Negro Housing Needs,* pp. 12-17.

60. Cole, "Voices and Choices," pp. 46-76.

61. Anderson, *A. Philip Randolph*, pp. 241-73; Reed, *Seedtime*, pp. 1-17; P.S. Foner, *Organized Labor*, pp. 239-42; Sitkoff, *New Deal for Blacks*, pp. 314-15.

62. Quote in Sitkoff, *New Deal for Blacks*, pp. 314-15.

63. Ibid.

64. Randolph, "March for a Fair Share," pp. 291-98.

65. Randolph, "Why Should We March," pp. 251-52.

66. Anderson, *A. Philip Randolph*, pp. 229-73; Reed, *Seedtime*, pp. 1-17; P.S. Foner, *Organized Labor*, pp. 239-42; Sitkoff, *New Deal for Blacks*, pp. 314-15.

67. Anderson, *A. Philip Randolph*, pp. 256-58.

68. P.S. Foner, *Organized Labor*, p. 256; Harris, *Harder We Run*, pp. 113-22; Foner and Lewis, *Black Worker*, pp. 251-300.

69. P.S. Foner, *Organized Labor*, pp. 242-43; Dickerson, *Out of the Crucible*, pp. 159-60; Kersten, "Publicly Exposing Discrimination," p. 14; Reed, "Black Workers," pp. 356-84; Reed, *Seedtime*, pp. 117-204.

70. Kersten, "Publicly Exposing Discrimination," p. 14; Bigham, *We Ask*, pp. 226-28.

71. G.C. Wright, *Blacks in Kentucky*, p. 16. Also see Dickerson, *Out of the Crucible*, p. 161.

72. Trotter and Lewis, *African Americans in the Industrial Age*, pp. 261-62.

73. Kersten, "Publicly Exposing Discrimination, pp. 18-19.

74. Trotter and Lewis, *African Americans in the Industrial Age*, pp. 261-62; Dickerson, *Out of the Crucible*, pp. 162-63.

75. Reed, *Seedtime*, pp. 219-20; Kersten, "Publicly Exposing Discrimination," pp. 16-18.

76. Reed, *Seedtime*, pp. 219-20; Kersten, "Publicly Exposing Discrimination," pp. 13-18.

77. The FEPC hearings also revealed deep-seated racial discrimination by labor unions. In Cincinnati, unlike most northern cities, the FEPC enabled blacks to make only a few inroads into better jobs. By July 1945, when Congress reduced funds for FEPC, it closed its Cincinnati office and left the discriminatory policies of most companies intact. During World War II, the segregationist editor of the *Louisville Courier-Journal* chaired the president's FEPC, which other southerners attacked as "Roosevelt racial experts" and "halo-wearing missionaries of New Deal Socialism."

78. Anderson, *A. Philip Randolph*, pp. 252-315; Harris, *Harder We Run*, pp. 95-122; Harris; *Keeping the Faith*, pp. 185-216; P.S. Foner, *Organized Labor*, quote, p. 249.

79. Burnham, "New Interracialism," pp. 267-68; Bigham, *We Ask*, pp. 217, 230; Dickerson, *Out of the Crucible*, pp. 146, 154-56. As St. Clair Drake and Horace R. Cayton noted in their study of Chicago during the period, "The Second World War broke the ceiling at the level of semiskilled work and integrated thousands of Negroes as skilled laborers in the electrical and light manufacturing indus-

tries, from which they had been barred by custom, and in the vast new airplane-engine factories. . . . They also began to filter into minor managerial and clerical positions in increasing numbers" (Drake and Cayton, *Black Metropolis*, pp. 214-62, 287-311).

80. Burnham, "New Interracialism," p. 268.

Epilogue

1. U.S. Department of Commerce, *Social and Economic Status*, pp. 4-18; Lemann, *Promised Land.*

2. W.J. Wilson, *Declining Significance of Race*, pp. 88-154; Broom and Glenn, "Occupations and Income," pp. 2-42; Ross and Hill, *Employment, Race and Poverty;* U.S. Department of Commerce, *Social and Economic Status*, pp. 60-81; Bigham, *We Ask*, p. 235; Landry, *New Black Middle Class*, pp. 43-93; Wallace, *Black Women*, pp. 1-9.

3. Bluestone and Harrison, *Deindustrialization of America;* W.J. Wilson, *Declining Significance of Race*, pp. 88-154; Jones, *Dispossessed*, pp. 205-92.

4. Dickerson, *Out of the Crucible*, pp. 183-86, 216-17, quote p. 194.

5. See note 3 above, W.J. Wilson, *Declining Significance of Race*, pp. 88- 154; Glenn and Bonjean, *Blacks in the United States*, pp. 2-42; Ross, *Workers on the Edge*, pp. 3-48; Marshall and Briggs, *Negro and Apprenticeship*, pp. 124-25; Dickerson, *Out of the Crucible*, pp. 194, 216-17; Jones, *Labor of Love*, pp. 260- 68.

6. Harris, *Harder We Run*, pp. 123-46; P.S. Foner, *Organized Labor*, pp. 274-331; Green, *World of the Worker*, pp. 210-34; Dubofsky, *State and Labor*, pp. 197-231; Nelson, Barrett, and Ruck, *Steve Nelson*, pp. 374-75.

7. Anderson, *A. Philip Randolph*, pp. 296-332; Dickerson, *Out of the Crucible*, p. 225.

8. Harris, *Harder We Run*, pp. 123-46; P.S. Foner, *Organized Labor*, pp. 274-331; Foner and Lewis, *Black Worker*, vols. 7 and 8.

9. Nieman, *Promises to Keep*, pp. 144-45; Massey and Denton, *American Apartheid*, pp. 42-57.

10. Wright, *History of Blacks*, pp. 220-21.

11. Bodnar, Simon, and Weber, *Lives of Their Own*, pp. 206-36; Weber, *Don't Call Me Boss*, pp. 270-76; Glasco, "Double Burden," pp. 69-109; Lubove, *Twentieth- Century Pittsburgh*, pp. 59-176.

12. Fairbanks, *Making Better Citizens*, pp. 164-71, and Fairbanks, "Cincinnati Blacks," pp. 193-208; *Cincinnati: The Queen City: Bicentennial Edition* (Eden Park, Cincinnati: The Cincinnati Historical Society, 1988), chs. 3-5.

13. Fairbanks, *Making*, pp. 164-71; Fairbanks, "Cincinnati Blacks," pp. 193-208; Casey-Leininger, "Park Town Cooperative Homes," pp. 36-52; G.C. Wright, *Blacks in Kentucky*, p. 223.

14. Mjagkij, "Behind the Scenes," p. 282.

15. Burnham, "Mayor's Friendly Relations Committee," pp. 258-279; Carmichael and James, *Louisville Story,* pp. 21-25; Glasco, "Double Burden," p. 93; Bigham, *We Ask,* p. 234.

16. Share, *Cities in the Commonwealth,* pp. 99-108; Wright, *Blacks in Kentucky,* pp. 191-226.

17. Share, *Cities in the Commonwealth,* pp. 99-108; Wright, *Blacks in Kentucky,* pp. 191-226.

18. Mjagkij, "Behind the Scenes," pp. 280-94.

19. Harris, *Harder We Run,* pp. 147-78.

20. Anderson, *A. Philip Randolph,* quote, pp. 328-29.

21. Lawson, *Running for Freedom,* pp. 31-65; Morris, *Origins of the Civil Rights Movement,* pp. 275-90; Anderson, *A. Philip Randolph,* pp. 320-32; Harris, *Harder We Run,* pp. 147-48; H. Hill, *Black Labor,* pp. 93-169; Marable, *Race, Reform, and Rebellion.*

Bibliography

Allen, Michael. *Western Rivermen, 1763-1861: Ohio and Mississippi Boatmen and the Myth of the Alligator Horse.* Baton Rouge: Louisiana State Univ. Press, 1990.

Anderson, Jervis. *A. Philip Randolph: A Biographical Portrait.* 1972. Reprint, Berkeley: Univ. of California Press, 1986.

Attaway, William. *Blood on the Forge.* 1941. Reprint, New York: Macmillan, 1970.

Baldwin, Leland D. *Pittsburgh: The Story of a City, 1750-1865.* 1937. Reprint, Pittsburgh: Univ. of Pittsburgh Press, 1981.

Balfour, Stanton. "Charles Avery, Early Pittsburgh Philanthropist." *Western Pennsylvania Historical Magazine* 43 (March 1960).

Banks, James. *The Pittsburgh Crawfords: The Lives and Times of Black Pittsburgh's Most Exciting Team.* Dubuque, Iowa: William C. Brown, 1991.

Bell, Thomas. *Out of This Furnace: A Novel of Immigrant Labor in America.* Pittsburgh: Univ. of Pittsburgh Press, 1976.

Berlin, Ira. *Slaves without Masters: The Free Negro in the Antebellum South.* New York: New Press, 1974.

Bernard, Richard M., ed. *Snowbelt Cities: Metropolitan Politics in the Northeast and Midwest since World War II.* Bloomington: Indiana Univ. Press, 1990.

Berry, Theodore M. "The Negro in Cincinnati Industries: A Survey Summary." *Opportunity* (Dec. 1930).

Berteaux, Nancy. "Structural Economic Change and Occupational Decline among Black Workers in Nineteenth-Century Cincinnati." In *Race and the City: Work, Community, and Protest in Cincinnati, 1820-1970,* ed. Henry Louis Taylor Jr. Urbana: Univ. of Illinois Press, 1993.

Berwanger, Eugene H. *The Frontier against Slavery: Western Anti-Negro Prejudice and the Slavery Extension Controversy.* Urbana: Univ. of Illinois Press, 1967.

Bigham, Darrel E. "River of Opportunity: Economic Consequences of the Ohio." In *Always a River: The Ohio River and the American Experience,* ed. Robert L. Reid. Bloomington: Indiana Univ. Press, 1991.

———. *We Ask Only a Fair Trial: A History of the Black Community of Evansville, Indiana.* Bloomington: Indiana Univ. Press, 1987.

Blackett, R.J.M. "Freedom or the Martyr's Grave: Black Pittsburgh's Aid to the

Fugitive Slave." *Western Pennsylvania Historical Magazine* 61 (April 1978).

Blakey, George T. *Hard Times and New Deal in Kentucky, 1929-1939.* Lexington: University of Kentucky, 1986.

Blockson, Charles L. *African Americans in Pennsylvania. A History and Guide.* Baltimore: Black Classic Press, 1994.

Bluestone, Barry, and Bennett Harrison. *The Deindustrialization of America: Plant Closings, Community Abandonment, and the Dismantling of Basic Industry.* New York: Basic Books, 1982.

Bodnar, John, Roger Simon, and Michael P. Weber. *Lives of Their Own: Blacks, Italians, and Poles in Pittsburgh, 1900-1960.* Urbana: Univ. of Illinois Press, 1982.

Bonosky, Philip. "The Story of Ben Careathers." *Masses and Mainstream* 6 (July 1953). Reprint, *The Black Worker from the Founding of the CIO to the AFL-CIO Merger, 1936-1955,* Vol. 2, ed. Philip S. Foner and Ronald L. Lewis. Philadelphia: Temple Univ. Press, 1983.

Bracey, John H., Jr., August Meier, and Elliott Rudwick, eds. *Free Blacks in America, 1800- 1860.* Belmont, Cal.: Wadsworth Publishing, 1971.

Brody, David. *Labor in Crisis: The Steel Strike of 1919.* 1965. Reprint, Urbana: Univ. of Illinois Press, 1987.

———. *Steelworkers in America: The Nonunion Era.* New York: Russell & Russell, 1970.

Broom, Leonard, and Norval D. Glenn. "The Occupations and Income of Black Americans," In *Blacks in the United States,* ed. Norval D. Glenn and Charles Bonjean. Chicago: Chandler Publishing, 1969.

Brown, Eliza, et al. *African American Historic Sites Survey of Allegheny County.* Harrisburg: Pennsylvania Historical and Museum Commission, 1994.

Buni, Andrew. *Robert L. Vann of the Pittsburgh Courier: Politics and Black Journalism.* Pittsburgh: Univ. of Pittsburgh Press, 1974.

Bunzel, Joseph H. *Negro Housing Needs in Pittsburgh and Allegheny County.* Pittsburgh: Pittsburgh Housing Association, 1946.

Burgoyne, Arthur G. *The Homestead Strike of 1892.* Pittsburgh: Univ. of Pittsburgh Press, 1979.

Burkett, Randall K. *Black Redemption: Churchmen Speak for the Garvey Movement.* Philadelphia: Temple Univ. Press, 1978.

Burnham, Robert A. "The Cincinnati Charter Revolt of 1924: Creating City Government for a Pluralistic Society." In *Ethnic Diversity and Civic Identity: Patterns of Conflict and Cohesion in Cincinnati since 1820,* ed. Henry D. Shapiro and Jonathan D. Sarna. Urbana: Univ. of Illinois Press, 1992.

———. "The Mayor's Friendly Relations Committee: Cultural Pluralism and the Struggle for Black Advancement." In *Race and the City: Work, Community, and Protest in Cincinnati, 1820-1970,* ed. Henry Louis Taylor Jr. Urbana: Univ. of Illinois Press, 1993.

——. "The New Inter-racialism: The Citizen's Committee for Human Rights and Restaurant Desegregation in Cincinnati." *Queen City Heritage* 52, no. 3 (Fall 1994).

——. "Reform, Politics, and Race in Cincinnati: Proportional Representation and the City Charter Committee, 1924-1959." *Journal of Urban History* 23, no. 2 (Jan. 1997).

Byers, William J., et al. *Black History of the Commonwealth of Pennsylvania, 1865-1976.* 1910. Reprint, Harrisburg, Penn.: Jas. H.W. Howard & Son, 1977.

Capeci, Dominic J., Jr., and Martha Wilkerson. *Layered Violence: The Detroit Rioters of 1943.* Mississippi: Univ. of Mississippi Press, 1991.

Carmichael, Omer, and Weldon James. *The Louisville Story.* New York: Simon & Schuster, 1957.

Carter, Dan T. *Scottsboro: A Tragedy of the American South.* 1969. Revised, Baton Rouge: Louisiana State Univ. Press, 1979.

Casey-Leininger, Charles F. "Park Town Cooperative Homes, Urban Redevelopment, and the Search for Residential Integration in Cincinnati, 1955-1965." *Queen City Heritage: Journal of the Cincinnati Historical Society,* 52 (Fall 1994).

Casto, James E. *Towboat on the Ohio.* Lexington: Univ. Press of Kentucky, 1995.

Cayton, Horace R., and George S. Mitchell. *Black Workers and the New Unions.* Chapel Hill: Univ. of North Carolina Press, 1939.

Chandler, Alfred D., Jr. *The Visible Hand: The Managerial Revolution in American Business.* Cambridge: Belknap Press of Harvard University, 1977.

Cheek, William, and Aimee Lee Cheek. "John Mercer Langston and the Cincinnati Riot of 1841." In *Race and the City: Work, Community, and Protest in Cincinnati, 1820-1970,* ed. Henry Louis Taylor Jr. Urbana: Univ. of Illinois Press, 1993.

Chudacoff, Howard P., and Judith E. Smith. *The Evolution of American Urban Society,* 4th ed. Englewood Cliffs, N.J.: Prentice Hall, 1994.

Chudacoff, Howard P., ed. *Major Problems in American Urban History.* Lexington, Mass.: Heath, 1994.

Clark, Peter H. *The Black Brigade of Cincinnati.* 1865. Reprint, New York: Arno Press, 1969.

Cole, Lori. "Voices and Choices: Race, Class, and Identity, Homestead, Pennsylvania, 1941-1945." Ph.D. diss., Carnegie Mellon University, 1994.

Collins, Ernest M. "Cincinnati Negroes and Presidential Politics." In *The Negro in Depression and War: Prelude to Revolution, 1930-1945,* ed. Bernard Sternsher. Chicago: Quadrangle Books, 1969.

Condit, Carl W. *The Railroad and the City: A Technological and Urbanistic*

History of Cincinnati. Columbus: Ohio State Univ. Press, 1977.

Couvares, Francis G. *The Remaking of Pittsburgh: Class and Culture in an Industrializing City, 1877-1919.* Albany: State Univ. of New York Press, 1984.

Cronon, William. *Nature's Metropolis: Chicago and the Great West.* New York: W.W. Norton, 1991.

Cunningham, Constance A. "Homer S. Brown: First Black Political Leader in Pittsburgh." *Journal of Negro History* 66, no. 4 (Winter 1981-82).

Curry, Leonard P. *The Free Black in Urban America, 1800-1850: The Shadow of the Dream.* Chicago: Univ. of Chicago Press, 1981.

Dabney, Wendell P. *Cincinnati's Colored Citizens.* 1926. Reprint, New York: Negro Universities Press, 1970.

Dalfiume, Richard M. "The Forgotten Years of the Negro Revolution." In *The Negro in Depression and War: Prelude to Revolution, 1930-1945,* ed. Bernard Sternsher. Chicago: Quadrangle Books, 1969.

Daniel, Walker C. *Black Journals of the United States.* Westport, Conn.: Greenwood Press, 1982.

Darden, Joe T. *Afro-Americans in Pittsburgh: The Residential Segregation of a People.* Lexington, Mass.: Lexington Books, 1973.

———. "The Effect of World War I on Black Occupational and Residential Segregation: The Case of Pittsburgh." *Journal of Black Studies* 18, no. 3 (March 1988).

Davis, George L. "Pittsburgh's Negro Troops in the Civil War." *Western Pennsylvania Historical Magazine* 36 (June 1953).

Davis, Mike. *City of Quartz: Excavating the Future in Los Angeles.* New York: Vintage, 1992.

DeBow, J.D.B. *Statistical View of the United States: Compendium of the Seventh Census.* Washington, D.C.: Beverly Tucker, Senate Printer, 1854.

Delany, Martin R. *The Condition, Elevation, Emigration, and Destiny of the Colored People of the United States.* 1852. Reprint, New York: Arno Press, 1968.

Dickerson, Dennis C. *Out of the Crucible: Black Steelworkers in Western Pennsylvania, 1875-1980.* Albany: State Univ. of New York Press, 1986.

Downey, Dennis B., and Francis J. Bremer, eds. *A Guide to the History of Pennsylvania.* Westport, Conn.: Greenwood Press, 1993.

Drake, St. Clair, and Horace R. Cayton. *Black Metropolis: A Study of Negro Life in a Northern City,* 2 vol. 1944. Reprint, New York: Harcourt, Brace & World, 1962.

Dubofsky, Melvyn. *The State and Labor in Modern America.* Chapel Hill: Univ. of North Carolina Press, 1994.

Du Bois, W.E.B. *Black Reconstruction in America, 1860-1880.* 1935. Reprint, Cleveland: Meridian Books, 1964.

Edmonds, Arthur J. *Daybreakers: The Story of the Urban League of Pittsburgh, the First Sixty-Five Years.* Urban League of Pittsburgh, 1983.

Epstein, Abraham. *The Negro Migrant in Pittsburgh.* Pittsburgh: Univ. of Pittsburgh Press, 1918.

Fairbanks, Robert B. "Cincinnati Blacks and the Irony of Low-Income Housing Reform, 1900-1950." In *Race and the City: Work, Community, and Protest in Cincinnati, 1820-1970,* ed. Henry Louis Taylor Jr. Urbana: Univ. of Illinois Press, 1993.

———. *Making Better Citizens: Housing Reform and the Community Development Strategy in Cincinnati, 1890-1960.* Urbana: Univ. of Illinois Press, 1988.

Faires, Nora. "Immigrants and Industry: Peopling the 'Iron City.'" In *City at the Point: Essays on the Social History of Pittsburgh,* ed. Samuel P. Hays. Pittsburgh: Univ. of Pittsburgh Press, 1989.

Fink, Leon. *Workingmen's Democracy: The Knights of Labor and American Politics.* Urbana: Univ. of Illinois Press, 1983.

Fishel, Leslie H. "The Negro in the New Deal." In *The Negro in Depression and War: Prelude to Revolution, 1930-1945,* ed. Bernard Sternsher. Chicago: Quadrangle Books, 1969.

Fitch, John A. *The Steel Workers.* 1911. Reprint, Pittsburgh: Univ. of Pittsburgh Press, 1989.

Fogelson, Robert M. *The Fragmented Metropolis: Los Angeles, 1850-1930.* Berkeley: University of California Press, 1993.

Foner, Eric. *Reconstruction: America's Unfinished Revolution, 1863-1877.* New York: Harper & Row, 1988.

Foner, Philip S. *Organized Labor and the Black Worker, 1619-1973.* New York: International Publishers, 1974.

Foner, Philip S., and Ronald L. Lewis, eds. *The Black Worker: A Documentary History from Colonial Times to the Present.* 8 vol. Philadelphia: Temple Univ. Press, 1978-1984.

Foster, William Z. *The Great Steel Strike and Its Lessons.* New York: B.W. Huebsch, 1920.

Franklin, John Hope, and Alfred Moss. *From Slavery to Freedom: A History of African Americans.* 1947. Reprint, New York: McGraw Hill, 1994.

Frazier, Thomas R., ed. *Afro-American History: Primary Sources.* Chicago: Dorsey Press, 1988.

Gerber, David A. *Black Ohio and the Color Line, 1860-1915.* Urbana: Univ. of Illinois Press, 1976.

Glasco, Laurence. "Double Burden: The Black Experience in Pittsburgh." In *City at the Point: Essays on the Social History of Pittsburgh,* ed. Samuel P. Hays. Pittsburgh: Univ. of Pittsburgh Press, 1989.

———. "Taking Care of Business: The Black Entrepreneurial Elite in Turn-of-the-Century Pittsburgh." *Pittsburgh History* 78, no.4 (Winter 1995-96).

Glenn, Norval D., and Charles M. Bonjean, eds. *Blacks in the United States*. Chicago: Chandler Publishing, 1969.

Goings, Kenneth W., and Raymond A. Mohl, eds. *The New African American Urban History*. Thousand Oaks, Cal.: Sage Publications, 1996.

Gottlieb, Peter. "Black Miners and the 1925-28 Bituminous Coal Strike: The Colored Committee of Non-Union Miners, Montour Mine No. 1, Pittsburgh." *Labor History* 28, no 2 (Spring 1987).

———. *Making Their Own Way: Southern Blacks' Migration to Pittsburgh, 1916-30*. Urbana: Univ. of Illinois Press, 1987.

Green, Constance McLaughlin. *American Cities in the Growth of the Nation*. New York: Harper & Row, 1957.

Green, James R. *The World of the Worker: Labor in Twentieth Century America*. New York: Hill & Wang, 1980.

Greenberg, Cheryl Lynn. *Or Does It Explode?: Black Harlem in the Great Depression*. New York: Oxford Univ. Press, 1991.

Greenwald, Maurine W. "Women and Class in Pittsburgh, 1850-1920." In *City at the Point: Essays on the Social History of Pittsburgh*, ed. Samuel P. Hays. Pittsburgh: Univ. of Pittsburgh Press, 1989.

Grossman, James R. *Land of Hope: Chicago, Black Southerners, and the Great Migration*. Chicago: Univ. of Chicago Press, 1989.

Gutman, Herbert. *Work, Culture, and Society in Industrializing America: Essays in American Working Class and Social History*. New York: Vintage Books, 1977.

Harlan, Louis. *Booker T. Washington: The Wizard of Tuskegee, 1901-1915*. New York: Oxford Univ. Press, 1983.

Harris, William H. *The Harder We Run: Black Workers since the Civil War*. New York: Oxford Univ. Press, 1982.

———. *Keeping the Faith: A. Philip Randolph, Milton P. Webster, and the Brotherhood of Sleeping Car Porters, 1925-37*. Urbana: Univ. of Illinois Press, 1977.

Hays, Samuel P., ed. *City at the Point: Essays on the Social History of Pittsburgh*. Pittsburgh: Univ. of Pittsburgh Press, 1989.

Hill, Herbert. *Black Labor and the American Legal System: Race, Work, and the Law*. Madison: Univ. of Wisconsin Press, 1985.

Hill, Robert A., ed. *The Marcus Garvey and Universal Negro Improvement Association Papers*. Berkeley: University of California, 1983-1986.

Hine, Darlene Clark. "Black Migration to the Urban Midwest: The Gender Dimension." In *The Great Migration in Historical Perspective*, ed. Joe W. Trotter. Bloomington: Indiana Univ. Press, 1991.

———, ed. *The State of Afro-American History: Past, Present, and Future*. Baton Rouge: Louisiana State University, 1986.

Hinshaw, John, and Judith Modell. "Perceiving Racism: Homestead from Depression to Deindustrialization." *Pennsylvania History* 63, no.1 (Winter 1996).

Hoerr, John P. *And the Wolf Finally Came: The Decline of the American Steel Industry.* Pittsburgh: Univ. of Pittsburgh Press, 1988.

Holt, Michael F. *Forging a Majority: The Formation of the Republican Party in Pittsburgh, 1848- 1860.* New Haven: Yale Univ. Press, 1969.

Horton, James Oliver, and Stacey Flaherty. "Black Leadership in Antebellum Cincinnati." In *Race and the City: Work, Community, and Protest in Cincinnati, 1820-1970,* ed. Henry Louis Taylor Jr. Urbana: Univ. of Illinois Press, 1993.

Houston, David. "A Brief History of the Process of Capital Accumulation in Pittsburgh: A Marxist Interpretation." In Joel A. Tarr, *Pittsburgh-Sheffield Sister Cities.* Pittsburgh: Carnegie Mellon Univ. Press, 1986.

Hunter, Barbara Jean. "The Public Education of Blacks in the City of Pittsburgh, 1920-1950: Actions and Reactions of the Black Community in Pursuit of Educational Equality." Ed.D. diss., University of Pittsburgh, 1987.

Ingham, John N. "Steel City Aristocrats." In *City at the Point: Essays on the Social History of Pittsburgh,* ed. Samuel P. Hays. Pittsburgh: Univ. of Pittsburgh Press, 1989.

Jackson, Kenneth T. *Crabgrass Frontier: The Suburbanization of the United States.* New York: Oxford Univ. Press, 1985.

———. *The Ku Klux Klan in the City, 1915-1930.* New York: Oxford Univ. Press, 1967.

Jacobson, Julius, ed. *The Negro and the American Labor Movement.* Garden City, New York: Anchor Books, Doubleday, 1968.

Jones, Jacqueline. *The Dispossessed: America's Underclasses from the Civil War to the Present.* New York: Basic Books, 1992.

———. *Labor of Love, Labor of Sorrow: Black Women, Work, and the Family from Slavery to Present.* New York: Basic Books, 1985.

Kelley, Robin D.G. *Hammer and Hoe: Alabama Communists during the Great Depression.* Chapel Hill: Univ. of North Carolina Press, 1990.

Kersten, Andrew. "Publicly Exposing Discrimination: The 1945 FEPC Hearings in Cincinnati, Ohio." *Queen City Heritage* 52, no. 3 (Fall 1994).

Kirby, John B. *Black Americans in the Roosevelt Era: Liberalism and Race.* Knoxville: Univ. of Tennessee Press, 1980.

Klebanow, Diana, Franklin L. Jonas, and Ira M. Leonard. *Urban Legacy: The Story of America's Cities.* New York: A Mentor Book, 1977.

Kleinberg, S.J. *The Shadow of the Mills: Working-Class Families in Pittsburgh, 1870-1907.* Pittsburgh: Univ. of Pittsburgh Press, 1989.

Kleppner, Paul. "Government, Parties, and Voters in Pittsburgh." In *City at the Point: Essays on the Social History of Pittsburgh,* ed. Samuel P. Hays. Pittsburgh: Univ. of Pittsburgh Press, 1989.

Knepper, George W. *Ohio and Its People.* Kent, Ohio: Kent State Univ. Press, 1989.

Koehler, Lyle. *Cincinnati's Black Peoples: A Chronology and Bibliography, 1797-1982.* Cincinnati: Center for Neighborhood and Community Studies, University of Cincinnati, 1986.

Kornbluh, Andrea Tuttle. "James Hathaway Robinson and the Origins of Professional Social Work in the Black Community." In *Race and the City: Work, Community, and Protest in Cincinnati, 1820-1970,* ed. Henry Louis Taylor Jr. Urbana: Univ. of Illinois Press, 1993.

Krause, Paul. *The Battle for Homestead, 1880-1892: Politics, Culture, and Steel.* Pittsburgh: Univ. of Pittsburgh Press, 1992.

Kusmer, Kenneth. "The Black Urban Experience in American History." In *The State of Afro-American History: Past, Present, and Future,* ed. Darlene Clark Hine. Baton Rouge: Louisiana State University, 1986.

———, ed. *Black Communities and Urban Development in America, 1720-1990.* Vol. 5, *The Great Migration and After, 1917-1930.* New York: Garland Publishing, 1991.

Landry, Bart. *The New Black Middle Class.* Berkeley: Univ. of California Press, 1987.

Lapin, Adam. "Negro America Acts to Build Steel Union." *Daily Worker* 8 (Feb. 1937).

Larsen, Lawrence H. *The Urban South: A History.* Lexington: Univ. Press of Kentucky, 1990.

Laurie, Bruce. *Artisans into Workers: Labor in Nineteenth-Century America.* New York: Noonday Press, 1989.

Lawson, Steven F. *Running for Freedom: Civil Rights and Black Politics in America since 1941.* New York: McGraw Hill, 1991.

Lemann, Nicholas. *The Promised Land: The Great Migration and How it Changed America.* New York: Alfred A. Knopf, 1991.

Leuchtenburg, William E. *Franklin D. Roosevelt and the New Deal, 1932-1940.* New York: Harper & Row, 1963.

Levine, Bruce. "Community Divided: German Immigrants, Social Class, and Political Conflict in Antebellum Cincinnati." In *Ethnic Diversity and Civic Identity: Patterns of Conflict and Cohesion in Cincinnati since 1820,* ed. Henry D. Shapiro and Jonathan D. Sarna. Urbana: Univ. of Illinois Press, 1992.

Lewis, Earl. "Expectations, Economic Opportunities, and Life in the Industrial Age: Black Migration to Norfolk, Virginia, 1910-1945." In *The Great Migration in Historical Perspective: New Dimensions of Race, Class, and Gender,* ed. Joe W. Trotter. Bloomington: Indiana Univ. Press, 1991.

———. *In Their Own Interests: Race, Class, and Power in Twentieth-Century Norfolk, Virginia.* Berkeley: Univ. of California Press, 1991.

Lewis, Ronald L. *Black Coal Miners in America: Race, Class, and Community Con-*

flict, 1780- 1980. Lexington: Univ. Press of Kentucky, 1987.

Litwack, Leon. *Been in the Storm So Long: The Aftermath of Slavery.* New York: Vintage Books, 1979.

Logan, Rayford. *Betrayal of the Negro: From Rutherford B. Hayes to Woodrow Wilson.* 1954. Reprint, New York: Macmillan, 1972.

Lubove, Roy, ed. *Pittsburgh.* New York: New Viewpoints, 1976.

————. *Twentieth-Century Pittsburgh: Government, Business, and Environmental Change,* vol. 1. 1969. Reprint, Pittsburgh: Univ. of Pittsburgh Press, 1995.

Lucas, Marion B. *A History of Blacks in Kentucky.* Vol. 1, *From Slavery to Segregation, 1760- 1891.* Frankfort: Kentucky Historical Society, 1992.

Machor, James. L. *Pastoral Cities: Urban Ideals and the Symbolic Landscape of America.* Madison: University of Wisconsin Press, 1987.

Marable, Manning. *Race, Reform, and Rebellion: The Second Reconstruction in Black America, 1945-1990.* Jackson: Univ. Press of Mississippi, 1991.

Marshall, F. Ray, and Vernon M. Briggs Jr. *The Negro and Apprenticeship.* Baltimore: Johns Hopkins Press, 1967.

Martin, Tony. *Race First: The Ideological and Organizational Struggles of Marcus Garvey and the Universal Negro Improvement Association.* Dover, Mass.: Majority Press, 1976.

Massey, Douglas S., and Nancy A. Denton. *American Apartheid: Segregation and the Making of the Underclass.* Cambridge: Harvard Univ. Press, 1993.

McBride, David, ed. *Blacks in Pennsylvania History: Research and Educational Perspectives.* Harrisburg: Pennsylvania Historical and Museum Commission, 1983.

McKenzie, Edna. "Pittsburgh's Daisy Lampkin: Her Life, a Labor of Love and Service." *Pennsylvania Heritage* 9, no. 3 (Summer 1983).

McLaughlin, Glen E. *Growth of American Manufacturing Areas: A Comparative Analysis with Special Emphasis on Trends in the Pittsburgh District.* Pittsburgh: Bureau of Business Research, University of Pittsburgh, 1938.

Meltzer, Milton, ed. *In Their Own Words: A History of the American Negro, 1916-1966.* New York: Thomas Y. Crowell, 1967.

Miller, Floyd J. *The Search for a Black Nationality: Black Colonization and Emigration, 1787- 1863.* Urbana: Univ. of Illinois Press, 1975.

Miller, Zane L. *Boss Cox's Cincinnati: Urban Politics in the Progressive Era.* New York: Oxford Univ. Press, 1968.

Mitchell, Patricia. *Beyond Adversity: African Americans' Struggle for Equality in Western Pennsylvania, 1750-1990.* Pittsburgh: Historical Society of Western Pennsylvania, 1993.

Mjagkij, Nina. "Behind the Scenes: The Cincinnati Urban League, 1948-63." In *Race and the City: Work, Community, and Protest in Cincinnati, 1820-1970,* ed. Henry Louis Taylor Jr. Urbana: Univ. of Illinois Press, 1993.

Mohl, Raymond A. *The New City: Urban America in the Industrial Age, 1860-1920.* Arlington Heights, Ill.: Harlan Davidson, 1985.

Monkkonen, Eric H. *America Becomes Urban: The Development of U.S. Cities and Towns, 1780-1980.* Berkeley: University of California Press, 1988.

Montgomery, David. *The Fall of the House of Labor: The Workplace, the State, and American Labor Activism, 1865-1925.* Cambridge: Cambridge Univ. Press, 1987.

Morris, Aldon D. *The Origins of the Civil Rights Movement: Black Communities Organizing for Change.* New York: Free Press, 1984.

Moss, Maurice. "The Negro in Pittsburgh's Industries." *Opportunity* 13, no. 2 (Feb. 1935).

Muller, Edward K. "Metropolis and Region: A Framework for Enquiry into Western Pennsylvania." In *City at the Point: Essays on the Social History of Pittsburgh,* ed. Samuel P. Hays. Pittsburgh: Univ. of Pittsburgh Press, 1989.

Myrdal, Gunnar. *An American Dilemma: The Negro Problem and Modern Democracy,* vol. 2. 1944. Reprint, New York: Harper & Row, 1962.

Naison, Mark. *Communists in Harlem during the Depression.* Urbana: Univ. of Illinois Press, 1983.

Nash, Gerald D. *The Crucial Era: The Great Depression and World War II, 1929-1945.* New York: St. Martin's Press, 1992.

Nelson, Steve, James R. Barrett, and Rob Ruck. *Steve Nelson, American Radical.* Pittsburgh: Univ. of Pittsburgh Press, 1981.

Nieman, Donald G. *Promises to Keep: African-Americans and the Constitutional Order, 1776 to the Present.* New York: Oxford Univ. Press, 1991.

Northrup, Herbert R. *Organized Labor and the Negro.* New York: Harper & Brothers Publishers, 1944.

Oak, Vishnu V. *The Negro Newspaper.* Westport, Conn.: Negro Universities Press, 1970.

Oestreicher, Richard. "Working-Class Formation, Development, and Consciousness in Pittsburgh, 1790-1960." In *City at the Point: Essays on the Social History of Pittsburgh,* ed. Samuel P. Hays. Pittsburgh: Univ. of Pittsburgh Press, 1989.

Painter, Nell Irvin. *The Narrative of Hosea Hudson: His Life as a Communist.* Cambridge: Harvard Univ. Press, 1979.

Proctor, Ralph. "Racial Discrimination Against Black Teachers and Black Professionals in the Pittsburgh Public School System, 1834-1973." Ph.D. diss., University of Pittsburgh, 1979.

Quillin, Frank U. *The Color Line in Ohio: A History of Race Prejudice in a Typical Northern State.* 1913. Reprint, New York: Negro Universities Press, 1969.

Randolph, A. Philip. "March for a Fair Share: The March on Washington Movement, 1941." Reprinted in *Afro-American History: Primary Sources,* ed. Thomas R. Frazier. Chicago: Dorsey Press, 1988.

———. "Why Should We March." Reprinted in vol. 7, *The Black Worker from 1900 to 1919: A Documentary History from Colonial Times to the Present,* 8 vol., ed. Philip S. Foner and Ronald L. Lewis. Philadelphia: Temple Univ. Press, 1978-1984. First published in *Survey Graphic* 31 (Nov. 1942).

Rayback, Joseph G. *A History of American Labor, Expanded and Updated.* 1959. Revised, New York: Free Press, 1966.

Reed, Merl E. "Black Workers, Defense Industries, and Federal Agencies in Pennsylvania, 1941-1945." *Labor History* 27, no. 3 (Summer 1986).

———. *Seedtime for the Modern Civil Rights Movement: The President's Committee on Fair Employment Practices, 1941-1946.* Baton Rouge: Louisiana State Univ. Press, 1991.

Reid, Ira de A. "The Negro in the Major Industries and Building Trades of Pittsburgh." M.A. thesis, University of Pittsburgh, 1925.

Reid, Robert L., ed. *Always a River: The Ohio River and the American Experience.* Bloomington: Indiana Univ. Press, 1991.

Roediger, David R. *The Wages of Whiteness: Race and the Making of the American Working Class.* London: Verso Press, 1991.

Ross, Arthur M., and Herbert Hill, eds. *Employment, Race, and Poverty: A Critical Study of the Disadvantaged Status of Negro Workers from 1865 to 1965.* New York: Harcourt, Brace & World, 1967.

Ross, Steven J. *Workers on the Edge: Work, Leisure, and Politics in Industrializing Cincinnati, 1788-1890.* New York: Columbia Univ. Press, 1985.

Ruck, Rob. *Sandlot Seasons: Sport in Black Pittsburgh.* Urbana: Univ. of Illinois Press, 1987.

Schnore, Leo F., ed. *The New Urban History: Quantitative Explorations by American Historians.* New Jersey: Princeton Univ. Press, 1975.

Schultz, Stanley K. *Constructing Urban Culture: American Cities and City Planning, 1800-1920.* Philadelphia: Temple University Press, 1989.

Schuyler, George S. "Union Drive Slows in Border Cities: Leaders Hostile." In vol. 7, *The Black Worker from 1900 to 1919: A Documentary History from Colonial Times to the Present.* 8 vol., ed. Philip S. Foner and Ronald L. Lewis. Philadelphia: Temple Univ. Press, 1978-1984. First published in *Pittsburgh Courier,* 11 September 1937.

Shapiro, Henry D., and Jonathan D. Sarna, eds. *Ethnic Diversity and Civic Identity: Patterns of Conflict and Cohesion in Cincinnati since 1820.* Urbana: Univ. of Illinois Press, 1992.

Shapiro, Herbert. *White Violence and Black Response: From Reconstruction to Montgomery.* Amherst: Univ. of Massachusetts Press, 1988.

Share, Allen J. *Cities in the Commonwealth: Two Centuries of Urban Life in Kentucky.* Lexington: Univ. Press of Kentucky, 1982.

Sherman, Richard B. "Johnstown v. the Negro: Southern Migrants and Exodus of 1923." *Pennsylvania History* 30 (Oct. 1963).

Sitkoff, Harvard. *A New Deal for Blacks: The Emergence of Civil Rights as a National Issue: The Depression Decade.* New York: Oxford Univ. Press, 1978.

Smith, Eric Ledell. "The 'Pittsburgh Memorial' of 1837: Allegheny County and the Fight for Black Suffrage." *Pennsylvania History* (forthcoming, ms. in author's possession, courtesy, E.L. Smith).

Spencer, Martin A. "The History of Blacks in Cincinnati Politics." *NIP Magazine,* Bicentennial Black History Edition, 1988.

Spero, Sterling D., and Abram L. Harris, *The Black Worker: The Negro and the Labor Movement.* 1931. Reprint, New York: Atheneum, 1968.

Spratt, Margaret. "Unity within Diversity: The Issue of Race and the Pittsburgh YWCA, 1918-1946." (Unpublished ms. in author's possession.)

Staudenrous, Philip J. *The African Colonization Movement, 1816-1865.* New York: Columbia Univ. Press, 1961.

Stave, Bruce M. *The New Deal and the Last Hurrah: Pittsburgh Machine Politics.* Pittsburgh: Univ. of Pittsburgh Press, 1970.

Stein, Judith. *The World of Marcus Garvey: Race and Class in Modern Society.* Baton Rouge: Louisiana State Univ. Press, 1986.

Sternsher, Bernard, ed. *The Negro in Depression and War: Prelude to Revolution, 1930-1945.* Chicago: Quadrangle Books, 1969.

Streater, John Baxter, Jr. "The National Negro Congress, 1936-1947." Ph.D. diss., University of Cincinnati, 1981.

Tarr, Joel A. "Infrastructure and City-Building in the Nineteenth and Twentieth Centuries." In *City at the Point: Essays on the Social History of Pittsburgh,* ed. Samuel P. Hays. Pittsburgh: Univ. of Pittsburgh Press, 1989.

———. *Pittsburgh-Sheffield Sister Cities.* Pittsburgh: Carnegie Mellon Univ. Press, 1986.

Tarr, Joel A., and Gabriel Dupuy, eds. *Technology and the Rise of the Networked City in Europe and America.* Philadelphia: Temple Univ. Press, 1988.

Taylor, Henry Louis, Jr. "The Building of a Black Industrial Suburb: The Lincoln Heights Story." Ph.D. diss., State University of New York-Buffalo, 1979.

———. "City Building, Public Policy, the Rise of the Industrial City, and Black Ghetto-Slum Formation in Cincinnati, 1850-1940." In *Race and the City: Work, Community, and Protest in Cincinnati, 1820-1970,* ed. Henry Louis Taylor Jr. Urbana: Univ. of Illinois Press, 1993.

———, ed. *Race and the City: Work, Community, and Protest in Cincinnati, 1820-1970.* Urbana: Univ. of Illinois Press, 1993.

Taylor, Henry Louis, Jr., and Vicky Dula. "The Black Residential Experience and

Community Formation in Antebellum Cincinnati." In *Race and the City: Work, Community, and Protest in Cincinnati, 1820-1970*, ed. Henry Louis Taylor Jr. Urbana: Univ. of Illinois Press, 1993.

Temin, Peter. *Iron and Steel in Nineteenth-Century America: An Economic Inquiry.* Cambridge: MIT Press, 1964.

Thornbrough, Emma Lou. *The Negro in Indiana before 1900: A Study of a Minority.* 1957. Reprint, Bloomington: Indiana Univ. Press, 1993.

Toker, Franklin. *Pittsburgh: An Urban Portrait.* University Park: Pennsylvania State Univ. Press, 1986.

Trotter, Joe William, Jr. "African Americans in the City: The Industrial Era." *Journal of Urban History* 21, no. 4 (May 1995).

———. "African-American Workers: New Directions in U.S. Labor Historiography." *Labor History* 35, no. 4 (Fall 1994).

———. *Black Milwaukee: The Making of an Industrial Proletariat, 1915-45.* Urbana: Univ. of Illinois Press, 1985.

———. *Coal, Class, and Color: Blacks in Southern West Virginia, 1915-32.* Urbana: Univ. of Illinois Press, 1990.

———. "Reflections on the Great Migration to Western Pennsylvania." *Pittsburgh History* 78, no. 4 (1995-96).

———, ed. *The Great Migration in Historical Perspective: New Dimensions of Race, Class, and Gender.* Bloomington: Indiana Univ. Press, 1991.

Trotter, Joe William, Jr., and Ancella Radford Bickley, eds. *Honoring Our Past: Proceedings of the First Two Conferences on West Virginia's Black History.* Charleston, W.Va.: Appalachia Educational Laboratory, 1991.

Trotter, Joe William, Jr., and Earl Lewis, eds. *African Americans in the Industrial Age: A Documentary History, 1915-1945.* Boston: Northeastern Univ. Press, 1996.

Tucker, Louis Leonard. *Cincinnati's Citizen Crusaders: A History of the Cincinnatus Association, 1920-1965.* Cincinnati: Cincinnati Historical Society, 1967.

Turner, Edward Raymond. *The Negro in Pennsylvania: Slavery-Servitude-Freedom.* 1910. Reprint, New York: Arno Press, 1969.

U.S. Bureau of the Census. *The Social and Economic Status of the Black Population in the United States: An Historical View, 1790-1978.* Washington, D.C.: U.S. Government Printing Office, 1979.

———. *Negroes in the United States, 1920-1932*, ed. Charles E. Hall. 1935. Reprint, New York: Arno Press, 1969.

———. *Negroes in the United States, 1790-1915.* 1918. Reprint, New York: Arno Press and *New York Times*, 1969.

Wade, Richard. "The Negro in Cincinnati, 1800-1830." *Journal of Negro History* 39 (Jan. 1954).

———. *The Urban Frontier: Pioneer Life in Early Pittsburgh, Cincinnati, Lexington, Louisville, and St. Louis.* Chicago: Univ. of Chicago Press, 1959.

Wallace, Phyllis A. *Black Women in the Labor Force.* Cambridge: MIT Press, 1980.

Warner, Sam Bass, Jr. *Streetcar Suburbs: The Process of Growth in Boston, 1870-1900.* 2d ed. Cambridge, Mass.: Harvard University Press, 1978.

———. *The Urban Wilderness: A History of the American City.* New York: Harper and Row, 1972.

Warren, Kenneth. *The American Steel Industry, 1850-1970: A Geographical Interpretation.* Oxford: Clarendon Press, 1973.

Watkins, T.H. *The Great Depression: America in the 1930s.* Boston: Little, Brown, 1993.

Weber, Michael P. *Don't Call Me Boss, David L. Lawrence: Pittsburgh's Renaissance Mayor.* Pittsburgh: Univ. of Pittsburgh Press, 1988.

Williams, Melvin D. *On the Street Where I Lived.* New York: Holt, Rinehart & Winston, 1981.

Williamson, Joel. *The Crucible of Race: Black-White Relations in the American South since Emancipation.* New York: Oxford Univ. Press, 1984.

Wilmoth, Ann G. "Pittsburgh and the Blacks: A Short History, 1780-1875." Ph.D. diss., Pennsylvania State University, 1975.

Wilson, Francille Rusan. *The Segregated Scholars: Black Labor Historians, 1895-1950.* Ph.D. diss., University of Pennsylvania, 1988.

Wilson, William J. *The Declining Significance of Race: Blacks and Changing American Institutions.* Chicago: Univ. of Chicago Press, 1978.

Wolseley, Roland E. *The Black Press U.S.A.* Ames, Iowa: State Univ. Press, 1990.

Wolters, Raymond. *Negroes and the Great Depression: The Problem of Economic Recovery.* Westport, Conn.: Greenwood Publishing, 1970.

Woodson, Carter G. "The Negroes of Cincinnati Prior to the Civil War." *Journal of Negro History* 1 (1916).

Woofter, T.J. *Negro Problems in Cities.* New York: Harper & Row, 1928.

Wright, George C. *A History of Blacks in Kentucky.* Vol. 2, *In Pursuit of Equality, 1890-1980.* Frankfort: Kentucky Historical Society, 1992.

———. *Life Behind a Veil: Blacks in Louisville, Kentucky, 1865-1930.* Baton Rouge: Louisiana State Univ. Press, 1985.

Wright, Richard R., Jr. *The Negro in Pennsylvania: A Study in Economic History.* 1912. Reprint, New York: Arno Press, 1969.

Wright, Richard, and Edwin Rosskam. *12 Million Black Voices.* New York: Thunder's Mouth Press, 1941.

Index